SIMPSONISTAS

Tales from the Simpson Literary Project

Vol. 2

SIMPSONISTAS

Tales from the Simpson Literary Project

Vol. 2

Storytelling is the foundation of a literate society.

Joseph Di Prisco, Editor

THIS IS A GENUINE VIREO BOOK

A Vireo Book | Rare Bird Books
453 South Spring Street, Suite 302
Los Angeles, CA 90013
rarebirdbooks.com

Set in Dante
Printed in the United States

10 9 8 7 6 5 4 3 2 1

CIP data available on request.

Dedicated to
Public Libraries, Librarians, and the People Who Sustain Them,
Especially
The Lafayette Library and Learning Center of
The Contra Costa County Library

CONTENTS

Girls Inc.

Contra Costa County Juvenile Hall

Northgate High School

Postscript

AN INTRODUCTION

BY JOSEPH DI PRISCO

Is the apocalypse upon us?

Bookstores are ghost towns, tumbleweed rolling around vacant shelves. The printed page is like the covered wagon of mass transportation. Poetry is approaching at warp speed an extinction event horizon. The novel? The novel! Seriously, what kind of person buys novels, not to mention what's a novel for anyway? And memoirs? Haven't we heard it all before, again and again and again? Authors are narcissists and social media strivers who serve the worst wine at the chaotic parties they throw to tediously promote themselves. Rest in peace, writers of books, not that you can or will.

Okay, not exactly *Mad Max* or *The Handmaid's Tale*, or even *Wall-E*, but still.

The doomsayers have been screeching from their virtual rooftops and clicketty-clacketting on their laptops and smartphones since the Big Dismal. And the literature obits have been flooding in, roughly since a certain "influencer" named Steve Jobs opined in 2008 that nobody reads anymore. (But while we're on that subject, who isn't concerned—even if only intermittently—about being reliant upon or distracted by that genius entrepreneur's diabolical invention, the personal computer that doubles as a telephone pinging in our pocket?) I probably have an ill-conceived, nonstrategic social life and have poorly chosen friends (especially on Facebook), and maybe the crunchers of numbers have, according to their own halogen lights, a point, but I'm not buying it. I don't know what the technological and demographic future holds, but I have confidence that storytellers, in all their multivarious incarnations, are not lurching among the walking dead. Long, long ago, William Faulkner famously took the very high road in his exhilarating Nobel Prize Address. His words from 1950 still resonate:

The poet's, the writer's, duty is...to help man endure by lifting his heart, by reminding him of the courage and honor and hope and pride and compassion and pity and sacrifice which have been the glory of his past. The poet's voice need not merely be the record of man, it can be one of the props, the pillars to help him endure and prevail.

The Simpson Literary Project is one bustling place in which to confirm that storytelling is anything but an afterthought, much less a quaint luxury. The Project is all the proof you may need that storytelling is a necessity, a tool for survival, a required weapon, and sometimes a shiny key, which in artful, skilled hands opens the door into the house of consciousness and imagination. True, sometimes that house is on fire, sometimes it drifts among the clouds, sometimes it is deep underground, beneath the bunkers. Sometimes it is anything but a constructed domicile; it can be more like a noisy carnival or a rushing river, a rain forest or a savannah, a cathedral or a mountain or a garden. Wherever the story takes us, its ultimate destination is a journey along an avenue unto mystery and wonder, accompanied by tears or laughter, and often in the case of our greatest storytelling achievements—looking at you, Chekov, O'Connor, Joyce, and your peers—simultaneously both.

Storytelling is the most serious sort of playful enterprise as well as the most playful sort of serious enterprise, and—as with the most complex games—if the stakes are not sky-high it is not worth the pursuit. One primary message teacher/writers leading workshops convey to students is: hold nothing back, risk everything, tell your story, share your truth, this game is for real. In this spirit, consider what Elena Ferrante, the prominent (and famously "anonymous") author of the Neapolitan novels, wrote recently, and emphatically, about the power of women's storytelling, and about the urgency these days for women to tell their stories, with insights applicable in general to all storytellers:

Telling stories really is a kind of power, and not an insignificant one. Stories give shape to experience, sometimes by accommodating traditional literary forms, sometimes by turning them upside down, sometimes by reorganizing them. Stories draw readers into their web, and engage them by putting them to work, body and soul, so that they can transform the black thread of writing into people, ideas, feelings, actions, cities, worlds, humanity, life. Storytelling, in other words, gives us the power to bring order to the chaos of the real under our own sign, and in this it isn't very far from political power. ("A Power of Our Own"; *New York Times*, 5/18/2019)

◆◆◆

One thing people who read and write know for certain is that making a book is not easy. For the artist, the psychic, emotional, and aesthetic expenditure in the service of such enterprise is maximal. Or as Joyce Carol Oates memorably remarked, writing the first draft of a novel is like pushing a peanut with your nose across a dirty floor—thereby garnering extra points yet again for unforgettable imagery. She means, in part, you don't know where you are going and you don't know why, and the process presents a menace to personal hygiene. What the magisterial Oates demonstrates, nonetheless, over the course of her some seventy-five novels, and still counting, is that, to our delight and edification, she inevitably and spectacularly arrives none the worse for wear. Writing, in other words, is not for the faint of heart, the squeamish, the recklessly timid, the perfectionistic. The writer's road is mapless and labyrinthine, replete with detours and distractions, with disappointments popping up around corners, and more than the occasional dead end or brick wall.

So yes, about *easy*? Well, writing a book may not be. But when I reflect upon the recipients and the finalists and the longlisted of the Simpson/Joyce Carol Oates Prize (2017, 2018, and 2019), many of them certainly make it *seem* that way, because the apparent effortlessness of their creations is the talented, enduring, hard-working writer's most magnificent illusion. Take, for example, the finalists for the 2019 Prize: Rachel Kushner, Laila Lalami, Valeria Luiselli, Sigrid Nunez, Anne Raeff, Amor Towles. Each of them has been justifiably, lavishly celebrated, and embraced by the Simpson Project, for their narrative command, depth of feeling, intellectual range, aesthetic power, and sheer human urgency. They are all very much worth reading right now. That previous sentence is what we English teachers like to call *understatement*.

◆◆◆

No one *compos mentis* would dismiss the gravity of the issues that weigh upon us, including (in alphabetical order) and not restricted to: artificial intelligence, Black Lives Matter, bullying, child abuse, climate change, election tampering, family separation, food security, gentrification, global autocracy, global warming, gun violence, homelessness, immigration, income inequity, media corruptibility, MeToo, nuclear proliferation, opioid proliferation, personal privacy, police misconduct, political polarization, poverty, prison reform, public health fails, racial inequality, racism, religious freedom, school safety, sexual diversity, sexual exploitation, the suicide epidemic, tariffs, terrorism, unemployment, vaccination denial, wealth disparity, white supremacy, women's rights, xenophobia. Little wonder that forebodings haunt our nights and days, infiltrate our monitors and screens, streets and schools.

Consequently, in the precarious twenty-first century, dystopian visions proliferate. Ferrante's op-ed, quoted above, references brilliantly the fourteenth-century author Giovanni Boccaccio, who wrote a great book called *The Decameron*. Ten young people flee Florence for the countryside. In the city, chaos has broken out—citizens are in abject panic over the plague, in fear of their neighbors and friends and family. And these ten storytellers converge to do something quite radical and ultimately sensible: they compose and tell each other over ten days a hundred stories of love and adventure and heroism. (As Ferrante trenchantly points out, seven of the ten storytellers are women.) In his book's first line he writes: "*Umana cosa è aver compassione degli afflitti.*" That is, it is (an essentially) human (thing) to have compassion for those in distress. But how to express compassion, sympathy, and empathy under such dire circumstances? For Boccaccio, it was to tell and attend to stories. History and literature have proven him and his book prescient. Storytelling is not an escape from the grimmest realities, but the subtly shifting, fluid foundation of our mutual humanity, which stories are uniquely positioned to illuminate—and fashion.

What we learn from centuries of writing is that the greatest storytelling is anything but an elitist diversion or preoccupation. At its heights and in its depths, it is intensely engaged with the turmoil and challenge of its times. As Oates writes: "Especially we crave radical and subversive art from the margins of society, that challenges the authority of the center. More quirky, stubborn, rebellious voices to counteract the ubiquitous drone of social media culture. More public support for all the arts—visual, musical, theatrical, dance, print—and not just the arts that reflect our own convictions. If our art sometimes provokes unexpected reactions this is the price we must pay for our commitment to bearing witness in a turbulent world." (*Simpsonistas: Vol. 1*; "'A Wounded Deer Leaps Highest': Motives for Metaphor")

Janet Burroway, novelist and author of the enduring *Writing Fiction*, refers to the fascinating, controversial *Sapiens: A Brief History of Humankind*, where she highlights the place of story in individual lives and in the culture at large:

Yuval Noah Harari points out that it is not language itself but the related capacity to imagine what is not immediately present *that distinguishes the human species. To imagine what is not immediately present allows us spirituality, nationhood, commerce, and law, and it is of course the essence of story. To write better and better stories may promote cooperation, gender equality, and the cementing of social bonds. If an aspiring writer has natural talent, so much the better. If she gets published, even paid—wonderful.... But in any case, it is good for a full-blooded life and good for the culture that human beings should continue to study the craft of fiction.* ("What It's Like to Teach Writing When Everyone's a Writer," Lithub; 6/3/2019)

◆◆◆

The nonprofit Simpson Literary Project has developed organically over time, implicated as it must be in this turbulent world of ours, and it continually grows in reach and impact ever since the founders initially gathered to dream and plan in summer 2015. We gradually conceived a multidimensional set of programs to serve writers and readers, teachers and librarians, across the generations. From the outset, the essential institutional partners would be the visionary Lafayette Library and Learning Center Foundation, which is our fiscal sponsor, and the University of California, Berkeley, English Department, long regarded as the leading English Department in the world.

All the pieces of the Project interconnect with, and reinforce and inform, each other. Workshop students learn from the prize winner and from Simpson fellows; the Writer-in-Residence is connected to the library and schools and the workshops; the prize winner is connected to the workshops, the libraries, and students at Berkeley; the Simpson fellows, professional writers themselves, teach our workshop students; *Simpsonistas* publishes participants across the entire spectrum, writers both professional and aspiring; the Project hosts events at UC Berkeley and the Lafayette Library featuring and celebrating all of them. In the broadest sense, everything and everyone is associated within the Simpson Literary Project. The teenager drafting her story, the incarcerated youth writing poetry, the distinguished midcareer novelist freed to finish a new book, the world-famous author speaking to librarians and inspiring everyone—all of them are connected, and for a sound, pragmatic reason. That reason is captured in our mantra: *Storytelling is the foundation of a literate society.*

We took pains to assure that this would not be all about one lucky writer receiving a meaningful prize benefit of $50,000—though, to state the obvious, we appreciate that writers can hardly afford to be blithe as to financial underpinning for work and survival. An appointed jury of professional readers considers a longlist of writers and determines a shortlist, which is then handed up to a panel of judges from the Simpson Literary Project Board. Each year, judges select a midcareer author of fiction, whose eligibility is defined as one who has published at least two distinguished works of fiction (novels and/or short stories). No age, geographic, or stylistic restrictions apply. The only other qualification is that this is a writer who has yet to receive capstone recognition, such as a Pulitzer or a MacArthur, though we might be forgiven for expecting it is likely just a matter of time for our finalists till that oversight is remedied.

While there are numerous prizes for emerging writers, this prize is for an already emerged author of national consequence—short stories and/or novels—at the relatively middle stage of a burgeoning career. Occasionally an intriguing question comes up in this regard. Unlike with the case of butterflies who emerge marvelous from their cocoon ordeals, the emergence of writers is more complicated still. A few geniuses do indeed spectacularly arrive one day on the scene, while others develop slowly, over time, often maddeningly and even perhaps erratically for authors and their fans. The arc of a writer's career can be long and it bends to—who would dare predict?

It's obviously fortunate for younger writers to feel the love and recognition, not to mention to enjoy the influx of real dollars. But writers at all stages feel that selfsame need. The fact is, there are precious few major prizes on the order of the Simpson Prize catering to midcareer writers. Insofar as we value the charms and challenges of storytelling, storytellers depend on our support. It's worth noting, too, that at the midpoint of writers' careers it's often a trial to publish or grow an audience. Only a tiny percentage of them will ever ascend the bestseller lists, or be able to care for themselves and their families on the proceeds, and effectively none will sell units like a Stephen King or a J. K. Rowling. Now that they have arrived at this juncture, occasionally they are invidiously saddled with the cruel label of "midlist"—a term to be used with extreme caution around any working writer you may bump into. The irony consists of this: midcareer is often when some writers are just hitting their stride, taking chances as they've never done before, sometimes after composing books that never saw the light of publication, or whose first published works found a limited albeit admiring audience. This all takes place at the precise moment when publishers' gaze is drawn instead to the gleam of flashy, younger, emerging writers. Again, at the risk of repetition: there's nothing wrong at all with embracing the *emerging*. Yet sign us up for the *emerged, still emerging.*

Over three years of prize-giving, 131 notable authors have been longlisted, fifteen shortlisted as finalists; decisions were never uncomplicated, and many of the longlisted could have easily been shortlisted, and some of the shortlisted could have been recipients. To respectfully acknowledge distinguished achievement, starting in 2019 we awarded each finalist $2,000.

That said, we are proud of our decisions. In 2017, the prize recipient was T. Geronimo Johnson; in 2018, Anthony Marra; in 2019, Laila Lalami. All three are represented in *Simpsonistas: Vol. 2*. In Spring 2019, we renamed the prize to honor the heroically philanthropic Barclay and Sharon Simpson in tandem with our dear friend and colleague. Henceforth, it will be known as The Simpson/Joyce Carol Oates Prize.

The Project always envisioned broader outreach and deeper influence upon communities at large. That is why our prize recipient takes up residency every spring in Berkeley and Lafayette for a circumscribed period, in order to stimulate and engage with the minds and hearts of college and high school students at the University of California, Berkeley, and elsewhere, as well as with the Lafayette Library and Learning Center and the general public. And that is why we make possible, at no charge, writing workshops for underserved younger people, led by professional writers who are graduate students in the English Department of the University of California, Berkeley. Seven Simpson Fellows have worked with nearly one hundred young writers over the last two years, 2018 and 2019, at Contra Costa County Juvenile Hall, Girls Inc. of Alameda County, and a comprehensive public high school, Northgate, in Walnut Creek, California.

In addition, we have also sponsored a Simpson Literary Project Writer-in-Residence at the Lafayette Library and Learning Center, who was there to speak and read to the public and to work with aspiring writers as well as librarians and teachers and the broader community; we have been incredibly fortunate to have been graced by the presence of Joyce Carol Oates as our Writer-in-Residence in 2018 and 2019. (Joyce also conducted a memoir workshop, offered at no cost, for aspiring adult authors associated with the Lafayette Library and Learning Center. Two of those authors are represented in this anthology.) And that is also why we cause to be published yearly volumes of *Simpsonistas: Tales from the Simpson Literary Project*, where previously unpublished authors across the generations appear for the first time in print alongside an outstanding group of professional authors, all of whom have been honored by the Project—as prize recipients, finalists, and longlisters. This book now in your hands makes tangible the wide range of accomplishment, aspiration, and idealism of everyone affiliated with the Simpson Literary Project.

I have been fleshing out our programs, but with this crucial caveat: programs are nothing if not, at heart, people. A plan is illusory without the people to animate them. And the Project has been fortunate in all the gifted individuals and institutions that have stepped up in support: donors, sponsors, authors, teachers, professors, librarians, workshop partners, board members, and so on.

In this vein, consider what Laura Ritland, devoted Simpson Fellow at Girls Inc. in 2018 and 2019, writes in her stirring "More Than Enough: Teaching with the Simpson Literary Project"; the complete essay may be found in this volume:

The road to calling oneself a "writer" without self-doubt and with a measured understanding of one's abilities is a long one. For students of these workshops, this is the beginning of what might be a much longer journey. However, wherever writing takes them, I hope that they find something in it that liberates the mind, body, spirit, and perception. For ultimately, writing is a way of attending to our environment and our places within it, of bringing consciousness and empowerment to our choices. With practice, attention, and kindness to ourselves, it can make us free.

And then there is this from renowned English teacher David Wood, of Northgate High School, whose impassioned essay in this volume is "Teaching Voice":

Nothing is more fun in an English classroom than hearing authentic voices come alive and expand. That is what the Simpson Literary Project gives to these young writers, a room of their own to express themselves. And so they did. What could be more indicative of the success of the Project than the vision that one of these young writers will be published in Simpsonistas *again down the line, only this time in the company of some of the finest writers in the country, as one of them. I hope I am here to see it.*

◆◆◆

We asked Anthony Marra to write a few words on how he spent his year as the 2018 Simpson/Joyce Carol Oates prize recipient. In his incandescent essay about the experience, Tony begins by wryly observing that "I came to realize that I would make a terrible memoirist."

I don't drink or smoke. I go to bed early enough that my mom, who lives on the East Coast, occasionally wakes me when she calls. I don't have a car, and my usual rounds take me no farther than I can walk. Just about every morning and afternoon, weekdays and weekends, I go to the same two coffee shops, order the same drink, and sit in the same seat and write. In October I went out of town for several days without telling the proprietor of my afternoon coffee shop and she worried some terrible accident had befallen me. I say this not in complaint but in gratitude. At the end of a perfect week, I look back without remembering what happened on any particular day—not because nothing happened, but because I was doing the same thing every day: getting good writing done. Thanks to the Simpson/ Joyce Carol Oates Prize, I'm having a year of those days.

I'm hesitant to speak directly about my current project. Needless to say, the work is going very well.

Recently, I watched the BBC nature documentary Blue Planet II, *an extraordinary series whose cast includes octopi armored in scavenged sea shells, sperm whales in vertical slumber, and bioluminescent creatures lighting the ocean floor miles below the last of the sun's rays. Beneath the seemingly monotonous surface of the ocean is a depthless underworld teeming with life.*

When asked, "What have you been up to?" I usually answer, "Not much," because to any casual observer, I'm simply in my coffee shops, working on the next page, writing these words. But to you, friend of the Simpson Literary Project, I will confess the truth: I'm swimming with the starfish and the sea anemones.

We are confident you will feel, as, we hope, a budding Simpsonista yourself, the elation experienced by our Project workshop students, the readers of all our prize winners, our Simpson fellows, along with the audiences for our readings and talks.

So by all means please dive in. The water, you will discover, is fine. And welcome to swimming with all the varicolored, diverse creatures flourishing and flashing beneath the surface, the shimmering starfish and sea anemones apocalyptically revealed to dazzle you in *Simpsonistas: Tales from the Simpson Literary Project: Vol 2.*

Joseph Di Prisco, Editor
Founding Chair, The Simpson Literary Project
jdp@simpsonliteraryproject.org
August 2019

NOTES & ACKNOWLEDGMENTS

Grateful thanks extended to

Authors and publishers for generous permission to print or reprint.

Institutional Partners of The Simpson Literary Project—

The Lafayette Library and Learning Center Foundation. lllcf.org/

The University of California, Berkeley, English Department. english.berkeley.edu/

The University of California, Berkeley. berkeley.edu/

The Contra Costa County Public Library. ccclib.org/

2017 Simpson/Joyce Carol Oates Prize Finalists—

T. Geronimo Johnson (Prize Recipient)

Valeria Luiselli

Lori Ostlund

Dana Spiotta

2018 Simpson/Joyce Carol Oates Prize Finalists—

Ben Fountain

Samantha Hunt

Karan Mahajan

Anthony Marra (Prize Recipient)

Martin Pousson

2019 Simpson/Joyce Carol Oates Prize Finalists—

Rachel Kushner

Laila Lalami (Prize Recipient)

Valeria Luiselli

Sigrid Nunez

Anne Raeff

Amor Towles

Simpson Project Writing Workshops—

Contra Costa County Juvenile Hall, Martinez, California; Noelle Burch, Contra Costa County Public Library; Mt. McKinley High School, Contra Costa County Office of Education; Ismail Muhammad & Rosetta Young, Simpson Fellows

Girls Inc., Oakland, Alameda County; Julayne Virgil, CEO; Courtney Johnson Clendinen, Jazmin Noble, Aja Holland, Carina Silva; Laura Ritland, Simpson Fellow; https://girlsinc-alameda.org/

Northgate High School, Mount Diablo Unified School District; David Wood, faculty; John James, Simpson Fellow; https://northgatehighschool.org/

Memoir Workshop at the Lafayette Library and Learning Center—

Joyce Carol Oates with Joseph Di Prisco;

Beth Needel, coordinator.

The Simpson Literary Project Board—

Diane Del Signore, Executive Director

Joseph Di Prisco, Chair; author and educator

Shanti Ariker, Attorney

Steven Justice, Professor of English, Chair of the English Department, UC Berkeley

Beth Needel, Executive Director, Lafayette Library and Learning Center Foundation

Joyce Carol Oates, teacher and author; Roger S. Berlind Professor of Humanities, Princeton University

Genaro Padilla, Professor of English; Vice Chancellor Emeritus; Chair Emeritus of the English Department, UC Berkeley

Vickie Sciacca, Manager, Lafayette Library and Learning Center

Pat Scott, Public Radio and Nonprofit Executive

Frank Starn, Finance Chair; CEO, PerceptiMed

David Wood, teacher, Northgate High School

Emeritus, Project Board—

Donald McQuade, author, English Professor, and Vice Chancellor Emeritus, UC Berkeley

Karen Mulvaney, Board Member, Lafayette Library and Learning Center Foundation

Scott Saul, author, English Professor, UC Berkeley

Project Team—

Diane Del Signore, Executive Director; diane@simpsonliteraryproject.org

Tyson Cornell, Rare Bird, Publisher, and Publicity; tyson@rarebirdlit.com

Christine McQuade Hsu, Digital Media; christine@simpsonliteraryproject.org

The Home Team—

Professor Ian Maloney, Saint Francis College, Brooklyn, New York; Noelle Burch; Professor Geoffrey O'Brien, UC Berkeley; Katharine Michaels; Kathi Bahr; Professor Scott Saul, UC Berkeley; Kim Dower; Anne Cain; Regan McMahon; Professor Donna Jones, UC Berkeley; Professor Joshua Gang, UC Berkeley; Professor Dora Zhang, UC Berkeley; Christine Raymond; Sarah Blumenfeld; Carrie Barlow

The Simpson Literary Project—

simpsonliteraryproject.org

With abundant, humble gratitude for the generous donors (as of this book release) who make possible the nonprofit Simpson Literary Project: https://www.simpsonliteraryproject.org/about

The Wood Family Foundation

Patti James

Simpson PSB Fund: Sharon Simpson

System Property Development Company

Richard Morrison; Mario & Jen Di Prisco; Janet & Norman Pease; Dodge & Cox; David Wood & Kathy Garrison; Karen & Tom Mulvaney; James & Katherine Moule; The McBurney Foundation; Tracey Borst & Robert Menicucci; Frank & Carey Starn; Mike & Ginny Ross

Ralph & Liz Long; Jim & Lela Barnes; Ellen & Joffa Dale; Anne & Marshall Grodin

Jacinta Pister & Richard Whitmore; Bill & Susan Caplan; A. R. Taylor; Katharine Ogden Michaels; Kathy & Anthony Laglia; Debbie Goldberg; Alice Breakstone; Eliot & Martha Hudson

PERMISSIONS

"'A Big, Beautiful Wall': Exclusion and Art along the US-Mexican Border," by Genaro Padilla, printed with permission of the author.

"Chinese Opera," by Anne Raeff, originally published in *The Jungle Around Us*, University of Georgia Press; reprinted with permission of the publisher and the author.

"La Florida," by Laila Lalami, excerpt from the novel *The Moor's Account,* published by Pantheon Books; reprinted with permission of the publisher and the author.

"The Grozny Tourist Bureau," by Anthony Marra, a story abridged from *The Tsar of Love and Techno,* originally published in *Zoetrope,* then published by Hogarth; reprinted with permission of the author.

"I Used to Be Brenda Starr, Reporter," by Beth Needel, printed with permission of the author.

Joyce Carol Oates & Anthony Marra: In Conversation, printed with permission of the participants.

"Little Albert, 1920," a poem by Joyce Carol Oates, printed with permission of the author.

"More Than Enough: Teaching with the Simpson Literary Project," by Laura Ritland, printed with permission of the author.

"Mussolini, McDonald's, and the Price of Happiness," by T. Geronimo Johnson, printed with permission of the author.

Lori Ostlund & Anne Raeff: In Conversation, printed with permission of the participants.

Poems by Kim Dower, from *Last Train to the Missing Planet* and *Sunbathing on Tyrone Power's Grave,* published by Red Hen Press; reprinted with permission of the publisher and the author.

Poems by John James, from *The Milk Hours,* published by Milkweed Editions; reprinted with permission of the publisher and the author.

"On Writing 'The Milk Hours,'" by John James, published on *Literary Hub* titled "Learning of My Father's Suicide from My Grandmother's Poetry"; reprinted with permission of the author.

"Teaching Voice," by David Wood, printed with permission of the author.

Where Night Stops, by Douglas Light, excerpt from the book published by Rare Bird Books; reprinted with permission of the publisher and the author.

"Worried Sisters," by Sigrid Nunez, published by *Prairie Schooner;* reprinted with permission of the author.

Student Workshop Writings: printed with permission of the authors.

THE STORY OF LA FLORIDA

BY LAILA LALAMI

2019 SIMPSON/JOYCE CAROL OATES PRIZE RECIPIENT

(Chapter 1, Excerpted from *The Moor's Account*)

It was the year 934 of the Hegira, the thirtieth year of my life, the fifth year of my bondage—and I was at the edge of the known world. I was marching behind Señor Dorantes in a lush territory he and Castilians like him called La Florida. I cannot be certain what my people call it. When I left Azemmur, news of this land did not often attract the notice of our town criers; they spoke instead of the famine, the recent earthquake, or the rebellions in the south of Barbary. But I imagine that, in keeping with our naming conventions, my people would simply call it the Land of the Indians. The Indians, too, must have had a name for it, although neither Señor Dorantes nor anyone in the expedition knew what it was.

Señor Dorantes had told me that La Florida was a large island, larger than Castile itself, and that it ran from the shore on which we had landed all the way to the Peaceful Sea. From one ocean to the other, was how he described it. All this land, he said, would now be governed by Pánfilo de Narváez, the commander of the armada. I thought it unlikely, or at least peculiar, that the Spanish king would allow one of his subjects to rule a territory larger than his own, but of course I kept my opinion to myself.

We were marching northward to the kingdom of Apalache. Señor Narváez had found out about it from some Indians he had captured after the armada arrived on the shore of La Florida. Even though I had not wanted to come here, I was relieved when the moment came to disembark, because the journey across the Ocean of Fog and Darkness had been marred by all the difficulties to be expected of such a passage: the hardtack was stale, the water murky, the latrines filthy. Narrow quarters made the passengers and crew especially irritable and almost every day a quarrel erupted. But the worst of it was the smell—the indelible scent of unwashed men, combined with the smoke from the braziers and the whiff of horse dung and chicken droppings that clung to the animal stalls in spite of daily cleanings—a pestilential mix that assaulted you the moment you stepped into the lower deck.

I was also curious about this land because I had heard, or overheard, from my master and his friends, so many stories about the Indians. The Indians, they said, had red skin and no eyelids; they were heathens who made human sacrifices and worshipped evil-looking gods; they drank mysterious concoctions that gave them visions; they walked about in their natural state, even the women—a claim I had found so hard to believe that I had dismissed it out of hand. Yet I had become captivated. This land had become for me not just a destination, but a place of complete fantasy, a place that could have existed only in the imagination of itinerant storytellers in the souqs of Barbary. This was how the journey across the Ocean of Fog and Darkness worked on you, even if you had never wanted to undertake it. The ambition of the others tainted you, slowly and irrevocably.

The landing itself was restricted to a small group of officers and soldiers from each ship. As captain of the Gracia de Dios, Señor Dorantes had chosen twenty men, among whom this servant of God, Mustafa ibn Muhammad, to be taken on one of the rowboats to the beach. My master stood at the fore of the vessel, one hand on his hip, the other resting on the pommel of his sword; the posture seemed to me so perfect an expression of his eagerness to claim the treasures of the new world that he might have been posing for an unseen sculptor.

It was a fine morning in spring; the sky was an indifferent blue and the water was clear. From the beach, we slowly made our way to a fishing village one of the sailors had sighted from the height of the foremast, and which was located about a crossbow shot from the shore. My first impression was of the silence all around us. No, silence is not the right word. There was the sound of waves, after all, and a soft breeze rustled the leaves of the palm trees. Along the path, curious seagulls came to watch us and departed again in a flutter of wings. But I felt a great absence.

In the village were a dozen huts, built with wooden poles and covered with palm fronds. They were arranged in a wide circle, with space enough in between each pair of homes to allow for the cooking and storing of food. The fire pits that dotted the perimeter of the clearing contained fresh logs, and there were three skinned deer hanging from a rail, their blood still dripping onto the earth, but the village was deserted. Still, the governor ordered a complete search. The huts turned up tools for cooking and cleaning, in addition to animal hides and furs, dried fish and meat, and great quantities of sunflower seeds, nuts, and fruit. At once the soldiers took possession of whatever they could; each one jealously clutched what he had stolen and traded it for the things he wanted. I took nothing and I had nothing to barter, but I felt ashamed, because I had been made a witness to these acts of theft and, unable to stop them, an accomplice to them as well.

As I stood with my master outside one of the huts, I noticed a pile of fishing nets. It was while lifting one up to look at its peculiar threading that I found an odd little pebble. At first, it seemed to me that it was a weight, but the nets had smooth stone anchors, quite unlike this one, which was yellow and rough-edged. Then I thought it might be a child's toy, for it looked like it could be part of a set of marbles or that it could fit inside a rattle; it might have been left on the fishing nets by mistake. I held it up to the light to get a better look, but Señor Dorantes saw it.

Estebanico, my master said. What did you find?

Estebanico was the name the Castilians had given me when they bought me from Portuguese traders—a string of sounds whose foreignness still grated on my ears. When I fell into slavery, I was forced to give up not just my freedom but also the name that my mother and father had chosen for me. A name is precious; it carries inside it a language, a history, a set of traditions, a particular way of looking at the world. Losing it meant losing my ties to all those things too. So I had never been able to shake the feeling that this Estebanico was a man conceived by the Castilians, quite different from the man I really was. My master snatched the pebble from my hand. What is this? he asked.

It is nothing, Señor.

Nothing?

Just a pebble.

Let me see. He scratched at the pebble with a fingernail, revealing, under the layer of dirt, a brighter shade of yellow. He was an inquisitive man, my master, always asking questions about everything. Perhaps this was why he had decided to set aside the comfort of his stately home in Béjar del Castañar and make his fortune in an uncharted territory. I did not resent his curiosity about the new world, but I envied the way he spoke about his hometown—it was, always, with the expectation of a glorious return.

It is nothing, I said again.

I am not so sure.

It must be pyrite.

But it might be gold. He turned the pebble around and around between his fingers, unsure what to do with it. Then, suddenly making up his mind, he ran up to Señor Narváez, who was standing in the village square, waiting for his men to complete their search. Don Pánfilo, my master called. Don Pánfilo.

I should describe the governor for you. The most striking thing about his face was the black patch over his right eye. It gave him a fearsome look, but it seemed to me his sunken cheeks and his small chin did not particularly reinforce it. On most days, even when there was no need for it, he wore a steel helmet adorned with ostrich feathers. Over his breastplate, a blue sash ran from his shoulder to his thigh and was tied with flourish over his hip. He looked like a man who had taken great pains with his appearance, yet he was also capable of the same coarseness as the lowliest of his soldiers. I had once seen him plug one nostril with a finger and send out a long string of snot shooting out of the other, all while discussing shipping supplies with one of his captains.

Señor Narváez received the pebble with greedy fingers. There was some more holding up to the light, some more scratching. This is gold, he said solemnly. The pebble sat like an offering in his palm. When he spoke again, his voice was hoarse. Good work, Capitán Dorantes. Good work.

The officers gathered excitedly around the governor, while a soldier ran back to the beach to tell the others about the gold. I stood behind Señor Dorantes, shaded from the sun by his shadow and, although I could not see his face, I knew that it was full of pride. I had been sold to him a year earlier, in Seville, and since then I had learnt how to read him, how to tell whether he was happy or only satisfied, angry or mildly annoyed, worried or barely concerned—gradations of feelings that could translate into actions toward me. Now, for instance, he was pleased with my discovery, but his vanity prevented him from saying that it was I who had found the gold. I had to remain quiet, make myself unnoticed for a while, let him bask, alone, in the glory of the find.

Moments later, the governor ordered the rest of the armada to disembark. It took three days to shuttle all the people, horses, and supplies to the white, sandy beach. As more and more people arrived, they somehow huddled around the familiar company of those closest to them in station: the governor usually stood with his captains, in their armor and plumed helmets; the commissary conversed with the four friars, all wearing identical brown robes; the horsemen gathered with the men of arms, each of them carrying his weapon—a musket, an arquebus, a crossbow, a sword, a steel-pointed lance, a dagger, or even a butcher's hatchet. Then there were the settlers, among whom carpenters, metalworkers, cobblers, bakers, farmers, merchants, and many others whose occupations I never determined or quickly forgot. There were also ten women and thirteen children, standing in throngs, surrounded by their wooden chests. But the fifty or so slaves, including this servant of God, Mustafa ibn Muhammad, were scattered, each one standing near the man who owned him, carrying his luggage or watching his belongings.

By the time everyone had congregated on the beach, it was late afternoon on the third day, and the tide was low. The waves were small, and a dark strip of shoreline was exposed. The weather had cooled; now the sand was cold and sticky under my feet. High clouds had gathered in the sky, turning the sun into a faint, distant orb. A thick fog drifted in from the ocean, slowly washing the color out of the world around us, rendering it in various shades of white and gray. It was very quiet.

The notary of the armada, a stocky man with owlish eyes by the name of Jerónimo de Albaniz, stepped forward. Facing Señor Narváez, he unrolled a scroll and began to read in a monotone voice. On behalf of the King and Queen, we wish to make it known that this land belongs to God our Lord, Living and Eternal. God has appointed one man, called St. Peter, to be the governor of all the men in the world, wherever they should live, and under whatever law, sect, or belief they should be. The successor of St. Peter in this role is our Holy Father, the Pope, who has made a donation of this terra firma to the King and Queen. Therefore, we ask and require that you acknowledge the Church as the ruler of this world, and the priest whom we call Pope, and the King and Queen, as lords of this territory. Señor Albaniz stopped speaking now and, without asking for permission or offering an apology, he took a sip of water from a flask hanging from his shoulder.

I watched the governor's face. He seemed annoyed with the interruption, but he held back from saying anything, as it would only delay the proceedings further. Or maybe he did not want to upset the notary. After all, without notaries and record-keepers, no one would know what governors did. A measure of patience and respect, however small, was required.

Unhurriedly Señor Albaniz wiped his mouth with the back of his hand and resumed speaking. If you do as we say, you will do well and we shall receive you in all love and charity. But if you refuse to comply, or maliciously delay in it, we inform you that we will make war against you in all manners that we can and shall take your wives and children, and shall make slaves of them, and shall take away your goods, and shall do you all the mischief and damage that we can. And if this should happen, we protest that the deaths and losses will be your fault, and not that of their Highnesses, or of the cavaliers here present. Now that we have said this to you, we request the notary to give us his testimony in writing and the rest who are present to be witnesses of this Requisition.

Until Señor Albaniz had arrived at the promises and threats, I had not known that this speech was meant for the Indians. Nor could I understand why it was given here, on this beach, if its intended recipients had already fled their village. How strange, I remember thinking, how utterly strange were the ways of the Castilians—just by saying that something was so, they believed that it was. I know now that these conquerors, like many others before them, and no doubt like others after, gave speeches not to voice the truth, but to create it.

At last, Señor Albaniz fell silent. He presented the scroll and waited, head bowed, while Señor Narváez signed his name on the requisition. Facing the crowd, the governor announced that this village would henceforth be known as Portillo. The captains inclined their heads and a soldier raised the standard, a green piece of fabric with a red shield in its center. I was reminded of the moment, many years earlier, when the flag of the Portuguese king was hoisted over the fortress tower in Azemmur. I had been only a young boy then, but I still lived with the humiliation of that day, for it had changed my family's fate, disrupted our lives, and cast me out of my home. Now, halfway across the world, the scene was repeating itself on a different stage, with different people. So I could not help feeling a sense of dread at what was yet to come.

My fears were confirmed early the next morning, when we heard a commotion behind the village storehouse. Señor Dorantes had wanted me to give him a haircut, and I had just begun to trim the edges of his thick, wheat-colored hair. His beard had grown, too, but he had not asked me to shave it. Perhaps he felt that he did not need to worry about matters of grooming now that he had reached the edge of the empire. Or he grew his beard because he could and the Indians, it was rumored, could not. I confess I did not ask him why; I was relieved to have fewer chores. But when we heard the cries of soldiers, Señor Dorantes shot to his feet, with the white linen cloth still tied around his neck, and ran across the square to see what had happened. I followed him, with the Sevillian scissors still in my hand. The soldiers, it turned out, had found some Indians hiding in the bushes and had captured four of them.

All four were men. All four were naked. I had seen Indians before, on the islands of Cuba and La Española, where the armada had stopped to purchase more supplies, but never at such close range. I was unused to seeing men walk about in their natural state, unashamed of their bodies, so my first impulse was to stare. They were tall and broad-shouldered, with skin the color of earth when it has rained. Their hair was glossy and long, and on their right arms and left legs, they had tattoos in shapes I did not recognize. One of them had a lazy eye, just like my uncle Omar, and he blinked in order to focus his gaze on his captors. Another was surveying the village, taking stock of all that had changed: a large cross had been set up by the temple; the governor's standard hung from a pole in the square; and, along the perimeter, horses were tethered to newly built posts. The stories I had heard about the Indians had me expecting something incredible, fire-breathing jinns perhaps, but these men looked harmless to me—especially next to the Castilian soldiers. Still, they were tied up and brought to Señor Narváez.

From his pocket, the governor retrieved the pebble of gold I had found. Holding it up in his palm, he asked them about it. Where did you find this gold?

The captives looked at him levelly and two of them said something in their mother tongue. I could not detect a pattern yet to the stream of sounds that emerged from their lips—where did one word end and another one begin? My upbringing in a trading town like Azemmur had instilled in me a love of language and, if I may be forgiven for this moment of immodesty, a certain ease with it. So I was curious about the Indians' tongue, even though it had none of the clues that had been helpful to me when I learned new idioms: familiar sounds, a few words in common, a similar intonation. But, to my surprise, the governor nodded slowly, as if he understood the Indians perfectly and even agreed with them.

Still, he repeated his question. Where did you find this gold?

Behind him, the soldiers watched and waited. Up in the trees, birds were singing, determined in their trills despite the oppressive heat. The soothing sound of waves came from the beach nearby and I could smell smoke in the air—someone had already started a fire for the almuerzo. Again, the Indians answered the governor in the same way as before. At least, I assumed they were answering; it was just as likely that they were asking the governor a question of their own, or challenging him to a fight, or threatening him with death if he did not release them.

The governor listened politely to their answers and then he turned to his page. Lock them up in the storehouse, he said, and bring me a whip.

Señor Dorantes returned to his seat, and again I had to follow. Neither one of us spoke. I finished cutting his hair, handing him a small mirror and holding another one behind him. I saw both of our reflections on these opposing mirrors. My master looked satisfied with the haircut, nodding appreciatively as he turned his face this way and that. His beard nearly hid the scar on his right cheek, a scar, I once heard him proudly tell one of his dinner guests, he had sustained years earlier in Castile, when he had helped put down a rebellion against the king. As for me, my bondage had taught me to keep an impassive face, but in the mirror I noticed that my eyes betrayed my anxiety. I told myself that I had merely been curious about the kind of fishnets the Indians used. I had not been looking for gold. Yet the pebble I had found had caused these four men, men who had done me no harm, to be whipped. I had to pretend, like my master, not to hear the cries that had begun to emerge from the storehouse. Within moments, they had turned into howls, so long and so filled with pain that I felt they were echoing in the depths of my own soul. And then, interrupted by the periodic and terrifying crack of the whip, there was only silence.

Later, when I was helping Señor Dorantes into his boots, I overheard his younger brother, Diego, a quiet lad of sixteen or seventeen years of age, ask him about the governor's encounter with the Indians. Diego was so different from Señor Dorantes it was a wonder to me that they were blood brothers. Where one was shy and guileless, the other was bold and crafty. Where one was selective in his friendships, the other was quick to love and quick to hate. And yet Diego patterned himself after his older brother in whatever way he could. He wore his doublet unbuttoned at the top and his helmet tilted back, like a weary soldier. He had tried to grow his beard, too, but so far only scattered patches of hair had sprouted on his cheeks. Hermano, Diego said. When did Don Pánfilo learn their language? Has he been to La Florida before?

Señor Dorantes gave Diego an amused look, but he must have thought the question harmless, for he answered it presently. No, this is his first time here, just like us. But he has a lot of experience with the savages. He can make himself understood quite well by them, and he rarely fails to obtain the facts he seeks.

This made no sense to me, yet I remained silent, for I knew that my master would not take kindly to being challenged about the governor's language abilities. The elders teach us: a living dog is better than a dead lion.

But why must he whip them? Diego insisted.

Because the Indians are known liars, Señor Dorantes replied. Take these four. They are likely spies, sent here to watch us and report on our movements. Slowly, almost imperceptibly, my master's tone had shifted from amusement to mild irritation. He stood up and ran a finger along the top edge of his boots, making sure his breeches were properly tucked in. To get the truth, he said, it is necessary to flog them.

The governor had whipped the four prisoners until he was satisfied that they had given him the whole truth. Armed with it, he called a gathering of all the officers that evening. They met in the largest lodge in the village, a kind of temple that could have easily accommodated a hundred people, though only a dozen high-ranking men had been invited: the commissary, the treasurer, the tax inspector, the notary, and the captains, among whom was Señor Dorantes. Wooden statues of panthers, their eyes painted yellow and their arms bearing war clubs, had been removed earlier in the day, along with the hand drums that, I imagined, were used in heathen ceremonies. So the temple was bare now. But the ceiling attracted my eye: it was decorated with a multitude of inverted seashells that cast a faint gleam on the ground.

One by one, the Spanish officers took their seats on Indian stools that had been arranged in a circle. The governor's page had covered a long bench with a white tablecloth and placed lit candelabras on either end of it. Now he served dinner—grilled fish, boiled rice, cured pork, and fresh and dried fruit from the village storehouse. At the sight of the food, I felt hungrier than I had in many days, but I had to wait until after the dinner before I could eat my meager rations.

Standing before his officers, Señor Narváez announced that the pebble of gold came from a rich kingdom called Apalache. This kingdom was located two weeks' march north of this village, and its capital city had great quantities of gold, as well as silver, copper, and other fine metals. There were large, cultivated fields of corn and beans around the city, and many people who tended them, and it was also near a river filled with fish of all kinds. The Indians' testimony, which the governor asked Señor Albaniz to record, had convinced him that the kingdom of Apalache was as rich as that of Moctezuma.

This word had the effect of a cannon shot. It seemed to me that the entire party greeted it with awe, and I admit that I, too, gasped with wonder, for in Seville I had heard many stories about the rich emperor whose palace was covered with gold and silver. The captains' excitement was so contagious that I found myself daydreaming. What if, I thought, the Castilians conquered this kingdom? What if Señor Dorantes were to become one of the richest men in this part of the empire? The reckless hope came to me that he might, as a gesture of gratitude or goodwill, or even as a celebration of his gold and glory, free the slave who had set him on this path. How easily I slipped into this fantasy! I would be able to leave La Florida on a vessel bound for Seville, and from there travel back to Azemmur, the city at the edge of the old continent. I would be able to return home to my family, to hold them and be held by them, to run my fingers along the uneven edge of the tiled wall in the courtyard, to hear the sound of the Umm er-Rbi' when it is swollen with spring runoff, to sit on the rooftop of our home on warm summer nights, when the air is filled with the smell of ripening figs. I would once again speak the language of my forefathers and find comfort in the traditions I had been forced to cast aside. I would live out the rest of my days among my people. The fact that none of this had been promised or suggested did not dampen my yearning. And, in my moment of greed, I forgot about the cost of my dream to others.

The officers raised their glasses to the governor, to thank him for the good tidings he had brought, and the slaves, including this servant of God, Mustafa ibn Muhammad, refilled them with wine. (Reader, it is not easy for me to confess that I served the forbidden drink, but I have decided in this relation to tell everything that happened to me, so I must not leave out even such a detail.) However, the governor said, raising his palms to quiet the assembly, there was one complication. The armada was too large: four caravels and one brigantine, six hundred men and eighty horses, fifty thousand arrobas of supplies and weapons. It was not suitable for the mission at hand.

So he had decided to split it into two contingents, each roughly the same size. The first of these was the sea contingent, with the sailors, the women and children, and anyone who suffered from a cold or a fever or was otherwise too weak to continue. These people would sail along the coast of La Florida to the nearest town in New Spain, which was the port of Pánuco, at the mouth of the Río de las Palmas. There, they would set their anchor and wait. The second contingent, that is to say, the able-bodied men who could walk, ride a horse, or carry food and water, weapons and ammunition, would march inland to Apalache, secure it, and then send forward a smaller group to meet the sea party. The governor invited the captains to select the best men from among those who had traveled on their ships.

Silence fell upon the assembly. Then, all at once, several captains raised their objections to this plan, particularly a young man who was a close friend of my master's. His name was Señor Castillo and he had joined the expedition on a whim, after hearing about it at a banquet in Seville. His voice had a nasal tone that made him sound like a child, and indeed he was a slight man who looked barely out of his teenage years. I remember he stood up from his seat and asked if it was not too risky to send all the ships and supplies away while we went on a mission to the interior. We have no map, he said. No means to resupply ourselves if the mission takes longer than we expect. And no agreement among our pilots about how far Pánuco is. Señor Castillo spoke with candor and without a hint of animosity; the others who had also objected to the plan were quiet now, tacitly allowing him to speak for them all.

We may not have maps, Señor Narváez replied pleasantly, but we have the four Indians. The padres will teach them our language, so that they can serve as guides and translators. As for the length of the mission, you have seen with your own eyes how poorly armed the savages are. It will not take us long to subdue them. The governor was not in his armor that night. He wore a black doublet, whose sleeves he periodically tugged and straightened. Now, he said, let us discuss how we will divide our numbers.

Señor Castillo ran his fingers through his mass of brown hair—a nervous habit. Forgive me, Don Pánfilo, he said. But I am still not convinced that we should send away the ships when the three pilots disagree about how far we are from New Spain.

We are not far from the port of Pánuco, the governor said. The chief pilot said it is only twenty leagues from here. The other pilots think it might be twenty-five. I would not call that a disagreement.

Surely you are not suggesting that we send the ships away, just like that?

Out of his good eye, the governor gave Señor Castillo a piercing look. That is precisely what I am suggesting.

What if the ships get lost on the way to the port? Some of us have invested large sums in these ships. We cannot afford to lose them.

I will not be lectured about the cost of the vessels, Castillo. I have put all my fortune in this expedition, too. The governor looked around him, enjoining all the officers who were present to share in his bafflement. Señores, my plan is simple. We march to the kingdom of Apalache, while the ships wait for us at a safe and secure port, where the crew can procure any supplies we might need. I used the same strategy in my Cuba campaign, fifteen years ago. Now the governor smiled nostalgically at the memory of his past glory and then, addressing himself only to Señor Castillo, he added: Probably when you were still a baby.

Señor Castillo sat down, his face the color of beets.

The governor's plan may have seemed bold to the young captain, but I knew that it had been tested. Before marching to Tenochtitlán to claim the riches of Moctezuma, Hernán Cortés had scuttled his ships in the port of Veracruz. And, seven centuries earlier, Tariq ibn Ziyad had burned his boats on the shores of Spain. In truth, Señor Narváez's plan was quite cautious, for he was only sending the ships to wait for us at the nearest port, where they could resupply. So I did not share Señor Castillo's fears, and a part of me even resented him for wanting to delay the journey to the kingdom of gold and thereby defer my dreams of freedom.

But Señor Castillo appealed to Señor Cabeza de Vaca, who sat across from him. Do you not agree that we are taking an unnecessary risk? he asked.

Señor Cabeza de Vaca was the treasurer of the expedition, charged with collecting the king's share of any wealth acquired in La Florida. Rumor had it that he was close to the governor, so most of the men feared him, even as they made jokes behind his back about his unusual name, calling him Cabeza de Mono, on account of his ears, which protruded like that of a monkey. Señor Cabeza de Vaca laced his fingers together; they were white and smooth and his nails were clean. He had the hands of a nobleman.

There is indeed a risk, he said. There is always a risk. But the Indians of this territory know about our presence now. We must start marching right away, before the king of Apalache can raise a large army against us or make alliances with any neighbors. We cannot squander a chance to take Apalache for His Majesty. Señor Cabeza de Vaca spoke with the innocence of a man in thrall to lofty ideas, ideas that could not be tainted by banal concerns about ships. Some of the captains nodded in agreement, for the treasurer was a thoughtful and experienced man who wielded a lot of influence among them.

The candles had burned down to their wicks and it was in the last, flickering light that the commissary lowered his rope belt below his paunch and began to speak. From the beginning, he said, this journey has been a trial. It has taken us nearly a year to travel from Castile, recruit pilots knowledgeable about the western seas, and secure enough weapons and horses. The expedition has already lost many members to defection or disease and it would be particularly sinful now that we have reached La Florida to delay the will of the Lord any longer. The sooner we find Apalache and begin a Christian settlement, the better.

The rest of the council was quiet now. Señor Narváez cleared his throat. I need someone to take charge of the ships while we march to Apalache. So if Castillo would rather not venture inland…

The insult in the governor's offer was barely hidden.

Don Pánfilo, Señor Castillo said, his manner completely changed. He stood up, ready to defend his honor. No, he said.

He will go, Señor Dorantes added, his hand on his friend's elbow, to stop him from saying anything to further damage his reputation.

So it was that the governor sent the ships to the port of Pánuco, while he led the officers and the soldiers, the friars and the settlers, the porters and the servants deep into the wilderness of La Florida—a long procession of three hundred souls looking for the kingdom of gold.

All around us, the land was flat and dense. In places where the sunlight penetrated the canopy of trees, it was colored a faded green, or sometimes a sickly yellow. The sound of the horses' hooves was muffled by the soft ground, but the soldiers' songs, coarse and loud, the creaking of the officers' armor, the clanging of the tools inside the settlers' bags—all these announced the passage of our company in the lush sea of green. Behind the trees, a quiet swamp often awaited, surrounded by exposed roots and overhung with slimy branches. After each crossing, I emerged covered with gray mud, which caked on my legs and in between my toes, making me nearly mad with the urge to scratch.

Once, when we were crossing a large swamp, a slave by the name of Agostinho—a man like me, whom greed and circumstance had brought from Ifriqiya to La Florida—called for help with the heavy burlap bag he was carrying over his head. I walked toward him, past a clump of white flowers whose fragrance I found intoxicating. The swamp bubbled around us, as if it were taking a deep, restful breath. My hands were almost on the burlap bag when a green monster leapt out of the water and sank its teeth into Agostinho. There was a clear snap of bones breaking, a gush of blood hitting the surface, and Agostinho went down with a gasp. I ran out of the swamp as fast as my legs could carry me, my heart consumed with the same boundless terror I had felt as a boy, when my mother told the ghoulish tales she reserved for the early evenings of winter, tales in which, unfailingly, children who dared to go into the forest were eaten by strange creatures. I reached dry land and collapsed, in time to see the beast disappear, beating its tail in the muddy water.

In the language of the Castilians, as in mine, there was no word yet for this animal, no way to talk about it without saying, the Water Animal with Scaly Skin, a cumbersome expression that would not work for long now that the Spaniards had declared their dominion over La Florida. So they gave new names to everything around them, as though they were the All-Knowing God in the Garden of Delights. Walking back to the edge of the swamp, the governor asked whose slave that was and what was in the burlap bag. Someone told him: the dead slave belonged to a settler; the bag was full of pots, dishes, and utensils. All right, the governor said, his voice tinged with annoyance. This animal, he announced, would be called El Lagarto because it looked like a giant lizard. It was not a name the expedition's notary needed to record. Everyone would remember it.

But the lagartos were not the only impediments to the governor's march. The rations he had assigned were not large: each man was given two pounds of biscuit and half a pound of cured pork, and each servant or slave, half that. So the men were always looking for ways to supplement their meals, particularly with hare or deer, but very quickly the governor forbade those who had bows or muskets from using them; he wanted them to save their ammunition in case the Indians of Apalache offered any resistance. I had no weapon; I had only my walking staff. With it, I could occasionally disturb a bird's nest and eat the eggs it held. Sometimes, I picked the fruit of the palm trees, which were smaller and thicker than those of my hometown, or I tried the berries of unfamiliar bushes, tasting only one or two before daring to eat them in greater quantities.

Señor Dorantes, of course, had no such troubles. Because he had invested some of his own money in this expedition, he and others like him received larger rations. He rode comfortably on his horse, Abejorro—a gray Andalusian with smart eyes, dark legs, and a good carriage—and tried to stave off the boredom by chatting with his younger brother Diego. On the whole, however, he seemed to prefer the company of Señor Castillo, often nudging his horse to keep up with his friend's white mare. As for me, I walked where Señor Dorantes had told me to: at all times, I was to be one step behind him. He was not satisfied just to travel through this wondrous land and to seek a share of its kingdom of gold, he wanted a witness for his ambitions; he felt himself at the center of great new things and so he needed an audience, even when there was nothing for him to do but march.

One fine morning, about two weeks into the march, we came upon a wide river. The sun glazed its surface a blinding white, but if you stood at the edge of the water you could see that it was very fast and so clear that you could count all the black pebbles at the bottom. The governor announced that this river would be called the Río Oscuro, on account of its multitude of black rocks, but the men barely paused to listen. Agua, por fin, they said, and Gracias a Dios and Déjame pasar, hombre!

Señor Dorantes dismounted, and I led Abejorro to the water, wading in myself to wash the gray mud off my legs and sandals. I thought we would rest on the riverbank for a while, but the governor ordered his carpenters to begin constructing rafts immediately, in order to transport those who could not swim—that is to say, most of the men—across the water. It was late spring and the days were longer, but sunlight had already begun to turn amber by the time the rafts were finally ready and the first groups of men crossed the river.

The other bank was flat and bare, with only a few tufts of grass jutting out here and there, but farther ahead a screen of green stalks showed where the wilderness began again. A cool breeze blew, rustling the edges of the pine trees in the horizon. I could feel it through the coarse fabric of my shirt as I adjusted the saddle on Abejorro and rubbed his neck. The officers and soldiers, who had been the first to be shuttled across the river, huddled together: the governor was having a long conversation with the commissary, his head inclined sideways toward the short friar, as if he could hear from only one ear; Señor Dorantes was showing Señor Castillo how to tie his cuirass so that it would not chafe against his skin; two men were arguing about a set of horse spurs.

Then a band of Indians emerged from behind the wall of trees, silently gathering on the field. Some were naked, but others wore, over their shameful parts, animal hides painted in patterns of blue and red. They held weapons made of animal bone and fire-hardened wood—lances, bows, or slingshots—but they did not threaten us. There were as many as a hundred of them. For a moment, each side regarded the other with the curiosity of a child who sees his reflection in the mirror for the first time. Then, unhurriedly, the governor climbed on his horse and the officers who had their mounts did the same. The page pulled the flagpole from the ground where it had been stuck and lifted it up; the standard of the governor whipped in the breeze.

Albaniz, the governor called.

In addition to being the official notary of the expedition, charged with the safekeeping of all its contracts and petitions, Señor Albaniz was also responsible for chronicling its progress for the next few months. His presence at this moment, our first encounter with an Indian nation, made me think of my father, who had dreamed of me becoming, like him, a notary public, a witness and recorder of major events in other people's lives. I felt as though my father's aspiration, which I had so easily and so carelessly brushed off many years ago, would never let go of me, that I would be reminded of it wherever I went, even here, in this strange land. But perhaps my father's dreams for me have come true in the end, for here I am setting down, for my own reasons, a relation of the Narváez expedition.

Tell the savages, the governor said, to take me to Apalache. He considered it beneath him to speak directly to the Indians.

With the look of a servant who has found himself chosen for a tedious chore, Señor Albaniz dismounted and stepped forward. This, he said, pointing behind him, is Pánfilo de Narváez, the new governor of this terra firma, by virtue of the bequest made to him by his Holy Imperial Majesty. He wishes to go to the kingdom of Apalache and to meet with its leader in order to discuss matters of great importance to our nations. He wants you to take him there.

Whether the Indians did not understand the notary's command or refused to comply with it, I could not guess. They remained silent. I looked for their leader, but I could not make out if it was the man who wore a headdress of stiff animal hair or the one who had the greatest number of tattoos.

Take us to the kingdom of Apalache, Señor Albaniz said, louder this time, his hands cupped around his mouth so that his voice could carry farther. One of the Indians sat on his haunches, enjoying the spectacle of this man in a metal costume and a feathered hat, crying and gesticulating before him.

Kingdom of Apalache! Señor Albaniz yelled again.

By then, the rafts had made another crossing, and more people disembarked—soldiers, settlers, servants, and captives. They joined our party without speaking; now we outnumbered the Indians.

You can stop, Albaniz, the governor said. He looked behind him. Bring me the captives.

The order was passed down, and a foot soldier brought forth the prisoners. Because I was always with my master, near the head of our long procession, I had not seen the prisoners since our departure from Portillo, the fishing village. They shuffled forward now, their hands bound by a length of rope that was tied to the soldier's belt. Their bodies were crisscrossed by lash marks and their limbs thinned down by the smallest of all the rations. One of the prisoners bowed his head in a way that struck me as unnatural until I noticed the hole where his nose should have been. Snot and blood caked at the edges of the gap. Flies darted around him relentlessly, but he could not swat them because his hands were tied. I averted my eyes from the horror, feeling as if I were witnessing something I should never have seen.

The prisoners came to stand next to Señor Albaniz, who spoke directly to one of them. Pablo, he said. Tell them to take us to Apalache.

The man Señor Albaniz had called Pablo, a lad whose long, glossy hair had been sheared and whose shoulders were covered with blisters, commenced to speak in his mother tongue, but almost immediately a lance surged in the air from the Indian side and the foot soldier who had been holding him by the arm lurched forward and tumbled to the ground, clutching his throat. An arrow had gone through his neck, its tip coming out on the other side. The soldier opened his mouth wide, but the only sound that came out was the bubbling of the blood inside. Now the Indians let out great howling cries, cries that sparked in me a nearly paralyzing fear.

My God, Señor Albaniz said, turning around and looking for his horse.

Ándale! the governor shouted.

Señor Dorantes nudged his horse forward and I felt Abejorro's tail swish across my chest as I turned to look for cover, though there was no place to hide. I tried to run back toward the river, but the crowd of Castilians who were moving forward pressed against me, their bodies bearing down on mine with such strength that I had no other choice but to sink to my knees. The air above me exploded with the sound of muskets. One of the soldiers next to me, a boy of no more than fifteen or sixteen years of age, raised his weapon and fired, but it was one of his own comrades who fell down. I could hear the Indian warriors advancing behind me, their unintelligible cries no longer in need of any translation.

Somehow, I made my way to a pack load, crates that held carpentry tools, and I cowered behind them. I would be safe here, I thought. Then I heard a labored grunt. Past a thicket of weeds on my left, not ten steps away from me, a settler was fighting an Indian. The settler had a trowel, which he was trying to land somewhere on the Indian. He missed. But the Indian's aim was unswerving and when he brought his hatchet down, he severed the settler's arm neatly at the elbow. Another blow to the head and the settler fell to the ground, eyes still open.

The Indian turned around, looking for another adversary. I flattened my back against the pack load. He seemed surprised when he saw me—a black man among white men. The color of my skin, so different from that of the others, made him pause. And I, as I said, had no weapon. He seemed unsure whether to leave me or kill me, but he decided on the latter, for he took a step forward with his hatchet raised. As he brought it down, I rolled to the side and he fell on top of me, his weight landing on my hip, his long hair falling on my eyes and blinding me. I could smell him—his sweat, his breathless anger, the snakeskin belt tied around his loins. We wrestled on the ground and I pressed the heel of my hand against his jaw, though my palm slipped against his hairless face. He punched me; I punched back. Still, he managed to right himself up and stand, with his hatchet drawn again. I thought my hour had come, but God willed that a stray musket ball brought him down. He fell forward and his hatchet grazed my leg, leaving a shallow cut along my shin. I cried out. I do not remember what I said; I imagine it was nothing at all, just the cry of relief at having survived the attack. Then I took the weapon by its handle and, trying to contain the fear inside me, I resolved to defend myself.

I raised myself upon my knees to peer over the stack of crates at the battlefield. Soldiers in armor were firing their crossbows and muskets, and the Indians were fighting back with their lances and arrows. Here and there, a few Indians had managed to inflict grievous harm—a Castilian in a rusty helmet tottered from his mount, his hands gripping the lance that had landed on his thigh; another had fallen from a slingshot strike—but more often, the Indians suffered injury. I remember that one of them, his bowels slipping out from his stomach, was holding on to himself with both arms. Another one screamed as a soldier straddled him and smashed his body with a mace.

I was not a man of arms and I knew nothing of battles, but I could see that this was not a fair match, that the Indians had no hope of winning. Soon, I found myself searching the dusty field for my master, the man to whom my mortal fate was tied. Where was he? Then I saw him, past the line of crossbowmen, riding on his horse. With his sword, he hacked an Indian on the shoulders until blood sprayed out from him. The man fell down to his knees, and Señor Dorantes trampled him as he moved on to the next. The other horsemen, too, had come upon the same solution; they crushed the Indians before them on the field in a wide stampede.

Then there came the sound of a horn and the Indians began to retreat. The sun had set now and it was difficult for me to make out the faces of all those who lay on the ground. As I walked, I was guided more by the sound of soldiers knocking the Indians about and the smell of dust and smoke than I was by sight alone. O Lord, I thought, what am I doing here in this strange land, in the middle of a battle between two foreign peoples? How did it get to this? I was still standing there, stunned and motionless, when torches were lit and names were called. Settlers and friars trickled in from wherever they had found some cover—a crate, a tree, or even a corpse. Behind us, the Río Oscuro rumbled, flowing unceasingly toward the ocean.

THE GROZNY TOURIST BUREAU

BY ANTHONY MARRA

2018 SIMPSON/JOYCE CAROL OATES PRIZE RECIPIENT

(A Story Abridged from *The Tsar of Love and Techno*)

The oilmen have arrived from Beijing. "It's a holiday for them," their translator told me, last night, at the Grozny Eternity Hotel, which is both the only five-star hotel and the only hotel in the republic. I nodded solemnly; he needn't explain. I came of age in the reign of Brezhnev, when young men would enter civil service academies hardy and robust, only to leave two years later anemic and stooped, cured forever of the inclination to be civil or of service to anyone. Still, Beijing must be grim if they're vacationing in Chechnya.

"We'll reach Grozny in ten minutes," I announce to them in English. The translator sits in the passenger's seat. He's a stalk-thin man with a head of hair so black and lustrous it looks sculpted from shoe polish. I feel a shared camaraderie with translators—as I do with deputies and underlings of all stripes—and as he speaks in slow, measured Mandarin, I hear the resigned and familiar tone of a man who knows he is more intelligent than his superiors.

The road winds over what was once a roof. A verdigris-encrusted arm rises from the debris, its forefinger raised skyward. The Lenin statue had stood in the square outside this school, arm upthrust, rallying the schoolchildren to glorious revolution, but now, buried to his chin like a cowboy sentenced to death beneath the desert sun, Vladimir Ilyich waves only for help. We drive onward, passing brass bandoliers and olive flak jackets, red bandannas and golden epaulettes, the whole palette of Russian invasion painted across a thunderstorm of wreckage. Upon seeing the 02 Interior Ministry plate dangling below the Mercedes's hood, the spies, soldiers, policemen, and armed thugs wave us through without hesitation. The streets become more navigable.

"A large mass grave was recently discovered outside of Grozny, no?" the translator asks.

I hesitate, unsure how to spin this. "It's an archaeology site," I venture. "Thousands of years old. Like Stonehenge."

The translator frowns. "I thought Human Rights Watch has pushed for it to be treated as a crime scene?"

I shrug him off. Who am I to answer for the barbarities of prehistoric man?

We pass backhoes, dump trucks, and jackhammers through the metallic dissonance of reconstruction—a welcome song after months of screaming shells. We drive to the central square, once the hub of municipal government, now a brown field debossed with earthmover tracks. Nadya once lived just down the road. The oilmen climb out and frown at each other, then at the translator, and then finally at me.

Turning to the northeast, I point at a strip of blue sky wedged between two fat cumuli. "That was Hotel Kavkaz. Next to that, picture an apartment block. Before '91, only party members lived there; and after '91, only criminals. No one moved in or out."

None of the oilmen smile. The translator leans to me and whispers, "You are aware, of course, that these three gentlemen are esteemed members of the Communist Party of China."

"It's OK. I'm a limo driver."

The translator stares blankly.

"Lloyd from *Dumb and Dumber*?"

Nothing.

"Jim Carrey. A brilliant actor who embodies the senselessness of our era," I explain.

The interpreter doesn't bother translating. I continue to draw a map of the square by narration, but the oilmen can't see what I see. They witness only a barren expanse demolished by bomb and bulldozer.

"Come, comrades, use your imagination," I urge, but they return to the Mercedes, and I am talking solely to the translator, and then he returns to the Mercedes, and I am talking solely to myself.

◆◆◆

Three months ago, the minister told me his idea. The proposition was ludicrous, but I listened with the blank-faced complacency I had perfected throughout my twenty-three years as a public servant.

"The United Nations has named Grozny the most devastated city on earth," the minister explained between bites of moist trout. "As you might imagine, we have an image problem."

He loomed over his desk in a high-backed executive chair, while across from him I listened from an odd, leggy stool designed to make its occupant struggle to stay upright. The minister's path had first crossed mine fifteen years earlier, when he had sought my advice regarding a recently painted portrait of him and his sons, and I had sought his regarding a dacha near my home village. The portrait, which still hung on the far wall, depicted the three of them heroically bestriding the carcass of a slain brown bear that bore a striking resemblance to Yeltsin.

"Foreign investment," the minister continued. "We're living off Kremlin subsidies—but only a mousetrap offers cheese for free. Most others don't agree with me, but I believe we need to attract capital unconnected to the Kremlin if we're to achieve a degree of economic autonomy, and holding the record for the world's largest ruin isn't helping. Rosneft and Gazprom are both eying us, but if we can get the Chinese to lease drilling equipment on the sly, we might have enough leverage to earn a seat at the table. Have you heard of Oleg Voronov? He's on the Rosneft board, the fourteenth richest man in Russia, and one of the hawks who pushed for the 1994 invasion. He's also a vampire and he won't be happy till he sticks his fangs in our oil fields."

The minister set down his silverware and began sorting through the little bones on his plate, reconstructing the skeleton of the fish he had consumed. "If we're to entice foreign investment, we need to rebrand Chechnya as the Dubai of the Caucasus. Think 'Switzerland, without the roads.' That's where you come in. You're what—the director of the Museum of Regional Art?"

"Deputy director, sir," I said.

"That's right, deputy director. You did fine work sending those paintings to Moscow. A real PR coup. Even British newspapers wrote about the Tretyakov exhibit."

With a small nod, I accepted the compliment for what was the lowest point of my rut-ridden career. In 1999, Russian rockets demolished the museum, and with my staff I saved what I could from the ensuing fires. Soon after, I was ordered to surrender the salvaged works to the Russians. When I saw that I'd been listed as cocurator of an exhibit of Chechen paintings at Moscow's Tretyakov Gallery, I closed my lids and wondered what had happened to all the things my eyes had loved.

The minister tilted the plate over the rubbish bin, and the ribs slid from the spine of the fish. "Nothing suggests stability and peace like a thriving tourism sector," he said. "I think you'd be the perfect candidate to head the project."

"With respect, sir," I said. "The subject of my dissertation was nineteenth-century pastoral landscapes. I'm a scholar. This is all a bit beyond me."

"I'll be honest, Ruslan, for this position we need someone with three qualifications. He must speak English. He must know enough about the culture and history of the region to convey that Chechnya is much more than a recovering war zone, that we possess a rich heritage unsullied by violence. Most important, he must be that rare government man without links to human rights abuses on either side of the conflict. Do you meet these qualifications?"

"I do, sir," I said. "But still, I'm entirely unqualified to lead a tourism initiative."

The minister frowned. He scanned the desk for a napkin before reaching over to wipe his oily fingers on my necktie. "According to your dossier, you've worked in hotels."

"When I was sixteen."

"Well," the minister beamed, "then you clearly have experience in the hospitality industry."

"I was a bellhop."

"So you accept?"

I said nothing, and as is often the case with men who possess more power than wisdom, he took my silence for affirmation. "Congratulations, Ruslan. You're head of the Grozny Tourist Bureau." And so my future was decided—as has become custom—entirely without my consent.

Over the following weeks, I designed a brochure. The central question was how to trick tourists into coming to Grozny voluntarily. For inspiration, I studied pamphlets from the bureaus of other urban hellscapes: Baghdad, Pyongyang, Houston. From them I learned to be lavishly adjectival, to treat prospective visitors as semiliterate gluttons, to impute reports of kidnapping and terrorism to the slander of foreign provocateurs. I tucked a notebook into my shirt pocket and raced into the street. Upon seeing the empty space where an apartment block once stood, I wrote, *Wide and unobstructed skies!* I watched as a pack of feral dogs chased a man, and noted, *Unexpected encounters with wildlife!* The city bazaar hummed with the sales of looted industrial equipment, humanitarian aid rations, and munitions: *Unparalleled shopping opportunities!* Even before reaching the first checkpoint, I'd scribbled, *First-rate security!* The copy was easy; the real challenge was in finding images to substantiate it. After all, the siege had transfigured the city. Debris rerouted roads through warehouses—once I found a traffic jam on a factory floor—and what was not rerouted was razed. A photograph of my present surroundings would send a cannonball through my verbiage-fortified illusion of a romantic paradise for heterosexual couples, and I couldn't find suitable alternatives of prewar Grozny within the destroyed archives. In the end, I forwent photographs altogether and instead used the visuals from January, April, and August of the 1984 Grozny Museum of Regional Art calendar. In the three nineteenth-century landscapes, swallows frolic over ripening grapevines, and a shepherd minds his flock backlit by a sunset; they portray a land untouched by war or communism, and beside them my descriptions of a picturesque Chechnya do not seem entirely dishonest.

◆◆◆

After depositing the troika of Chinese oilmen at the Interior Ministry, I go home. I knock on the door of the flat adjacent to mine and announce my name. Nadya appears in a headscarf and sunglasses. Turning her unscarred side toward me, she invites me in. "How was the maiden voyage?"

"A great success," I say. "They dozed off before we reached the worst of the wreckage."

Nadya smiles and takes measured steps to the Primus stove. She doesn't need her white cane to reach the counter. I scan the room for impediments, yet everything is in order. Nothing on the floorboards but the kopek coins I'd glued down in paths to the bathroom, the kitchen, the front door so her bare feet could find their way in her early months of blindness.

The kettle whistles in the kitchen. We sip tea from mismatched mugs that lift rings of dust from the tabletop. She sits to hide the left half of her face.

"The tourist brochures will be ready next week," I say. "I'll have to send one along to our Beijing comrades, if the paintings come out clearly."

"You used three from the Zakharov room?"

"Yes, three Zakharovs."

Her shadow nods on the wall. That gallery, the museum's largest, had been her favorite, too. The first time I ever saw her was there, in 1987, on her first day as the museum's restoration artist.

"You'll have to save me one," she says. "For when I can see it."

Her last sentence hangs in the air for a long moment before I respond. "I have an envelope with five thousand rubles. For your trip. I'll leave it on your nightstand."

"Ruslan, please."

"St. Petersburg is a city engineered to steal money from visitors. I know. I'm in the industry."

"You don't need to take care of me," she says with a firm but appreciative squeeze of my fingers. "I keep telling you—I've been saving my disability allowance. I have enough for the bus ticket, and I'm staying with the cousin of a university classmate."

"It's not for you. It's for movies, for videocassettes," I say, a beat too quickly. Slapstick and romantic comedies have been my favorite genres in recent years.

She's looking straight at me, or at my voice, momentarily forgetting the thing her face has become. We were together when rockets turned three floors of our city's preeminent works of art into an inferno she barely escaped. The third-degree burns hardened into a chapped canvas of scar tissue wrapping the left side of her skull. That eye is gone, yet the other was partly spared; sometimes, her right eye can sense the faintest flickers of light. There is the possibility, an ophthalmologist has told her, that sight could be restored. However, any optical surgeon clever enough to perform such a delicate operation was also clever enough to have fled Grozny long ago for a city like St. Petersburg, where she has several appointments arranged.

"If it happens, the surgery, if it's successful," I say, "you don't need to leave."

"What I need is sleep," she says.

When I return to my flat, I rinse my hands in the sink and let the water run even after they're clean. Indoor plumbing was restored six months ago. Above the doorway hangs a bumper sticker of a fish with *WWJCD?* inscribed across its body, sent by an American church along with a crate of Bibles in response to our plea for life-saving aid.

I take a dozen scorched canvases from the closet and lay them on the floor in two rows of six. They were too damaged for the Tretyakov exhibit. Not one was painted after 1879, and yet they look like the surreal visions of a psychedelic-addled mind. Most are charred through, some simply mounted ash, more reminiscent of Alberto Burri's slash-and-burn than the Imperial Academy of Arts's classicism. In others the heat-melted oils have turned photo-realistic portraits into dissolved dreamscapes.

My closet holds one last canvas. I set it on the coffee table to examine by the light of an unshaded lamp. The seamless gradation of color, the nearly invisible brushstrokes—not even the three years I spent writing my dissertation on Pyotr Zakharov could diminish my fascination with his work. Born in 1816, on the eve of the Caucasian War that Tolstoy and Pushkin would later memorialize in their narrative cycle, he was an orphan before his fourth birthday. Yet his brilliance so exceeded his circumstances that he went on to attend the Imperial Academy in St. Petersburg, and despite exclusion from scholarship, employment, and patronage due to his ethnicity, he eventually became a court painter and a member of the Academy. He was a Chechen who learned to succeed by the rules of his conquerors, a man not unlike the minister, to be admired and pitied.

A meadow, an apricot tree, a stone wall in a diagonal meander through the grasses, the pasture cresting into a hill, a boarded well, a dacha. It's among the least ambitious of all Zakharov's work. Here is an artist who painted the portraits of tsars, duchesses, and generals, even the famed depiction of Imam Shamil's surrender, and this, in my hands, portrays all the drama its title suggests: *Empty Pasture in Afternoon.*

I grew up in the southern highlands, just a few kilometers from the pasture. Though the land was technically part of a state farm, nothing was ever planted, and flocks were banned from grazing because no one liked the idea of sheep relieving themselves on Zakharov's soil. During secondary school, on a class trip to the Grozny Museum of Regional Art, I finally beheld the canvas that existed with greater vibrancy in village lore that it ever could on a gallery wall.

More than anything, it was that painting that led me to study art at university, and there I met and married my wife. We lived with my parents in cramped quarters well into our twenties, and found the privacy to speak openly only in deserted public areas: on the roof of the village schoolhouse, in the waiting room of the shuttered clinic, in Zakharov's pasture. After I received my doctorate and a position at the museum, we relocated to a Grozny flat, where we learned to talk in bed.

The USSR fell. We had a son. With the assistance of the minister, I purchased the dacha in Zakharov's pasture amid the frenzied privatization of the post-Soviet, prewar years. When the First War began, I stayed in Grozny to protect the museum from the alternating advances of foreign soldiers and local insurgents. My wife and son fled to the dacha, far from the conflict.

In my research for the tourist bureau, I've learned that the First and Second Chechen Wars have rendered the republic among the most densely mined regions in human history. The United Nations estimates that five hundred thousand were planted, roughly one for every two citizens. I was unaware of this statistic when I visited the dacha during the First War, taking what provisions I could from the ruined capital, a few treats for which I paid dearly—tea leaves for my wife, sheets of fresh drawing paper for my son—but I knew enough to warn my family never to venture into the pasture. Initially, they heeded my words.

I don't know how it happened, on that May day in 1996, if they were pursued by depraved men, if the perilous field were a relative sanctuary, if they were afraid, if they called for help, if they called for me. I'd like to believe that it was a day so beautiful they couldn't resist the crest of the hill, the open sky, that radiance. I'd like to believe that my wife suggested a picnic, that their penultimate moment was one of whimsy, charm. I'd like to believe anything to counter the more probable realities at the edge of my imagination. With terror or joy, with abasement or delight, they remained my wife and child to the end—I must remind myself of this, because in the mystery that subsumes those final moments they are strangers to me. I was in Grozny, at the museum, and never heard the explosion.

◆◆◆

For the two weeks Nadya is in Petersburg, my evenings stagnate. Twice I go to Nadya's flat to clean her bedroom closet, the back corners of shelves, behind the toilet, the little places that even in her fastidiousness she misses. I must make myself into a crutch she cannot risk discarding.

One Wednesday night, feeling unusually alert given the hour, I contemplate Zakharov's pasture. It's the least ruined of the canvases, the principal damage—aside from the stains of ash and soot—being the burn hole at its center, upon the hill, which I see as the aftermath not of the museum fire but of the mine blast, the crater into which everything disappeared. A few years ago, Nadya could have restored it in days.

I let myself back into her flat to retrieve her restoration kit. Back home I set the kit beside the Zakharov. Plastic bottles of emulsion cleaner, neutralizer, gloss varnish, conditioner, varnish remover. A tin of putty. Eight meters of canvas lining. A depleted packet of cotton-tipped swabs. A dozen disposable chloroprene gloves. I'd taken a yearlong course in conservation at university, but my real education came from Nadya, when in the months after my family died, I neglected my duties as deputy director and spent most afternoons in her office, watching her work.

Every evening for the next week I snap on the gloves and wash away the surface dirt with cotton balls dampened in neutralizer. The emulsion cleaner smells of fermented watermelon, and I apply it with the swabs in tight circles until the tips gray and the unadulterated color of Zakharov's palette is revealed. Employing the repair putty as sealant, I patch the burn hole with a square of fresh canvas. Then I paint.

The totality of my attention is focused on an area the size of a halved playing card. The grass, turned emerald by sunlight, must be flawless, and

I spend several hours testing different blends of oils. As I apply them with delicate brushstrokes, I realize that even in his rendering of a distant field, Zakharov is beyond imitation, and that were Nadya here to witness my final infidelity, she would never forgive me.

With precise, strong lines, I draw them as silhouettes. The boy's arms are raised, his body elongated as he makes for the crest, his head thrown back in rapture. The woman hurries a step behind, animated by his anticipation. Their backs are to me. The sun rakes the grass, and ripe apricots bend the branches. No one chases them. They run from nothing.

◆◆◆

Nadya has returned, and the white tea has cooled in our cups, and still she hasn't mentioned the Petersburg eye surgeons.

"What did the doctors say, Nadya?"

The pause is long enough to peel a plum.

She delivers her reply with a downcast frown. "Reconstructive surgery is possible."

I force as much gusto as I can muster into my congratulations, slapping a palm on the table while my spine wilts. What will I be if Nadya no longer needs me? This is truly good news, though, of course it is, but her face is joyless. "What's wrong? Is there a long wait for the operation?"

"There won't be one."

"What? Why not?"

"Too expensive." She's facing the empty chair across the table, thinking that I'm still sitting there. "One hundred and fifteen thousand."

One hundred and fifteen thousand rubles. A huge yet not impossible sum. Years to save for, but within the realm of possibility. I'm already scheming ways to defraud the minister when she says, "Dollars."

My heart spirals and crash-lands somewhere deep in my gut. At thirty-three rubles to a dollar, the figure is insurmountable. Nadya reaches for her purse and pulls out an envelope.

"What I owe you for the trip. Help me count it out," she says. For a moment her instinct to trust anyone, even me, is infuriating. Isn't suspicion the natural condition of the blind? Haven't I warned her, told her to be careful, cautioned that she can't rely on anyone? But by some perversion she's become more credulous, more willing to believe that people aren't by nature hucksters and scoundrels.

"It's nothing," I say.

"I'm paying you back."

"If you want to be a martyr, go join them in the woods."

"Help me count it out," she insists, her voice stern, cool, serious. "I still have money left from the disability fund. I'm not a charity."

Of course there's no disability fund. Of course the government isn't providing her a stipend or subsidizing the flat adjacent to mine. The cash delivered in the Interior Ministry envelope on the first of the month comes from me, as does her rent.

"I'm waiting," she says. We both know this is a farce. But I sit beside her. I play my part in the lie that preserves the illusion that our friendship, our romance, whatever this is, is based in affection rather than dependence. I count the bills that I will return to her, and we shake hands as if our business is concluded, as if there is nothing left that we owe one another.

In bed I run my fingers through what remains of her hair, press my fingertips to her cheeks, slowly scrolling to decipher the dense braille scrawled across her face. I slide my hand down her torso, over the bulge of her left breast, the hook of her hip bone, to thighs so smooth and unmarked they're hers only in darkness. She turns away.

Lying here, I nearly forget the falling rockets, the collapsing museum, the cinder blocks shifting like ice cubes in a glass, the air of a clean sky impossibly distant. The Zakharov was in my hands when I found her, her face halved, her teeth chattering. I nearly forget how I lifted her cheek to cool it with my breath, how her broken eyes searched for me as I held her. So many times I've warned her of monsters, ready to prey on the vulnerable, and as she turns, I nearly forget to ask myself, *What monster have I become today?*

◆◆◆

In the morning I return to my flat and find the paintings on the floor where I left them. Daylight grants the scorch and char an odd beauty, as if the fires haven't destroyed the works but revised them into expressions of a brutal present. I pick up the nearest one, a family portrait commissioned by a nobleman as a wedding present for his second son. The top third of the canvas has been incinerated, taking with it the heads of the nobleman, his wife, the first son, and the newly betrothed, but their bodies remain, dressed in soot-stained breeches and petticoats, and by their feet sits a dachshund so fat its little legs barely touch the ground, the only figure—in a painting intended to convey the family's immortal honor—to survive intact.

I hang the canvas on the wall from a bent nail and step back, marveling that here, for the first time in my career, I've displayed a work of modern art. After pulling the furniture into the kitchen, I hang the remaining canvases throughout the living room, finally coming to the restored Zakharov, which I consider returning to the closet, where it would exist in darkness for me alone, but my curatorial instincts win out, and I mount it beside the others, where it is meant to be. I scrawl a sign on a cardboard shingle and nail it to the door: *Grozny Museum of Regional Art.*

Over the following weeks, I bring all my tours through the museum. A delegation from the Red Cross. More Chinese oilmen. A heavyweight boxing champion. A British journalist. *This is what remains*, the canvases cry. *You cannot burn ash! You cannot raze rubble!* As the only museum employee, I give myself a long overdue promotion. Henceforth, I am director.

◆◆◆

The newly installed telephone rings one morning, and the gloomy minister greets me. "Well, we're properly fucked."

"Nice to hear from you, sir," I reply. I'm still in my sleeping clothes, and even for a phone conversation I feel unsuitably dressed.

"The Chinese backed out and Rosneft is backing right in."

I nod, grasping why Beijing didn't sent its shrewdest or most sober representatives. "So this means Rosneft will drill?"

"Yes, and it gets even worse," he heaves. "I may well be demoted to deputy minister."

"I was a deputy for many years. It's not as bad as you think."

"When the world takes a dump, it lands on a deputy's forehead."

I couldn't deny that. "What does this mean for the Tourist Bureau?"

"You should find new employment. But first, you have one final tour. Oleg Voronov. From Rosneft."

It takes a beat for the name to register. "The fourteenth richest man in Russia?"

"Thirteenth now."

"With respect, sir, I give tours to human rights activists and print journalists—people of no power or importance. What does a man of his stature want with me?"

"My question precisely! Yet apparently his wife, Galina Something-or-other-ova, the actress, has heard of this art museum you've cobbled together. What've you been up to?"

"It's a long story, sir."

"You know I hate stories, but do show him our famed Chechen hospitality—perhaps with a glass of unboiled tap water. Let's give the thirteenth richest man in Russia an intestinal parasite!"

◆◆◆

Three weeks pass and here he is, Oleg Voronov, in the back seat of the Mercedes, with his wife, the actress Galina Ivanova. Sitting up front is his assistant, a bleached-blonde parcel of productivity who takes notes even when no one is speaking. Still, try as I might, I'm unable to properly hate Voronov. So far he's been nontalkative, inattentive, and uncurious—in short, a perfect tourist. Galina, on the other hand, has read Khassan Geshilov's *Origins of Chechen Civilization* and recites historical trivia unfamiliar to me. As the office doors of dead administrators clatter beneath us, she asks thoughtful questions, treating me not as a servant, or even as a tour guide, but as a scholar. I casually mention the land mines, the street children, the rape and torture and indiscriminate suffering, and Voronov and his wife shake their heads with sympathy. Nothing I say will turn them into the masks of evil I want them to be; and when the oligarch checks his watch, a cheap plastic piece of crap, I feel an affinity for a man who deserves its opposite.

The tour concludes at my flat. As I open the door, I say, "This is what remains of the Grozny Museum of Regional Art."

Voronov and Galina pass the burned-out frames to the pasture. "Is this the one?" he asks her. She nods.

"A Zakharov, no?" he inquires, fingering his lapel as he turns to me. "There was an exhibit of his at the Tretyakov, if memory serves."

Only now do I recognize clearly the animals I have invited into my home. "When the museum was bombed, the fires destroyed most of the original collection. We sent what was saved to the Tretyakov."

"But not this?"

"Not this."

"Rather reckless, don't you think, to leave such a treasure on an apartment wall?"

"It's a minor work."

"Believe it or not, my wife has been looking for a Zakharov. She collects art from every region I drill."

"Could I offer you a glass of water?"

"You could offer me the painting."

I force a laugh. He laughs, too. We are laughing. Ha-ha!

"The painting is not for sale," I say.

His mirth disappears. "It is if I want to buy it."

"This is a museum. You can't have a painting just because you want it. The director of the Tretyakov wouldn't sell you the art from his walls just because you can afford it."

"You are only a deputy director, and this isn't the Tretyakov." There's real pity in his voice as he surveys the ash flaking from the canvases, the dirty dishes stacked in the sink; and yes, now, at last, I hate him. "I have a penthouse gallery in Moscow. Temperature- and moisture-controlled. First-rate security. No one but Galina and I and a few guests will ever see it. You must realize that I'm being more than reasonable." In a less-than-subtle threat, he nods out the window to the street below, where his three armed Goliaths skulk beside their Land Rover. "What is the painting worth?"

"It's worth," I begin, but how can I finish? What price can I assign to the last Zakharov in Chechnya, to the last image of my home? One sum comes to mind, but it terrifies me. Wouldn't that be the worst of all outcomes, to lose both the Zakharov and Nadya in the same transaction? "Just take it," I say. "You took everything else. Take this, too."

Voronov bristles. "I'm not a thief. Tell me what it's worth."

My gaze floats and lands upon the bumper sticker: *WWJCD?* What would he do? Jim Carrey would be brave. No matter how difficult, Jim Carrey would do the right thing. I close my eyes. "One hundred and fifteen thousand dollars. US."

"One fifteen?"

I nod.

"That's what—three-point-seven, three-point-eight million rubles?" Voronov fixes me with a venomous stare, then turns to his wife, who still hasn't glanced away from the painting. I look into it, too, to its retreating figures, wondering if we might be reunited soon.

A single, fleshy clap startles me like a gunshot, and I spin to find Voronov smiling once more. "Let's make it an even four," he says expansively.

The assistant unyokes herself from a mammoth purse and spills eight stacks of banded five-thousand-ruble bills onto the floor.

"Never trust banks," Voronov says. "You can have that advice for free. It's been a pleasure." He slaps my back, tells the assistant to bring the canvas, and heads for the door. Then he's gone.

Galina remains at the Zakharov. Even as I'm losing it, I'm proud my painting can elicit such sustained attention. She smiles apologetically, touches my shoulder, and follows her husband out.

I'm left with the assistant, whose saccharine perfume reeks of vaporized cherubs. "And you'll have to give us a curatorial description," she says. "Something we can mount on a placard." She passes me the notepad, and I stand before my painting for a long while before I begin.

Notice how the shadows in the meadow mirror the clouds in the sky, how the leaves of the apricot tree blow with the grass. No verisimilitude escapes such a master. The wall of white stones cuts an angle across the composition, both establishing depth and offsetting the horizon line. Channels of turned soil run along the left flank of the hill, as if freshly dug graves, or recently buried land mines, but closer inspection reveals the furrows of a newly planted herb garden. The first shoots of rosemary already peek out. Zakharov portrays all the peace and tranquility of a spring day. The sun shines comfortingly, and hours remain before nightfall. Toward the crest of the hill, nearing the horizon, you may notice what look to be the ascending figures of a woman and a boy. Pay them no mind, for they are merely the failures of a novice restoration artist, no more than his shadows. They are not there.

.

.

.

MUSSOLINI, MCDONALD'S,
AND THE PRICE OF HAPPINESS

BY T. GERONIMO JOHNSON

2017 SIMPSON/JOYCE CAROL OATES PRIZE RECIPIENT

Keynote delivered on June 14, 2019, at the Rendezvous with Risk Literary Festival, sponsored by the Oregon State University-Cascades Low-Residency MFA Program.

There is a widespread refusal to let children know that the source of much that goes wrong in life is due to our very own natures—the propensity of all men for acting aggressively, asocially, selfishly, out of anger and anxiety. Instead, we want our children to believe that, inherently, all men are good. But children know that they are not always good; and often, even when they are, they would prefer not to be. This contradicts what they are told by their parents, and therefore makes the child a monster in his own eyes.
—Bruno Bettelheim

About race and racism there isn't anything I can tell you that you don't already know, even if you deny it. So I'm not going to talk at length of race, even though I write about it. I'm not going to say things that make you feel the perfect amount of guilt and help me feel the perfect amount of righteousness. I'm not going to advise as to how you can improve the world so that you can check that box that you check after attending the obligatory church event or political rally. In short, today we will not perform a ritual of outrage that would result in nothing but us psychically patting ourselves on the back.

And in fact, when I say I write about race, that is not exactly true. I write about friendship, love, war, natural disaster, the challenge of creating a meaningful life, the revolutionary effect that love can have on the soul and the psyche. I write about what it means when young men find themselves facing the disorienting truth that much of what they have been told about being a man is false, and the parts that are true are often only valued when they are convenient for others. I write about what it means to try to live a well-intentioned life, to try to live in accord with your beliefs. I write about what it means to be a human who is aware, but some of my characters are black, and so it's sometimes said that I write about race and only about race, which is not what we are going to talk about.

I want to tell a little story about Italy. My first week at the American Academy in Rome, I attended a PowerPoint presentation on the state of affairs. Politically and economically, it was said, Italy is buried alive under a millennium of mismanagement and corruption. Along with the other Americans in the audience, I learned that Italy has three Mafias, that Northern Italians look down on Southern Italians, and that Italians rarely move. (Italy is stickier than Louisiana, which is the stickiest state in the Union.) The political parties, we were told, were shamelessly courting fascism, and their Internet technology is decades behind (web no-point-o). The rest of the world was on the cloud and the Italians were using floppy disks. The rest of the world was using PS4s and Xboxes while the Italians were still playing Atari 2600s and Commodore 64s. The situation, we were told, was and is bleak. Then, at the end of the talk, the presenter, an American attorney who had only weeks before retired to Rome to live out his golden years, segued into a discussion of the metrics of health. The Italians were happier, ranked high in health care and life satisfaction, and lived longer. They were, despite the alleged economic and political ineptitude, rich in everything we here in American were dying to acquire, such as time, for example.

In America, if you are an important person, you are busy, and you don't have time for people, including your family. In Italy, if you are an important person, you have nothing but time, because if you are important, why would you make yourself busy?

So I resolved to think about not being busy all the time, and I thought about it, and it didn't quite work. I'm a writer. No one cares whether I write or not, but if I don't write, I don't eat. So I'm accustomed to working through happy hour, so to speak. But I did try to spend some time with the other fellows in the fallow hours between dinner and whatever activity would occupy the night.

One evening behind the Academy, I was smoking[1] with Alessandro di Pietro, a Milanese artist who was a guest of the Academy for six months. At the American Academy, the idea was that by mixing Americans and Italians, some inspiration would arise that could lead to a novel and exciting collaboration. That happened on occasion, but for the most part the Italian fellows—especially those from Rome—were an invaluable resource when an American needed to know where to find the best coffee or a reasonably priced enoteca (wine shop), why Sicilian pizza isn't always thick, or if the carbonara we were eating at that moment was indeed the very best carbonara in all the world. It was always the second-best carbonara in all the world.

So, few spontaneous inspirations.

Until that evening chatting with Alessandro.

The air was crackling, and the stone walkway that ran parallel to the rear of the MMW building was lit by ghostly yellow squares projected from the few rooms where the lights were on but the shutters weren't yet down. All of the exterior-facing windows have these articulated shutters that you can lower to block all light. Behind us in the Bass Garden, unseen sprinklers switched on, announcing their good intentions with that stuttering ratchet sound sprinklers love to make. The leafy crests of the olive grove were haloed by the streetlights that peeked through the arrow slits near the top of the wall. The Academy's land is bordered by a section of the original wall of Rome, close to Porta San Pancrazio. Through the kitchen windows only ten feet away we could see the cooks skate around in their Crocs as they played the percussive music that accompanied cleaning up the kitchen after the last meal of the day. It was an evening like every other evening: pleasant, unthreatening, and entirely unremarkable.

For some reason I can't now recall, the subject of Mussolini came up. I forgot to tell you that during the PowerPoint presentation on Italy, we were told that many Italians pined for the days of Mussolini because they grieved the loss of strong-willed men, and that was why Berlusconi had been so popular. When this subject came up, a look of disappointment

---

1   I don't smoke. Cigarette inserted for cinematic effect.

marked my companion's face. And Alessandro felt that Mussolini's corpse shouldn't have been displayed upside down in public. He felt that there is, or should be, a limit to the degradation one human visits upon another, even after death. I was surprised because I had seen this image of Mussolini in my history textbooks in high school and again in college, and it had never occurred to me that suspending the *fully clothed* and intact dictator's body upside down was a particularly heinous act.

After our cigarettes fizzled down to smoldering filters, we parted. Alessandro went back inside to the MMW building where he was staying, and I made my way to 5B where the families are housed.

On the way home to a building that was once a monastery, I watched my step because the large red stones underfoot were uneven. The walkway was bordered by a perfectly trimmed hedge, and so with the light overhead and the sprinkler in the distance throwing a silver arc of water, it looked like a path to the Garden of Eden, but the path was treacherous. Though it did indeed lead to a garden. I passed the brick-lined plot where the cooks (i cuochi) grew many of the vegetables (verdure) they served every day: chard, kale, broccoli, leeks. I passed the rosemary and thyme plants. I passed branches that suspended tantalizing neon citrus at eye level, inviting you to partake.

But I thought about Mussolini. What did I know about Mussolini? I had forgotten that he had qualified as an elementary school master. But that certainly was not why Alessandro objected to his treatment. I wondered about this as I blindly passed the landscaped beauty around me.

Because after you have been exposed to idyllic beauty long enough, it becomes a backdrop. This beauty, this rolling lawn, the sheltering trees, the pomegranate shrub, the majestic umbrella pines that tower overhead like spectacular specimens taken from the pages of a Dr. Seuss book, are all a backdrop. They are a backdrop to the same concerns you had when the path home passed by a 7-Eleven, a McDonald's, and a Walmart.

My puzzlement. Why did he care? I realized that night I didn't think human bodies should be publicly desecrated, but since early childhood I had seen images of black bodies hung, burned, and dismembered, and, more recently, shot without regard, and none of these people were dictators, and often the corpses were surrounded by a crowd of cheerful white people.[2]

So just like I was desensitized to the pomegranates, the umbrella pines, the scented whisper of rosemary and thyme. So I was desensitized to this idea of any kind of sacred constraint of the body. Further, in my studies of Buddhism I had learned that in some communities monks toss corpses to the vultures in what they call a "sky burial." And living in San Francisco, growing up near Washington, DC, and shooting a film on gentrification in Seattle meant that I was exposed to thousands and thousands of people without permanent homes forced to live a humiliating public existence.

Though I wouldn't want to desecrate a body, it was beyond my imagination that it was beyond anyone else's imagination to do so. And the black body in particular has no rights. And growing up watching the films that I did, meaning mainstream American films, the female body, be it white, black, Asian, or any race and combination thereof, was protected by no limits either. Remember Black Dahlia, let alone the serial killers like Ted Bundy who monopolized the news. And we won't even talk about Juarez.

And it occurred to me that in America, the body can be a source of pain, but it is not always respected as the site of legitimate feelings, depending on who you are. So to lynch or to rape is to cause pain, but it's the pain of a starving dog kicked to death on the side of a road, not the pain of a human being with a network of feelings, and even now you may feel more sympathy from the image of the dog than you did at the gestures toward human suffering.[3]

And this brings me, of course, to the Declaration of Independence. We understand intuitively life and liberty. Happiness is another matter altogether. We hold these truths to be self-evident, that all men are created equal, that they are endowed by their Creator with certain unalienable Rights, that among these are Life, Liberty and the pursuit of Happiness.

How happy can we be with suffering of others?

- Can you be happy if 12k people in Seattle are without housing?
- Can you be happy if 15k people in San Francisco are without food?

---

2   Cheerful, yes. Happy? Maybe? Maybe not?

3   Several people nodded here.

- Can you be happy if hundreds of thousands of kids in the US are without adequate education?
- Can we be happy if violence against trans people continues to rise?
- Can we be happy if during the time we are in this room six people are killed by gun violence and a half dozen more injured? (Ninety-six Americans die by firearms daily.)
- Can we be happy if during this same time nine women are raped (a reported rape every six minutes)?

The sad truth: Yes, we can.

That's how it looks to me. The #metoo movement is not an enlightenment, nor is the #blacklivesmatter movement. These movements are in the news, but there is nothing new about them.[4] All they have done is challenged us to ask ourselves an easy and direct question: Can we be satisfied with our unalienable right to pursue happiness if it comes at the expense of others' rights to pursue happiness?

Can men be satisfied with our right to pursue happiness if it comes at the expense of women's rights to pursue happiness? The answer is yes.

Can whites be satisfied if their right to pursue happiness comes at the expense of nonwhite's rights to pursue happiness? The answer again is yes.

Can able-bodied people be satisfied if their right to pursue happiness comes at the expense of disabled people's rights to pursue happiness?

What would you say the answer is? The answer is yes.

The reason this is possible is that in our laissez-faire free market economy so-called happiness is available to anyone who can afford the bill. Be it a new electric sports car, a larger home with the perfect bathroom-to-occupant ratio and radiant heating in the floors, or an ideal tech status symbol, such as the latest smart watch.

And in our economy, the prevalent myth tells us that good people are rewarded. And poor people suffer from fatal flaws of character, never

---

4   The West has been engaged in a series of both hot and cold race wars since colonialism's earliest incursions, and women have been willfully and intentionally displaced by men using tools as varied as literacy and religion, allegedly net-positive, value-neutral developments. Consider, for example, the peculiar history of midwifery. As for the hot-and-cold race war, some combatants have been conscripted unknowingly, while others have volunteered.

from low wages, and so of course they are not rewarded and thus not happy. The poor are lazy.

While at the same time we know our possessions are precisely that: things that possess us. We know that the stress of maintaining our lifestyles cuts short our very lifespans. We know that we are trapped in a system that depersonalizes people. So can be we happy[5] while others suffer?

The obvious answer is YES, so long as we can convince ourselves that happiness is a consumable product, as long as we convince ourselves that happiness is best preserved and enjoyed in isolation, and as long as we believe that happiness is reserved for the financially secure and financially successful because only they have earned it. The answer is yes if we believe that the right to the pursuit of happiness is earned and not, as the founding architects wrote—inalienable.

But the inalienable is not earned.

The challenge is that the most common alternative model under which we operate, the concept most frequently invoked as the vaccination for the disease of "laissez-faire capitalism" is what I call "conscriptive altruism." This is the idea that you can only be a good person by subverting your will and your needs to others. This is the idea that you can only excel through service, and through submission. In the West, because of the influence of Christianity, we receive conflicting messages that hobble us. We're told that financial success is admirable, but we're also told that financial success is evil and inhuman and is only possible at the expense of others.

These conflicting philosophies leave people with no way out, and no clear path to a life that can embrace material and spiritual and communal satisfaction, unless that life involves some economic segregation, which usually results in cultural and racial segregation as well. Because who wants to park their Tesla next to a shopping cart apartment?

In other words, we are told to be all that we can be, as long as it is not too much more than anyone else. Black people are supposed to be authentic as long as they do not frighten nonblack people. White people are invited to engage in open conversations about race as long as they

---

5   What of extreme sadism, you ask? As a side note, I want to explain that cross-burning and sexual assault, for example, may bring perverse pleasures to the perpetrators but are not a happiness of the legitimate and profound sort under discussion here.

do not say anything offensive (which, by the way, is like trying to learn a foreign language without making mistakes). People can dress attractively, but only if for themselves. Men can be "brave" only so long as that is confined to killing people in other countries. Trans people should be quiet. People without homes should find jobs.

This is not a catalogue of despair; it is more so an acknowledgement of the utterly ridiculous state of being in which we find ourselves because we humans have given away too much of our personal power and look to answers from so-called experts who themselves haven't even resolved the mystery of their own human condition.[6] So what can we do?

I think that we can accept that self-interest is a rational pursuit and not inherently evil. Unless we accept that reality, we cannot move forward. No man can stand for women or trans people if he cannot acknowledge that sexism benefits all men. No white person can stand for a nonwhite person unless they can acknowledge that racism and white supremacy benefit all white people. But the self-interest inherent in these systems isn't inherently evil; it's the denial that is the problem, because denying it feeds it and makes it stronger.

Consider this: parents usually think of their own children before they consider the needs of the children of others. This does not make them evil; this makes them rationally self-interested people.[7] And as rationally self-interested people we can also acknowledge that happiness may be a dish best shared widely, but that we cannot share what we do not have.

My suggestion for making the world better is twofold. Embrace a cause you believe in that empowers people who have less social capital than you. Embrace your inalienable right to be happy and make that happen in an authentic way; perhaps then you can see clearly how to support others and be an ally without falling into paternalism.

By happiness I mean the right to pursue your fully exalted self without the impediment of undue social burdens that hinge on accidents of birth, and the process of achieving that state of exalted selfhood at no expense to others. I mean to be fully present in your own life. This is the greatest gift we can give anyone with whom we ally, support in clearing the way for them to be free to engage in their pursuit of happiness.

6   In other words, a sizeable percentage of the population is looking for easy answers to hard-bred misery.

7   Yes, North Carolina, there is such a thing as rational and enlightened self-interest.

The world will not be made better by each of us embracing our own cause. The world will be made better by each of us embracing the cause of another and accepting that because happiness is not a product, but a process, we cannot be happy when another suffers for our benefit—we can only be blind, and being blind to the reality of life does not make us happy, it makes us rabid consumers of distraction. Because the real answer is that we are not happy with the suffering of others; we are distracted from others, and from ourselves.

We have too many of us become like the idyllic garden I passed on the walk home that evening after the discussion with Alessandro. We have become desensitized to ourselves. For many of us, our deepest dreams and desires have become the ignored backdrop of our own lives.

Be important—make time for yourself. Find your true happiness because you cannot give what you do not have. If you fail to embrace yourself with joy, fail to embrace the miracle of existence, fail to be open to all the possibilities of love, your unhappiness becomes another's suffering.

I am ending with a quote from Irvin Yalom, the existential psychotherapist:

We cannot say to them you and your problems. Instead, we must speak of us and our problems, because our life, our existence, will always be riveted to death, love to loss, freedom to fear, and growth to separation. We are, all of us, in this together.

◆◆◆

[This keynote was part of an ongoing series of formal and informal conversations about happiness and social justice, mindfulness, the relationship between self-acceptance and prejudice, and, the most urgent question: *Why should any so-called disenfranchised community stake their social, economic, or spiritual enlightenment on the practices, habits, or even the beneficence of the very people who have kept them sidelined and who benefit from their continued estrangement?*]

LITTLE ALBERT, 1920

BY JOYCE CAROL OATES

SIMPSON PROJECT WRITER-IN-RESIDENCE
AT THE LAFAYETTE LIBRARY AND LEARNING CENTER

I was Little Albert.
Nine months old in the famous film.
In a white cotton nightie, on a lab
table sitting upright
facing a camera.
Remember me? Sure.
You do.

First, you saw that I was a "curious" baby.
You saw that I blinked and stared
with all the intensity of an infant-brain
eager to suck into its galaxy of neurons
all of the world. You saw that
I was *you*.

You saw that I was a "fearless" baby.
You saw that I was not frightened
of a burning newspaper held before me
at an alarmingly close range.
Though indeed my rapt infant-face
expressed the classic *wariness* of our race.

Next, you saw that I was not frightened
of a frisky monkey darting close about me
on a leash. You saw
that I was not frightened

by a large dog brought close to me
nor by a quivering rabbit, nor
a small white rat—
nor even a Santa Claus mask
worn by a menacing male figure
clad in white, shoved close
to my infant face.

You saw that I was attracted to the small white rat.
You saw that I reached out to touch the small white rat.
And as I reached for the small white rat
behind my head came an explosion of noise—
the shock of it sent me sprawling, cringing,
face contorted in terror, mouth
a perfect O of anguish, howling—
as the experimenter John Watson struck
a metal pipe with a hammer.
What a shock!—how terror
rushed through me. How
desperately I crawled
to escape almost toppling
off the edge of the table—
>   except adult hands restrained me.
>   *Children naturally fear loud noises.*
>   *Children naturally fear surprises.*
>   *Children naturally fear the unknown.*
>   *Children can be taught to fear the known.*

The second experiment was one month later.
No escape for me for I was Little Albert.
Grim as a little gargoyle
in white cotton nightie able
to sit upright though now wary,
distrustful. No joy in my little body
as (again) a small white rat
was introduced to me. You saw
how this time I shrank away. How

this time there was terror in my face.
How this time I did not reach
with infant eagerness for the small white rat
        for I'd learned to fear and hate
        the small white rat. And again
        (you saw) how the very presence
of the small white rat
precipitated a deafening clamor
as John Watson another time
        struck a metal pipe
        with a hammer again, again and
        again behind my head for
who was there
to stop him? In this way
establishing on film
        how (baseless) fear can be instilled
        in a subject where fear had
        not previously existed and
how memory of this (baseless) fear
will endure contained
in the unfathomable brain.

How I cried and cried! As if
I'd known that my mother had
received but one dollar for
the use of me in John Watson's psych lab
in the experiment that would destroy me
and make John Watson famous.
For in the alchemy of my brain
my fear of a small white rat
had become *generalized*
and now (as Watson ably demonstrated)
I feared the monkey, the dog, the rabbit
equally though each was unaccompanied
by a clanging hammer.
Now I feared the menacing figure
in the Santa Claus mask as if

understanding that Santa Claus
was my tormentor. Cried
and cried and could not be
consoled, even a woman's
fur coat terrified me for
how could I trust *softness*?
Sudden movements, sounds
behind my head—
the unexpected...

Classic Pavlovian conditioning.
Bedrock of behavioral psychology.
Brilliant pioneer John Watson!

You are wondering: did John Watson
de-condition me? No. He did not.
Did another experimental psychologist
de-condition me? No. He did not.
Ask me what was the remainder of my life.
Ask me did I adjust to life after the
infamous experiment. Ask me
did I overcome my terror of animals?—
the answer is not known for
I died of hydrocephalus at age six.

All this was long ago. Things are different now.
John Watson would not be allowed to terrorize
Little Albert in his famous experiment now.
Ours is an *ethical* age.

Or was it all a bad dream? Were you deceived?
You were Little Albert? You were conditioned
to fear and hate? You were conditioned to
thrust from you what you were meant to love?
You were the victim? You were the experimental subject?
You were Little Albert, who died young?

[See page 90 for the author's remarks about her poem.]

JOYCE CAROL OATES & ANTHONY MARRA
IN CONVERSATION

BETH NEEDLE (BN), JOE DI PRISCO (JDP), JOYCE CAROL OATES (JCO), ANTHONY MARRA (AM)

Joyce Carol Oates and Anthony Marra joined Joseph Di Prisco for conversation at the Lafayette Public Library on the evening of March 5, 2019. Their selected remarks are lightly edited for clarity. Beth Needel, Executive Director of The Lafayette Library and Learning Center and Founding Board Member of the Simpson Literary Project, welcomed everyone.

BN: I love libraries. I love books. I love their smell. I love their texture, their covers and the magic between their pages. I love to see people, all people come through the library doors seven days a week and I love watching the different ways that people love and use the library, our library.

And, I believe that libraries are perhaps the most important institutions on earth, for they exist for all people and they are all-inclusive and always, all the time. So, welcome to the Lafayette Library and Learning Center. I just wanted to take a minute to thank generous donors, friends of the library, the foundation or foundation board members, the librarians, my amazing staff and volunteers. Without you, evenings like this would not take place.

So, I leave you in the now, always very capable, humorous hands of Joe Di Prisco, author, library lover, Simpson Family Literary Project chairman, and tonight's moderator. Thank you.

JDP: Thank you, Beth. It's so great to see everybody here on a rainy night and, is there a better place to be on a rainy night? I don't think so. And, this gorgeous library, and I've said this before, I'm always ... I've been in the library a million times, and every time I come here, I think, "This is the most gorgeous place in the world." And, I think we're very fortunate to have this in our community.

So, here we are tonight, a very special event. It's also Fat Tuesday, and that means that this is our version of Mardi Gras. Our version of Bourbon Street right here. That also means that tomorrow is Ash Wednesday, and as you may not know, it's Mercury retrograde, which I don't understand, but I know it's very important for a lot of people.

The Simpson Project, in case you don't know much about it, you're going to hear more than you can imagine, directly and indirectly. We teach writing workshops at places like Martinez Juvie, in the boys-identified wing and the girls-identified wing. We teach at Girls Inc. in downtown Oakland, and we teach at Northgate High School in Walnut Creek. We have taught about a hundred kids, free of charge, financed by generous donors, many of whom are here tonight. The Project is funded by altruistic individuals, family foundations, and some corporate sponsors, a couple of dozen generous donors. We do the teaching. We cause a book to be created and published called *Simpsonistas*, which is an anthology of work connected to the Simpson Project, and it includes these distinguished guests tonight, and also the distinguished young people who are incarcerated in Martinez and who come to Girls Inc. from traumatized family situations, and they're in this book too, along with Northgate High School kids.

And we award yearly the Simpson Literary Prize and you're going to hear a little bit more about that tonight. And we also have a writer-in-residence, an obscure, emerging writer whom I'll be very happy to introduce to you in a minute. The Prize goes to an important mid-career writer of fiction, you might say to an emerged and still emerging writer. I'm going to share some breaking news with you right now before it goes public tomorrow morning at 8:00 a.m. There will be a national press release announcing the short list for the 2019 Simpson Prize. I'm going to tell you who they are, but don't tell anybody until the morning, okay?

The short list includes Rachel Kushner, the author most recently of *The Mars Room*; Laila Lalami, author of *The Moor's Account*; Valeria Luiselli, author most recently of *Lost Children Archive*; Sigrid Nunez, author most recently of *The Friend*, which was awarded the National Book Award; Anne Raeff, whose most recent novel is *Winter Kept Us Warm*; and Amor Towles, whose most recent novel is *A Gentleman in Moscow*.

That's a murderer's row of authors, just like every other list we've put out in three years, but with pretty interesting range of diversities here, including writers from LA, from New York City, one from San Francisco. And, across generations, writers in their thirties, forties, fifties, and sixties on the shortlist. So, that's very interesting, I think.

And now, for tonight, the big show, Anthony Marra. Anthony is the 2018 Simpson Prize Winner, and the recipient of numerous awards, and been honored by widespread recognition, and richly deserved recognition. I have personally lost count of the number of times people have told me they love Anthony Marra's books. Now, what makes it even worse is that he's the nicest guy in the world. You are going to give writers a very bad name if you keep this up, Anthony, I'm telling you that.

He may share a few thoughts with you tonight about what it means to be a Simpson Prize winner. But I know I speak for everybody in the Project when I say it's been just a tremendous pleasure working with Tony. In fact, yesterday began his two-week residency as part of the Simpson Project, where he's teaching at Cal, doing some public events. He's at Northgate High School tomorrow, working with the kids there, and this is an essential part of what the project does. As you can tell, it's not just a prize for one lucky writer. It's a prize that we think has impact across the entire community.

And now, Joyce Carol Oates. Joyce Carol Oates is, well, Joyce Carol Oates. How rare it is for somebody in my capacity to say accurately, truthfully, "This is somebody who needs no introduction," but I'm sorry, Joyce, I'm going to introduce you just a little tiny bit with your kind forbearance.

It would take up most of our scheduled time for me to enumerate all the prizes and recognitions that Joyce has enjoyed, but a few items come to mind. Her most recent honor is that she was named in January the winner of the 2019 Jerusalem Prize. It's a most prestigious prize, given only to the greatest writers in the world. And her most recent novel, her forty-sixth, is *Hazards of Time Travel*, which has been released to widespread acclaim.

We're grateful that she's taken a leave of absence from Princeton in the spring and winter to be here in Berkeley. She teaches at Cal, and here she is the Simpson Project Writer-in-Residence at the Lafayette Library. Thank you, Joyce.

So, we appreciate so much everything that both Tony and Joyce do for the Project and I hope they don't regret this evening, as we're going to talk about a few things. I have a few questions, and I do hope that you'll be able to talk to each other. I'm happy to be the third wheel here. That won't be the first time I was the third wheel, and I'm hoping that we'll have a real conversation.

I just shared some news about the Simpson Prize, so I'm wondering, Tony, Joyce, as being the recipients of recognition and awards, I wonder if you could reflect on what awards have meant to you, whether there's some way in which this recognition by your peers or by the public has been validating, has been encouraging, has been helpful?

JCO: Well, it's an interesting question, because I think in a philosophical sense, the prize has to come at the right time, and sometimes when people have instant celebrity and they're enormously successful very young, it's actually a kind of curse. We all think of, for instance, Ralph Ellison, whose *Invisible Man* is one of the great novels in American literature, and of course, for him, it was an enormous, joyous experience, I think, at first.

But then, as time went on, it became a burden. Harper Lee's *To Kill a Mockingbird* has the same reaction in the world. These novels were so incredibly well received and so honored, that the writers then became somewhat blocked or paralyzed, and as I said, the prize should maybe come at the right time. I think a quintessentially ideal career is something like William Faulkner.

William Faulkner began, he began very modestly. His first novel was a failure, and the second novel was a failure, and his third novel was a failure, but maybe he's building his own style. And then, finally when he was about twenty-eight years old, he acquired this astonishing voice. He worked his way through, I think many different styles. He was trying to imitate Hemingway at one point.

Anyway, when he was twenty-eight years old, he had this remarkable trajectory, maybe eight years or so of creating incredible works, some of the greatest novels in the English language. But, I think if he had won, let's say, the Simpson Prize, and the Pulitzer Prize, and the National Book Award for one of those first novels which were not his own style, and really dead ends, they were novels that were imitations of other people's novels, then I think it would've been a curse, and I think he might not have even had the career of Faulkner.

So, in my own life, I was very fortunate and I think prizes come in a contingent way. I don't think we exactly deserve them. You have to have a committee or jurors who like your work. Somebody on the committee has to promote the work and a lot of that is really just accident. And so, I was lucky. I think it's a matter of luck, when I was about nineteen years old, I won a *Mademoiselle* fiction contest award, and that allowed me to be published in a national magazine. And then, I was always working on stories, which I sent out to little magazines.

But I think that initial little bump or giving a lift to a bird or a butterfly or something, it just somehow lifted my heart and gave me hope, so that writers do have many rejections, and years can go by when everything seems very depressing and not working out well. But you can think back upon that early boost, and I think it's very encouraging.

AM: Yeah, I think that rejection is the resting state of most writers, that you wake up in the morning and you look in the mirror and you say, "I don't like what I see." So I think that receiving ... certainly an award of this stature and magnitude is an incredible boom and blessing. But I think along the way, I think back to when I was an undergraduate and I got third place in my English department creative writing contest, and just the feeling of affirmation, and of course, it is as you said, largely luck.

I think most things in writing, stumbling upon the right material at the right time, reading the right books at the right time to give you the benchmarks that you're aiming for, so much of that is just a matter of timing and good fortune. I certainly feel like this one came at the right time.

JDP: So, one of the key things about the Project, of course, is the teaching, and both Tony and Joyce are dedicated teachers. In fact, if you don't mind my saying this, Joyce, I think you list as your occupation, teacher.

JCO: I have, yes.

JDP: And so, I'm wondering: you hear writers who complain about schedules and teaching and if you're an adjunct, it's a pretty tough life, no question about it. Or, teaching high school can be very tough, too. But I'm wondering how do you approach teaching? What's in it for you? I'm trying not to make this a big question. I'm trying to make it a small question, that is, how do you approach the work of teaching? What is significant for you when you're in the classroom?

AM: I think for me it forces me to clarify what I actually think about things, that there's nothing like a group of distractible eighteen-year-olds to make you really sharpen your sensibilities, to describe why do you think certain things work in fiction. Why are certain stories or certain writers or certain flights of sentences in a particular piece, why is that meaningful? Why is it something to aspire toward? And, I feel like so much of writing and reading is this very solitary endeavor, that when you're writing, at least I am just mainly staring at my computer screen and trying not to watch any more YouTube cat videos.

But when you're teaching, it suddenly becomes this communal experience where your own, at least I've felt quite frequently that my own sense of what is worthwhile literature is expanded, and just being peppered with very simple questions about something that's complex as a novel, forces a kind of refinement that has been really useful for my own writing.

JCO: Well, when I began teaching, I think I probably needed a job and was quite really grateful to be a teacher. When I was really a very little girl, literally very little, I just loved my teachers. I loved my first grade teacher and I loved, when I was in junior high school and high school, it was an emerging sense of wanting to join a community of likeminded people.

I had such reverence for them. I also loved librarians, and I loved libraries. And, this library, I was saying to Joe, this is a library that's most distinctive in that one can never really find the front door. It's wonderful. You become creative in your movements around. So, to me, being a librarian would have been, made me just as happy as being a teacher, and so, then I was in college and I wanted to be a college teacher, it just kept moving up.

When I teach creative writing, I feel that I'm meeting young people who are not unlike myself. I identify with the young writers much more than I do with my own self. I don't have much interest in my own self, but I have a lot of interest in the young writers. They're working with material that can be very raw and very sincere and painful and candid, and they're trying to figure out ways to express themselves.

A student I have, with wonderful story to tell, but he or she hasn't begun it, at the right point, or the wrong character's perspective is being emphasized, and so, we try to find out what the best way to present it is, and I find that really exciting, that kind of collaborative work.

JDP: Well, it's very interesting that you said you're not interested in yourself as a teacher and a writer. Tony, you said something, I can't find it, I wrote it down, you said, one interview, the great pleasure is that you don't know who you are as a writer. You don't know who you are. That gives you all the freedom to write. I know, everybody in law enforcement would be very interested in that position. You don't know who you are.

AM: I'm trying to think where I said that. Yeah, I think that people write for all sorts of reasons, and I think that one reason people write and I think it's a very important and worthwhile reason, is self-expression. I recently finished reading *Educated*, which I thought was an incredibly beautiful book, and it's a book that you could tell with every word that she needed to write this book, and that it was a book that, I would imagine that the very act of writing it was transformative.

I, as a writer, I feel like I'm always trying to approach the work that I'm composing as I approach the books that I want to read. And, ever since I was a little kid, I feel like reading has been just this wonderful form of escapism, where I want to go to different planets, to different time periods. I want to open a book and feel like I'm falling through a window, not looking into a mirror. And, I supposed that that sense of being stuck with myself, within a book over the course of years, that kind of self-examination just doesn't particularly appeal to me.

I think that one of the things, along with show don't tell, that we always are taught in creative writing classrooms, at least I was, was that you should write what you know. And I remember at some point somebody said that rather than writing what you know, why don't you write what you want to learn, or write what you want to know. And that just had a pretty profound impact on me. It suddenly meant that my canvas could be the entire world. And, so much of what I work on, I think, is a way for me to try to understand what it is that I am interested in, rather than a way of trying to understand myself. And so, that necessarily takes the work quite far from my personal life, and I can tell you my parents are thrilled with that.

JCO: Yes.

AM: So every time I talk to my mom on the phone, she signs off by saying, "Don't write about us." Good luck, Mom. Okay.

JDP: And Joyce, you've quoted Toni Morrison approvingly as, write the book that you want to read, and I think that's probably good advice. Not that any writer or aspiring writer is interested in advice. No writer is interested in advice, or they're never taking it.

AM: Writers are very interested in dispensing advice.

JDP: But to get into this, relating to not being interested in yourself or using this escape for literature, both of you are very interested— in *Hazards of Time Travel*, and in *The Tsar of Love and Techno*—in deletion, which is a big motif. Deletion, vaporization, and these characters, this wonderful thing you do with the brother who is working with the paintings in Chechnya. And then, with your protagonist, Joyce, the threat of being deleted is so poignant and powerful, and she's moving ... so I'm wondering if ... it reminds me, and I'm not going to step on your joke, Tony, but it's what people told you all the time when you visited Chechnya. They had a running joke with you, do you remember? ... I'll step on the line if you want.

AM: I can't remember what...

JDP: You said, "Their continual joke with me was they wanted to kidnap me."

AM: Oh yeah, yeah.

JDP: A pretty serious joke. So, I'm wondering, what's the fascination with deletion, in your works?

AM: I suppose for me, it was in *The Tsar of Love and Techno*, one of the main characters is this censor, and throughout the Soviet Union during Stalin's reign, I'm not sure if anybody saw the *Death of Stalin*. During the credits, you see the various actors, the various historical figures being airbrushed out, and that was a common way of how people were dealt with in photographs and paintings, that once you fell from favor you were erased. And, it was the idea that a person could not only be imprisoned or assassinated, but they could literally be obliterated from history. And, that idea of a state actor viewing reality, viewing his country the same way that a novelist views a novel, that you can rewrite certain characters, you can delete lines, you can entirely cut someone expendable out, is a very creepy and horrific idea and it's a way of, I think, looking at that particular time period that I hadn't quite seen as the center of a novel before. And so, it was a way of, in that book, of tracing the legacy of this particular censor and the people that he censored over the course of about a century and seeing the ways in which despite the overwhelming machinery of the Soviet apparatus to erase all of these individual dissidents and innocent people, that over time their ghosts live in the machine as it were, and eventually emerge on the back end.

JDP: This is a real-world dystopia.

AM: Mm-hmm [affirmative]. Yeah, yeah.

JDP: So Joyce, could you tell us about your setup for *Hazards of Time Travel*, the dystopia that you created?

JCO: I should begin by saying that the original title, which I was working for years, was *Vicissitudes of Time Travel*, and so actually that title got partially deleted.

JDP: Hard to spell.

JCO: I guess people felt that they couldn't pronounce it. They had no idea what it was or what it meant. *Vicissitudes of Time Travel*, but to me that was the real title of the novel, then my editor and the marketing people...as soon as marketing people are on the scene, you know in your heart, you know it's all over at that point.

So, *Hazards of Time Travel* doesn't have quite the same ring. I guess we're always living in precarious present tense and things are being deleted in the sense that things are being forgotten. So, I often read about memory in works of fiction, assuming that the reader is the repository of memories that some of the characters are forgetting, so that the reader knows more than some of the characters. They're entering into relationships that partially eclipse or occlude or erase parts of their own personality, especially perhaps a young woman who is the protagonist of *Hazards of Time Travel*. And so, even though I wrote the novel, when I have reread it or read it to an audience, I notice near the end of the novel, that the young woman has actually forgotten a number of things that we know she experienced.

In other words, the erasure being forced upon her by her society to make her a conformist, to bend her to the will of people who are invisible, when I began working on the novel in 2011, we did not have a United States tyrannically run by a demagogue. I think Obama may have been president at the time. And, I was thinking as I created the novel, I was thinking more of the surveillance state, what I see coming in the future. I would not have guessed that we would have a populist demagogue president, because that somehow is more of an old-fashioned ... it's like a reversion to another, earlier America.

But I think in the long run, the danger will be a totalitarian international, global surveillance state where something you do is recorded on your cell phone, like right now, and it's sent all around the world and somewhere in China it's being recorded, and it's somewhere hearing that and then, when you go to present yourself at an airport or something, this will all be waiting for you. It's a huge web, a huge mesh of identifications that you don't know anything about, you didn't give any permission for.

So, my novel is about, really, that kind of reality that's closing in upon us, rather than a populist political reality. People have asked me if I've been writing about the Trump administration, but I actually wasn't. There are some things in common, the distrust of science, and shutting down bureaus of inquiry and shutting down national parks and just taking away the budget from things that mean a good deal to people in the humanities and people who are interested in science. That would be a typical totalitarian move, which the Trump administration has been trying to do, or perhaps already has done. So, there are some things in common.

JDP: Well, this makes me think about what you're doing in *Tsar of Love and Techno*, Tony. I've heard you speak about how you don't consider yourself an expert on Russia or the Soviet Union or Chechnya. But you are an expert on these characters. And so, I'm wondering when people say, "Well, this is a dystopian kind of vision," I'm wondering how you ... What are you putting in its place in the story? What does the novel do that, for you, isn't happening on the ground in Chechnya?

AM: Well, it's interesting. The idea of dystopia, there's that famous phrase from, I think, William Gibson, that the future is here, it's just unevenly distributed, and I think that's true with dystopia as well, that you don't need to look into a *Hunger Games* future necessarily to see what a postapocalyptic world would look like, and I think that one of the things in both *Constellation* and *Tsar* that I really tried to draw upon was some of the tropes from dystopic literature, but put it within this very historical context.

So, *The Road* and *Blindness* were two books ... *The Road* by Cormac McCarthy and *Blindness* by Jose Saramago, are both these really incredible visions of apocalyptic human ruin, and those were two books that I was reading very closely as I was working, particularly on *Constellation*, and thinking of how some of those grotesque fantasies we have about the future we can find in the present and in the recent past.

JCO: Was *The Road* published when you were working on *Constellation*?

AM: Yeah, it was published a couple years ahead of mine.

JCO: I'm surprised. I thought it was more recent.

AM: I think it was 2006, 2007, something like that.

JDP: Wonder if this would be a good time for some reading?

JCO: Okay.

JDP: Just an idea.

JCO: What an original idea.

JDP: Who wants to go first? Tony?

AM: Sure, yeah, should I sit here? Go up there?

JDP: Wherever you want to be. You require musical accompaniment?

AM: Please.

JDP: Okay.

AM: Well, I was telling Joe beforehand that tomorrow I'm visiting Northgate High School and I found a bunch of poems that I wrote when I was in high school that I'm going to read to them. And, as soon as I said that, I wish that I had brought them here.

JDP: Thank you for not bringing them.

AM: Yeah, yeah, no worries. No worries. One is a love sonnet to Ralph Nader. I was deeply enamored with him. But I'm going to read two very short things. This is a very brief, little notice that I wrote for the Simpson's website a couple of weeks ago.

When Joe asked me to write a few words on how I've spent my year as the Simpson Prize recipient, I came to realize that I would make a terrible memoirist. I don't drink or smoke. I go to bed early enough that my mom, who lives on the East Coast, occasionally wakes me up when she calls. I don't have a car, and my usual rounds take me no farther than I can walk.

Just about every morning and afternoon, weekdays and weekends, I go to the same two coffee shops, order the same drink and sit in the same seat and write. This is literally the most exciting thing I've done in weeks. In October, I went out of town for several days without telling the proprietor of my afternoon coffee shop and she worried that some terrible accident had befallen me.

I say this not in complaint, but in gratitude. At the end of a perfect week, I look back without remembering what happened on any particularly day. Not because nothing happened, but because I was doing the same thing every day, getting good work done. Thanks to the Simpson Prize, I'm having a year of those days. I'm hesitant to speak directly about my current project, needless to say, the work is going quite well.

Recently, I watched the BBC nature documentary, Blue Planet Two, *an extraordinary series whose cast includes octopi armored in scavenged sea shells, sperm whales in vertical slumber, and bioluminescent creatures lighting the ocean floor miles below the last of the sun's rays. Beneath the seemingly monotonous surface of the ocean is a depthless underworld, teeming with life.*

When asked, "What have you been up to?" I usually answer, "Not much," because to any casual observer, I'm simply sitting in my coffee shops, working on the next page, writing these very words. But to you, dear friend of the Simpson Literary Project, I will confess the truth. I am out there swimming with the starfish and the sea anemones.

JDP: Beautiful. That's so beautiful.

AM: Thank you. So, I was going to also just read this very brief section. I thought I would read literally what I've been writing. This is what I had been working on up until yesterday, so it covers Sunday and Monday, and I thought I would give you just a snapshot of a work in progress.

This is the first time I've read anything from this book, so here we go. Just as context, this is set in 1926, '27 Italy, right at the point where Mussolini had begun the dictatorship, but where you still had these last few gasps of socialist dissident and it's about a brother and sister. The brother is a college-age socialist who's running an underground newspaper, and he gets his little sister to become his courier. And, this comes at a point after you realize the aftermath of this, obviously, terrible idea, and so it's written with, I guess, the nostalgia one might, when looking back at the point in one's life before everything went wrong.

[He read a short draft piece from his new novel, forthcoming from Hogarth. The novel is set in Italy and in what immigrants called Los Angeles, "Sunny Siberia."]

JDP: That's pretty spectacular devastation and color … The secret pages, that's a marvelous touch. With the heels…

AM: Oh. The imperious heights of her heels.

JDP: Very Italian. Joyce, would like to read something, please?

JCO: Yes. The most distinct feature of this is that I wrote it very recently. It was meant to be funny. We thought, both Tony and I, that we would read new work rather than old work. So, this is a poem. It's divided into stanzas. I will just pause between the stanzas. As some of you know, if you've read my novel, *Hazards of Time Travel*, formerly *Vicissitudes of Time Travel*, it's very much about B. F. Skinner and the behaviorist psychology.

The idea of managing, manipulating people's minds, making people do things that are maybe against their own best interest, best exemplified, I suppose, in insidious ways of politicizing elements that are really not political, and dividing people and maneuvering large masses of people for political reasons, or for other reasons.

Originally, John Watson, who's, I guess you could say, the protagonist of this poem, John Watson is called the father of American psychology, of behaviorist psychology. He was the person who really worked out a strategy for advertising that has descended to us today, that's all around us. The idea being that you manipulate people unconsciously, to arouse in them a craving for purchasing something that maybe they don't need or don't particularly want, or it's overpriced and you do that by manipulating symbols and things that have various kinds of meanings.

The most obvious being a very beautiful expensive car, and there's a beautiful woman standing next to it, so the promise seems to be if you could buy the car, then the woman somehow comes along with it. Or, a woman who is anxious about her beauty and she has all array of cosmetics and things, or people being worried about their natural body odors and their deodorants for them, and so forth and so on.

I remember seeing ads that are no longer allowed, where someone in a white coat pretending to be a doctor is smoking a cigarette and saying, "Nothing tastes quite so good as a cigarette should," or something like that. So, my novel is about, really the twenty-first-century consequences of mind manipulation, particularly politically and in every way, and culturally.

B. F. Skinner is not a character in my novel, but he was alive at the time of the novel. The novel is time travel, so they're either going back, people are sent back to the 1950s. Skinner was alive at that time. He was a professor at Harvard. And, my husband Charlie Gross is not actually that old. He was a freshman at Harvard when Skinner was in his prime, and Charlie was actually in one of Skinner's laboratories.

But my poem is not about Skinner, it's about John Watson, who comes before Skinner, and this is called Little Albert 1920. Many of you know who little Albert was. This is a very famous psychological experiment. Many of you, if you have taken psychology in universities, you've seen the film of a little baby who was put on the table and then these various things are brought to him, like a white rat and a monkey and different things, and his reactions to them.

This was all filmed. You can look it up on Google. Just type in Little Albert, John Watson 1920, it will all come up. Little Albert 1920.

[*Oates reads her poem "Little Albert," which appears on page 71*]

JDP: So, speaking of truths that are lost there, truthfulness over time and scientific theories that are then debunked, I'm wondering in a larger sense, when … Well, for instance, Mark Twain thought he was living in very perilous times. He was the first great anti-imperialist American writer, though maybe W. E. B. Du Bois qualifies, or Frederick Douglass, those two.

But Homer, of the Odyssey and the *Iliad*, thought that things were pretty good back in the day. He missed the past. So, I'm wondering, and if you watch enough TV, and it's tempting to watch TV these days, you hear talking heads talk about inflection points, moments of change that we're in, the post-Skinnerian Age, the post-Soviet Age that we're in.

I'm wondering if you have any thoughts about whether we are at an inflection point for literature. For instance, it was commonplace to observe that *Uncle Tom's Cabin* changed the world when it was published. It made people think about slavery in a whole new way. I don't think it's a news flash that we're still struggling with these same issues today. But when you think about the big issues, race, gender, sex, immigration, all the burning issues, are we at an inflection point, and what are writers doing to help us get through this moment, or illuminate us in this moment? I'm not saying that they have responsibility to do that, but are they doing that?

JCO: Well, I think one of the most profound changes in maybe the last fifty years or so is that there's a kind of egalitarianism in literature. It didn't used to be, and I'm saying this apologetically. So, the straight white male literature was the mainstream, really the only literature. And then, there were peripheral people who may be allowed in the club so to speak, Willa Cather, Edith Wharton, Emily Dickinson, very few of these brilliant women were allowed in that club. However, in the last fifty years or so, really beginning in the 1960s, that kind of pyramid situation, I think, has really been struck down.

We have many, many perspectives. We have people who are writing from all sorts of different ethnic identities, gender identities, people who are this, that and trans and this. And, all of that was really totally unknown when I was, say, in high school.

And so, if you were a young girl who wanted to be a writer, the main writers were someone like Ernest Hemingway or William Faulkner and some others, with, as I say, a few women on the side, and many of the women, maybe they might be bestsellers, but they weren't considered literature.

So, that is the most obvious and most profound change in my lifetime, has been the decentralization of literature as reflected in bookstores, and, I'm sure, library and bookstore both, just the categories you see when you going in a store now. They didn't really exist. Now you see many, many different categories and I thought that was really exciting and very wonderful. There are negative things about our society too, but to me, that seems like a really wonderful positive thing.

JDP: In fact, you addressed this in the essay that you published in *Simpsonistas*, "A Wounded Deer Leaps Highest," which is a marvelous essay treating this very thing, in which you reference this obscure author, Anthony Marra. What do you have to say for yourself, Mr. Marra?

AM: Honestly, I feel like I've been pulled on stage to play with Bruce Springsteen. I feel like there's little I can add to that. I'm thirty-four years old and so I feel like most of my reading has been in the period after that flowering of different experiences and voices and the doors being opened to more people, more narratives, all of that, and I feel like it has certainly, profoundly affected how I became a writer. I'm not sure if writing about a place like Chechnya would be something that I necessarily would have been interested in, or felt capable of or even seen within the realm of possibility had I really grown up only on stories about divorce in Connecticut.

JDP: Or, as your publisher said, "We were not waiting on the next great Chechnyan novel." Okay, we're going to take questions in a few seconds, but let me just raise this issue about social media and tracking pop culture. I wonder if you both … Joyce is kind of a star on Twitter, and my favorite tweet, in addition to all the cat stuff, is … and I don't even have a cat, but her stuff is pretty cool. No disrespect to cats. Cats are wonderful. Some of my best friends are cats, honest. Okay, you bust me. So, one of the things, my favorite tweet of yours is, "Sure was glad to get out of there alive. Favorite line from Bob Dylan song. Applicable to virtually every experience we are likely to have anywhere," including, I hope, tonight. We will be glad to get out of here alive.

So, Tony, there you are, you're thirty-four. Aren't you living in this ether of social media?

AM: I don't.

JDP: No, you don't.

JCO: I think of Twitter as completely vaporous and fleeting and just a scroll that's like clouds in the sky. I really don't think there's much permanence. And, from the very first, when I went on Twitter, in the very beginning, it wasn't so politicized. It was more for jokes and surreal, goofy things and Steve Martin was one of the people who was quite prominent, whom I followed. It's only with the campaign of 2016 that everything got so embittered and so politicized. So, in the beginning, Twitter was much more of an innocent place and people would post where they were, what they were reading, or if they like the movie, or recommended something, some music or something, and then they had these jokes. And so, to me basically, that was the great appeal of it. But, I wouldn't say that it's like Paradise Lost. It's not anything that's going to abide very long. People who are on Twitter, I don't think they themselves remember what they've tweeted forty-eight hours ago.

AM: Yeah, I have a Twitter account.

JDP: I saw that. Four years ago…

AM: Four years ago, no, but I still go on almost every day just to look at the news. And, I've noticed just … it used to be I'll go on and just see what's happening out in the world and now it feels like every time I go onto Twitter, it's like the internet or technological version of the *Morning Joe* set. The doors have been locked and they haven't been fed for days, and they're fighting over who's going to get Willie Geist. And I feel like it's Twitter and social media as an environment, I feel like, is not conducive to my own mental health.

JDP: And you don't have a TV.

AM: I don't, no. But I have a computer and Netflix and everything.

JCO: Well, I say one thing about Twitter that is very positive. It opens doors or windows to many people who didn't know other people like them existed. And, if you're interested, for instance in say, animal rights or animal shelters, or no-kill shelters, there's a community there of people who are like-minded. All sorts of women's issues, battered women, victims of sexual abuse and so forth, people who might have languished away or even committed suicide far away in some rural area in northern Idaho, they suddenly have a community of people that they can write to, and I think that's just really, really wonderful.

It's analogous to the first telephones that were introduced in the United States. In rural areas, where women were all alone and people were very isolated, like in New England, then they had something called the party line, where the phone rang and you heard it ring. Your ring was two rings, somebody else's three rings, and suddenly people were connected with other people. That made a tremendous difference to these lonely people.

JDP: Anybody have any questions for Joyce or Tony?

A1: [Audience Member 1] I'd love to compliment the Simpson Project for the teaching aspect. Even though you were discouraged with young people who didn't seem to be ready for your work, they don't remember that always in precious time when they get a little older. So, thank you for that section of the Simpson Project.

JDP: Thank you. So Tony, good luck teaching at Northgate tomorrow. Any other questions or comments?

A2: [Audience Member 2] In working with younger students, or even hopeful writers to be, do you ever sense a new emerging turn or a fresh emergence of a kind that hints of remarkable changes?

JDP: Tony, Joyce, the question is whether or not you're seeing in your students evidence of some social movement, some artistic movement broadly conceived, an aesthetic movement, a technical advance. I'll keep going.

AM: I've only worked with undergraduates, and I think usually you see similar stages where often they're beginning by bringing in a lot of personal material, stuff that's clearly drawn from their family or their personal life. You see a lot of campus dramas, and maybe over the course of a couple of years, it will begin to move into other arenas of their life, or their interests.

Something that I always try to do is try to get them interested in social and historical and political, the context around which they are writing. And so, we always do these exercises where they have to write these biographies of their settings, where they have to include all of that and then see how the individual characters ricochet off of all of that. But, in terms of any formal artistic movement, I don't think there's been any sort of unified theory of what's happening in literature that you can necessarily see through sophomores in college who are really just trying to get the nuts and bolts of the craft.

JCO: No, I would agree with that. I think some years ago, minimalism swept through universities, but today, people write in very different ways. I've taught at Princeton University for quite a long time, and I always teach at NYU in the graduate writing program, and at UC Berkeley undergraduate, so I have a wide range of students, and yet the interesting thing is that whether one is teaching right now, in 2019, or has been teaching say, since, in 1975, that there's a wide range of time and wide range of kinds of students. But the odd thing is that a writing student, a poet or a fiction writer, is almost ahistorical. A student who … a young writer of 1957 or 1931, would have a lot in common with a young writer of 2011, or 2019. There's just a feeling of a kind of camaraderie of people who love books, people who are not necessarily conformist or trendy, or a person who is a poet, who is in love with poetry.

I've always had students like that, individuals rather than parts of movements. And, the great drama for most of my students, particularly at Berkeley, well, also at Princeton, the great drama's actually for the ethnic minority students, whose parents came to this country or grandparents, where they are the generation, they are thoroughly American, but their parents and grandparents may still be speaking another language and identify with a foreign culture, that to me is the big change. When I first started teaching, writing teachers didn't have that drama, but almost every one of my students presents that drama which is profound. It's profound because the young Americanized student, whose parents and grandparents are from another country, is like a pioneer. They are making their way in uncharted waters. They are very anxious and fearful of hurting or wounding their parents, but they don't want to do what their parents want them to do. They don't want the old rituals. They don't want the old food. They are Americans and they're very much focused on the future and on one another. And, that drama plays out in their writing and it's very dramatic.

A3:   [Audience Member 3] Tony, I wonder in your case, what is the appeal in historical fiction for you?

AM: Well, I feel like this present project that I'm working on now is the first historical work I've really sunk my teeth into. Both of my books, *Constellation* and *The Tsar of Love and Techno*, have both been, I feel like, shoehorned in historical fiction, which I've never entirely understood, because *Constellation* is set in 2004 and aside from the opening story, *The Tsar of Love and Techno* is set during the nineties to the present day.

But, there you have it. But, I find history just gives you these kinds of, almost these currents of narrative that you can draft behind a little bit. It presents all of these fascinating narrative arcs. If you set a story on the day the Titanic sets sail, you have a pretty clear end point. And, I think that there's all kinds of reasons to read, but one of the things that I've always found really fascinating is seeing how a novel can map out a place, map out a point in time.

One of the writers that meant a lot to me was Mario Vargos Llosa, and he's somebody who always writes historical fiction, even if he's writing in the present day, that he's presenting the world in terms of these historic forces and these structures of power and poverty and all the rest of it. And, he animates Proust and Latin America in a way that feels so much more vibrant and alive to me than any history book ever could. And so, I suppose I'm drawn to what I want to read, I suppose, and that has put me in that category, I guess, at least from my present book.

A4: [Audience Member 4] Let's see if I can articulate this. I was wondering if either of you have had the experience of, because of the way society's constantly changing its attitudes about the MeToo, or whatever, whether people are reevaluating characters from Joyce, say, your earlier books and having different opinions about those characters that might not necessarily reflect how you made them when you wrote the—

JCO: Well, that may be happening. We know that has certainly happened with Mark Twain and *Huckleberry Finn*, where a novel that seemed to us, when we were fairly young, sort of incontestably a great work, is now challenged because of its language and because of accusations of racism and so forth. So, there's an ever-shifting set of standards that surely we're all going to fail at some point. We live in our own time, and we say things and do things in our own time that seem acceptable, and then in some other era, they're brought into question.

The MeToo movement is a very good example. There are people whom I know, and I respect their sensitivity. They really don't want to read novels about sexism. They don't want to read novels in which women are victims or willing victims, or subservient, playing subservient roles, even though at the time those were written, none of that was intended at all. It was more like a portrait, like a mirror held up to the society at that time.

I had an interesting conversation with Mary Gaitskill when I was visiting Claremont College recently, and Mary Gaitskill, who is quite a feminist as you probably know, Mary Gaitskill says she almost preferred, or she did prefer, reading a really sexist writer, like John Updike, because she felt that that was expressing what people really thought, whereas today, when people are very politically correct and very sensitive, there may be a kind of hypocrisy or fraudulence, and it's not really as deep or as profound. And, I thought that was an interesting point of view. At the same time, she said she was very bored and her students hated these novels. It was kind of a complex thing.

JDP: But, if I remember your very famous short story, "Where Are You Going, Where Have You Been," which was written in 1975, and made into a wonderful movie. Much written about, this is a fantastic story. It's aged very well. It's a story of shocking sexual exploitation, a visionary story in all sorts of ways.

JCO: Well, where I think about women and girls, I think, which I've done for much of my life, did seem to be a way of moving into a future that now seems very contemporary. At the time, it may have seemed excessive or unlikely, or people would get angry with me. They would say, "Joyce, what are you writing about? Why is your writing so violent?" I was asked many times. But the world is so violent. It's just that women were not expected to express it. Men would be expected to, but not women.

JDP: A story that is dedicated to Bob Dylan as it happens.

JCO: Yeah, coming around full circle.

JDP: It is coming around full circle. I'm working really hard to do that. Any other comments or questions?

A5: [Audience Member 5] Speaking of John Updike, I'm a huge fan and I know you were a peer and friend of his. Where do you place him in the pantheon of great American writers?

JCO: Well, I don't really think placing people in any rank, in any way of ranking. To me, John Updike was just such a gifted, wonderful stylist. I always loved just his language. His early short stories are just beautiful and very, actually autobiographical. He's not pretentious. He's not trying to do a kind of writing that was necessarily shocking. For John Updike, just opening the door and showing a middle-class household, that was, to him, absolutely beautiful, and I think he had a religious element to his writing. He may have been, in fact, religious. I'm not so sure how he developed when he became older, but he felt that God expressed himself in the beauty of the natural world and of people, of sexuality and people's bodies and so forth. There was a transcendental value in these things. So, if John is just describing a sunset or snow falling, or a woman's face, or a child, he's infused with this radiance, and I think that's what we really liked.

Another element of John Updike was his humor. He was very funny, extremely witty. Some of his poetry is really witty poetry and there are jokes here and there in his writing that tend to be maybe lost. He is actually disdained and really hated by some people because it's perceived, I think maybe unjustly, that he was the sexist. It's just the word, which I think is unfortunate.

JDP: Maybe we could take one more question or comment? Yes, please.

A6: [Audience Member 6] Thank you both for your presentation. Joyce, I started *The Man Without a Shadow* just the other day, and I'm hearkening back to your poem. Where does your genesis of exploration of the mind begin?

JCO: Well, specifically with that novel I was interested in the phenomenon of losing memory and how our personalities are really dependent upon our memories, the associations of people whom we know and all the memories going back to when we're children that constitute our personalities. If we start to lose those memories, the personality starts to deteriorate, and we see as people are getting older in our culture, generally of course, the phenomenon of Alzheimer's and dementia is not just an idea or a philosophical notion, it's actually very clinical and very immediate.

So, I wanted to write a novel about a woman scientist, who's working with the most famous amnesiac in the history of neuroscience, who really did exist. His initials were HM, and he's immortalized in a book by Suzanne Corkin called *Permanent Present Tense*, the amazing history of HM. Now, the reason that I had this book, it actually came in the house because my husband's a neuroscientist. So, I started reading this.

This is so amazing because this woman, Suzanne Corkin, worked with HM from the time she was quite a young woman scientist. She worked with him for something like thirty or forty years. But, every time they met, every time she met him, he never remembered her. She, of course, knew all about him. She was working, experimenting with his memory. And, my novel is based on … It's different from her experience, because in my novel, she actually does fall in love with him, and he expands her life even as his memory's failing, he's always the same age and she gets older. He doesn't understand that he is not also getting older. But that, by the end of the novel, she is really so much in love with him and so devoted to him, that though he never remembers her ... It's like a parody of a marriage. Where are my car keys and where is my cell phone and all this, that you don't really judge the person any longer by that part of the conscious personality, but by something deeper. She loves him on that deeper spiritual level, even though the person he is doesn't know who she is. So it seemed to me kind of a beautiful phenomenon, which I think is actually happening in many people's relationships.

JDP: That's fascinating.

Our time together is now up. I want to make sure you have the opportunity to frequent the Great Good Place for Books store out there in the lobby. There are lots of books that Tony and Joyce will sign for you. Support your local independent bookstore. I'll just leave with one thought, one last tweet of Joyce's that's my favorite of hers. Actually, it's a quotation of Augustine of Hippo. It's slightly amended, and Joyce writes, "Love and do what you will," quoting Augustine. "Best advice at any time," she tweets. So love and do what you will. Thank you so much for being here tonight.

WORRIED SISTERS

BY SIGRID NUNEZ

2019 SIMPSON/JOYCE CAROL OATES PRIZE FINALIST

Our sister has always caused us grief. A dyspeptic baby; a nervous, accident-prone little girl, abnormally (so we, at least, thought, even if the doctor pooh-poohed this) sensitive to germs. Sneezing and hacking through every winter. (And where we lived, winters were long.) Everything went into her mouth. Take your eyes off her one instant and she'd surely hang or choke or poison herself. Twice it ended in the emergency room. It was all we could do to pull her through childhood. Not a lovable child, but we loved her, of course: she was our sister.

As she grew bigger, her problems grew too. She might have been a difficult, clumsy little girl, but at least she was happy. In her teens, she was never happy. The beauty of the family, to her own eyes she was grotesque. She tortured her hair till it began to fall out, tortured her blemishes so that they left tiny scars. She ate too much, and then too little. Grew fat, grew thin, but of course never thin enough. Once, she punched a mirror into shards. Tears at the drop of a hat. Rage at the merest suggestion of criticism. Countless absences from school. Not normal: this time, the doctor agreed. Now there would always be doctors in her life, and medications, new kinds of which kept coming on the market but none of which seemed to help.

She wanted to be an artist—but why put it that way? Were we out to *destroy* her? She didn't want to be an artist; she *was* an artist. And it was true that she won a full scholarship to art school, that soon after graduation she was awarded a prestigious young artist's prize. But after this, encouraging signs were few. We could see for ourselves what a hard life it was, especially for one as sensitive to rejection and failure as she was. How would our baby ever survive?

We tried to be supportive, turning the other cheek when she lashed out. We, with our ordinary lives and concerns—we who listened to the wrong bands and read the wrong books and made the mistake of calling paintings pictures—we could hardly be expected to understand her: nothing to do with blood. She often seemed just one long nose of disapproval. We confess that at times she scared us. In those days she affected a drastic look, always in black, her dyed black hair stiffened into porcupine-like quills that said back off, or we'll shoot. She accused us of not caring whether she became a famous artist or not—and what could we say since it was true?

Nobody was more selfish or narcissistic than the male artist, she always said. But that was the only kind of man she went for, and always so recklessly that when the relationship fell apart she fell apart too. And then it was just as it had been when she was a child: she had to be watched every minute.

When she turned forty she kept a promise she had made to herself at thirty: she gave up her studio and stopped making art. She took a job as a fundraiser for a small local museum. Though we would never have told her so, this change gave us hope. For the first time, she began dating someone who was not an egotistical young buck of an artist but a soft-spoken man a few years older than she, who worked for a company that sold office furniture. We could see how much our sister wanted things to work out. She tried not to compare her new boyfriend too much with the other, more exciting men she had been with and to temper her disdain for his job. But the thought that she had settled for this man out of fear that she couldn't do better tormented her. He had no conversation, and certain personal habits that had always annoyed her turned out to be more than she could bear. One day she found a nail clipper and a pile of dirty toenails on the coffee table.

Although she was sure she had made the right decision, the man was no sooner out of her life than she fell into her worst depression ever. Yet another new drug had recently become available, and her doctor urged her to try it. To everyone's surprise, it worked. Before our eyes, our sister passed from frantic despair to ordinary sadness. She got up every day and went to work, she ate, she slept, she went out with friends, like any normal unhappy person. A year passed, during which we caught up on our sleep and our reading, finished various projects and played with our grandchildren, and then one day our sister ran into her old, ditched boyfriend on her way home from work. Now they are back together again. In fact, she says, they have never gotten along so well. The things that bothered her the first time around? Those habits that took such a toll on her nerves? They now roll right off her back. He is no longer a man who never has anything to say, but the strong, silent type.

We see. We knew that this was one of the effects of the miracle drug: a mellowing effect, enabling the depressive for the first time in her life to take daily annoyances and simple frustrations in stride. Not till now, however, did we understand that another effect of the drug was to protect the depressive from this very knowledge. Not being medicated ourselves, and knowing our sister as we do, we can see clearly that if she were not taking the drug, her feelings for this man would be the same as they were before. We know it's the pills talking when she tells us how much she wants to get married.

We have discussed the matter between ourselves, but never with our sister. We don't want her to be alone, but we are troubled by the thought of her marrying someone that she would never agree to marry if she were not on the medication. We don't like to think what might happen if, for some reason, she were to stop taking it. We are relieved that at least she is past having children. No children will suffer, whatever happens. However, the man in question is a fine, decent human being whom we have always liked, and we are uncomfortable with the idea of his making such a life-changing decision when he is lacking all the information.

Together we compose a letter to the columnist who answers questions from readers in various moral quandaries for our local newspaper. We explain that the doctor has said there is no reason our sister shouldn't be able to stay on the medication for the rest of her life. But we have also heard of studies that say that this might not be possible; the medication could lose its effect over time, or staying on it for too long might turn out to be in some way harmful. This, now, has become our new worry. We take our responsibilities seriously, but we don't know what is the right thing to do, whether to speak now or forever hold our peace. We do not sign our real names, of course, but rather, Her Loving Sisters.

ESSAY & POEMS

BY JOHN JAMES

SIMPSON FELLOW 2019

.

ON WRITING "THE MILK HOURS"

At the age of twenty-four, I had the bizarre but enlightening experience of learning from a poem that my father had committed suicide. In a sense, I'd known this for a long time. I was six when he died, and the explanation I'd been given was that he was "sick," that he suffered from a disease called "depression." A priest gave me a card with haloed Jesus on the front. After that, my family was reticent. I filled in details for myself.

I was in college when a letter from my paternal grandmother arrived. At that point, we'd been estranged almost my entire life. After my father's death, my family moved from Long Beach, California, where I'd been born, to Louisville, Kentucky, an hour's drive from the tobacco farm where my mother's parents lived. Pretty quickly, we lost touch—less out of habit than by design. When a person commits suicide, you look for someone to blame. Sometimes that blame is justified. My mother sought geographic and emotional distance.

This wasn't the first letter. They'd arrived throughout my life—sometimes with my grandmother's return address, sometimes in the guise of advertisements for activities I'd been interested in at the age of four or five. One appeared to be a letter from a Tae Kwon Do studio. I was passively discouraged from replying, though the option was never barred. When I grew older, I became curious.

My grandmother and I corresponded in general terms for several years. I cultivated the relationship, but held her at a distance. I gave my email address and sent updates, but never shared my phone number. She was never on social media, but if she were, I probably would have avoided her. But the messages grew deeper, closer, and as I made my way through college, then moved to New York for graduate school, I began to share details: photos, poems.

As it turned out, my grandmother was an amateur poet, and the latter became a point of connection. She sent pieces she'd written, usually by hand. When my first poems appeared in journals, she bought copies and shared them with the family. She was a good grandma, in that way.

By this point, I'd been writing obliquely about my father's death for a long time. My poems were vaguely elegiac, usually without mentioning their subject. They danced around what they suspected but never stated—what on some level I knew, but was afraid to admit.

After my MFA, I moved back to Kentucky, where I lived cheaply teaching adjunct at my alma mater and wrote many of the poems that became *The Milk Hours*. I had a dog, a garden, and twice the space I'd had in Brooklyn—for half the price. Around that time, my grandmother offered to share a poem that, she said, might trouble me. She also noted that I was an adult and could decide for myself whether to read it. I told her to send.

I'm sure I saved the poem, though at the moment, it's tucked away in a basement somewhere. I remember the curved scrawl of her pen. Something about crystals and pain. There was also a rhyme: a "son," who "took his life with a gun." There it was, what I'd suspected. I felt a pain in my gut.

The information sent me reeling. I needed to know more—the facts, the events, the days leading up to his death. I was consumed by a totalizing urge to pin down the minutia, to set it all straight. Now that I knew the *what*, I needed to know *why*.

Of course, there were no explanations. Only mitigating circumstances. My mother provided the details. I learned that he'd experienced serious bouts of depression from a young age—that it was paralyzing, keeping him in bed for days on end. He'd lost several jobs because of it. He'd taken medication, which evened him out—until he went off of it. That's when the worst happened.

In hindsight, better drugs and more information about their effects could have saved my father's life. Circumstances in his childhood might have prevented his illness, or kept it from becoming the monster it became. The rest I already knew. His mother had been an alcoholic. He and his siblings were severely neglected. According to family lore, he changed his own diapers—at the age of four, since no one had potty-trained him.

Once when he was in high school, his parents moved without telling him. It took several days to locate an address.

The experience also helped me understand what could have eased my own grief. Talking about it from a younger age, within context, might have helped me properly mourn his death rather than avoid the awful fact. Only by confronting the situation, and writing my way through it, was I able to move on.

It's still a wound, but no longer a festering one.

A year or two later, I received a message from a cousin in California. My grandmother had been diagnosed with lung cancer, and it was very advanced. She didn't have much time.

I had continued to write to my grandmother, sharing my life as it developed. My daughter was born, making her a great-grandmother. I was in a relationship, bought a house. But I still held her at a distance. I had never talked to her as an adult—not in person, nor on the phone. I immediately bought a ticket to Los Angeles.

When I arrived at the hospital, I was ushered to my grandmother's side. She lay in bed, a plastic mask allowing her to breathe. She could hear, but couldn't talk, and wrote on a dry-erase board to communicate. When I came close, she touched my face. I gave her a limp hug.

Flying out there, I was afraid she'd interpret my presence as absolution. Maybe she did, but it was the only resolution I was going to get. I stood there awkwardly while my cousins cried, watching them mourn a grandmother I basically didn't know—and who, to be honest, I still resented.

When she died a few hours later, I was relieved. I was glad she was no longer suffering—and happy for the both of us that we reunited before she passed. I spent the afternoon dazed, staring at the pink azaleas spotting my cousin's yard. It was spring and seventy degrees. My aunt offered to drive me to the beach.

Not long after that, back in Kentucky, I sat on my front porch, across the street from the cemetery where my father is buried, which sounds more morbid than it is. It occurred to me that he and my daughter never met—that their lives were separated by a twenty-year gap, and that, despite their shared genetics, I was the only connective tissue between them.

That moment condensed into a punctum, a point of realization wherein past and future collide. When I sat down to write it, it formed the title poem of my book: the single piece that combines the temporal strands of my life, which vector forward and back, acknowledging the hard fact my other poems only dance around, and admitting the terrible truth to the reader and to myself.

THE MILK HOURS

for J.E.J., 1962-1993
and C.S.M.J., 2013-

We lived overlooking the walls overlooking the cemetery.
The cemetery is where my father remains. We walked
in the garden for what seemed like an hour but in reality must
have been days. Cattail, heartseed—these words mean nothing to me.
The room opens up into white and more white, sun outside
between steeples. I remember, now, the milk hours, leaning
over my daughter's crib, dropping her ten, twelve pounds
into the limp arms of her mother. The suckling sound as I crashed
into sleep. My daughter, my father—his son. The wet grass
dew-speckled above him. His face grows vague and then vaguer.
From our porch I watch snow fall on bare firs. Why does it
matter now—what gun, what type. Bluesmoke rises. The chopped
copses glisten. Snowmelt smoothes the stone cuts of his name.

HISTORY (N.)

"I didn't make these verses because I wanted to rival that fellow, or his poems, in artistry—I knew that wouldn't be easy—but to test what certain dreams of mine might be saying and to acquit myself of any impiety, just in case they might be repeatedly commanding me to make this music."
— Plato, *Phaedo*

Viewed from space, the Chilean volcano blooms.

I cannot see it. It's a problem of scale. History—the branch

of knowledge dealing with past events; a continuous,

systematic narrative of; aggregate deeds; acts, ideas, events

that will shape the course of the future; immediate

but significant happenings; finished, done with—"he's history."

—

Calbuco: men shoveling ash from the street.

Third time in a week. And counting.

Infinite antithesis. Eleven

miles of ash in the air. What to call it—

just "ash." They flee to Ensenada.

—

The power of motives does not proceed directly from the will—

a changed form of knowledge. Wind pushing

clouds toward Argentina. *Knowledge is merely involved.*

Ash falls, it is falling, it has fallen. *Will fall.* Already flights

cancelled in Buenos Aires. I want to call it snow—

what settles on the luma trees, their fruit black, purplish black,

soot-speckled, hermaphroditic—*if this book is unintelligible*

and hard on the ears—the oblong ovals of its leaves.

Amos, fragrant. Family name *Myrtus*. The wood is extremely hard.

—

Ash falling on the concrete, falling on cars, ash
on the windshields, windows, yards. *They have lost
all sense of direction. They might as well be deep
in a forest or down in a well. They do not comprehend
the fundamental principles. They have nothing in their heads.*

— .

The dream kept
urging me on to do
what I was doing—
                                                 .
to make music—
since philosophy,
in my view, is
the greatest music.

—

History—from the Greek *historía*, learning or knowing by

inquiry. *Historein* (v.) to ask. *The asking is not idle.* From the French *histoire,* story. *Hístor* (Gk.) one who sees. *It is just a matter of what we are looking for.*

METAMORPHOSES

what was it this
morning : you said

redgrass glistens
in surf : the pine

board fence collapsed
along the line : after

the storm a kestrel
in headwind : sand

accumulates on your
feet : puckered seal

skin : the salt-washed
flesh : wreckage towing

upshore : when the
gulls came out I saw

them circling in air :
saw them pecking

seals' eyes from
torn skin : a boy

downstrand rolling
in dunes : I could see

the stomach's red
wall : the small hairs

on its flippers : blubber
wretched by shark

bite from the belly's
swell : later seen

from a dune : black
water : fish spit

pooling : mouth open
enough to see teeth

trailing in sand : his lips
limp : there in

the storm's wake
I wanted something

to say : the ocean
scraped his insides clean

POEM AROUND WHICH EVERYTHING
IS STRUCTURED

On his third night of dreams the boy turning in his bed
        hums about goodness & trees. He sees the berries
in his palm, which are the final berries of the season,

        so he squeezes them to watch their juice bleed through
the dim crevasses of his hand. Something's missing
        in this song & I don't know what it is. A shadow, maybe,

or a light between trees. Tonight, as the stars seep
        through his window & touch the dusty water he keeps
in a glass by his bed, the boy wonders what it would be

        to touch the body of another. I search his eyes
for mutual absence. And maybe as I map the freckles
        on his wrist, as the song crescendos, as the night fades into

dull purples & blues—maybe the lights go out & I feel
        his breath on my hand. Or maybe that's wrong, too.
Maybe I become the delicate prison he attends to, the cold

        thread wending in & out his chest, the rapture he feels
when he dangles me from the wood post of his gallows.
        Suppose I wrote this song in another key entirely.

I could cast it in a way that doesn't care about touching
        & hips. The boy could carry a spade out into the yard
& drop it down into the soil, where the earth would dance

        around it & the stars shrink into the distance until they
disappear between hills. This is how I think, Love,

about you. This is how I structure everything around me

that needs to be structured—the taste buds on your tongue,
        the salt of your wrist, the shape of your mouth as you
tell me every little thing you ever wanted me to know.

        I want to give him a name, that boy. I want to call that name
on nights when the ceiling hangs low above my bed,
        & the plaster cracks, & the sky pokes through the minute

slits between blinds. I want to feel his hands, not my hands,
        shivering in the wool sleeves of my coat, anything
but the same shaking of the leaves, the orchid dying bloom

        by bloom in the window while its naked stem bends
a single blossom toward the sun. It delights in a small
        cool mist. Let me speak plainly. Let me get to the dark

heart of the matter. The thing is, Love, that when I watch
        the squash buds wither, when the June sun makes them
shrivel into themselves, it's almost too much for me to bear.

        I see them—& that is all. I hear an emptiness in the wind,
& wrap my mind around it, & think of the king snake coiled
        in the grass. Soon he will be skin & bones. Already he is but

skin & bones. He rubs his head against a rock. The sun shines.
        Wood lice creep from the open dirt. Tonight, as the boy
turns in his bed, & wrestles with the prospect of his own

        approaching dusk, I bend myself above you, or below, whichever
way it is that you prefer. I breathe the clean grasses
        of your skin & unpack each assorted item you keep hidden

in a travel-sized box by your purse. And I, & the boy, sit
        blinking in the dark, staring off at the wall & the dead stars
beyond it throwing cold light through the black matter

        of millennia. It rests inside his palm. It rests in mine. At times,
looking out at the bare sky, & watching those stars fizzle

in the map of still time, I want to crawl up into its stillness,

& feel obsolete, distant from my father & the warm bodies
      I've touched, & watch through a tree so lovingly hollowed
their vague shapes flit between leaves. It's a problem

      in philosophy & form, each hand's different twenty-
seven little bones reaching out to hold the cloth
      draped upon the shoulders of another. Slowly,

those shapes come into focus, & the dawn light, which is
      not dead light, seeps into the room. In it, in the yard,
where the boy throws down his spade, & a mule-tailed deer

      licks dew from his palm, the apple trees shine, collard
stalks stiffen, the paper-white bark of an aspen
      quivers, Love, & the grasses shudder in unison, in wind.

AT ASSATEAGUE

The sun is a thin line of red
broadening over the bay.
It slices the horizon, strikes light
into a darkness poised
to disclose some secret the night
couldn't shake out of it.

Trout smokes over hot coals.
Wild ponies in the distance
charge along the strand, kick sand
up behind them, an inelegant cloud
that smears the dawn's gouache.

It's unbearable, this scene,
its sickening romance.

Still I want to hold it, to freeze
its sudden architecture
in the flotsam of the beach—
to suck the ichor from its rib.

It wouldn't sustain me, I know.
The gulls turning their circles
would grow dull.
I'd berate the sand flea's itch.
The gravitation of the tide's pull
would choke me with ennui.

Pear blossoms soon give way to pears,
I'll never stop eating them.

WHERE NIGHT STOPS

BY DOUGLAS LIGHT

2019 LONGLIST, SIMPSON/JOYCE CAROL OATES PRIZE

(EXCERPTS)

CHAPTER ONE

She smells of lemons and warm cinnamon and isn't very pretty. Sliding onto the barstool next to me, she says, "Can I sit here?"

The bartender, the woman, and I—we're the only people in the bar.

She can sit anywhere. It's not just a seat she wants.

I study her a moment then catch the bartender's eye; the order is placed without a word. Whatever the woman wants. Alcohol, like long marriages, has a language of its own, one not composed of speech.

Tuesday. The hard light of the Florida morning pours into Charm's Tavern, bleaching everything to its true ugliness. Open daily from 8:00 a.m. to 2:00 a.m., Charm's is anything but charming. *Providing hangovers and alibis since 1968*, the sign above the cash till reads. The oak bar cutting the length of the space looks whittled from a tree felled on the spot. The barstools wobble, their seats swaddled in duct tape, while stalactites of grime dangle from the exposed wires crisscrossing the ceiling. Everything in the place is warped from decades of spilled drinks. Covering the wall opposite the bar are photographs. Hundreds, if not thousands. Floor to ceiling, people smile, shout, and hold drinks up in moments they'll never remember.

The bartender pours a gin on ice and walks it down to where we sit.

The key ring looped on his belt jangles with each step.

She nods thanks.

He turns on the TV and mutes it.

She lifts the glass to her lips, downs a solid swallow. The weight of the drink seems to strain her narrow wrists. "Gin," she says, catching me with a direct stare. Her eyes are a broken blue, muted light through scratched stained glass. "A beautiful, brutal creation," she says, then touches my arm. "Was a time I could tell you everything about gin, its history, the different types, medicinal uses, even its effect on the British fertility in the mid-seventeen hundreds. Now," she says, "all I can tell you about it is how I like to drink it—cold." She tilts her head to one side then the other, like a goldfinch at the feeder. "You don't like to talk?"

"I like to talk," I say. "I like to listen, too." *And I like to be left alone*, I think. It was a mistake buying this woman a drink.

She leans to me, her breath charged with loneliness. "I'm not pretty," she says. "I know I'm not pretty. I've come to accept that, and it isn't an easy thing to accept." She sways back, takes in the rest of her drink. "Now you know my problem. What's yours?"

I gauge her face, sidelong. She has me by a solid two decades, mid-forties. "What makes you think I've got a problem?"

She taps her wrist where a watch should be. "It's just past eight a.m. You're drinking at Charm's," she says.

Touché. "I'm working," I say, leaving it there. I'm not positive I could say what it is I do exactly, but even if I could, I wouldn't. People's perceptions change the moment you're defined. The weight of your words changes. The phrase *I can help* means something different coming from a lunch lady and a doctor.

The woman smiles. "Work." She considers me, then nods slightly, a small dip of confirmation. "You're not a hard one to figure out," she says. "I know your problem—or at least one of them." She touches her lips as though to reassure herself, ready to serve. "Gin and people. The two things I know. And what I know is that this gin"—she holds her glass up—"is French, ninety-eight proof, and the cause of many car wrecks and failed marriages. I also know," she says, "that you don't have friends."

"How's that a problem?"

She lifts her chin. "Maybe it's not," she says, clattering the ice in her glass. "Other people need them to feel they have a purpose." She folds her arms across the bar, lays her head on them. "Maybe you don't need that." Her voice is distant, longing. She closes her eyes. "You know what the problem with problems is? It's *not* solving them. You'd think that'd be the hard part but it's not. The hard part is living with the solution. It's like you spend the first part of your life trying to figure it all out. Then you spend the second part just trying to forget all the stupid things you did to figure it all out."

"You're a mess," I tell her. "Keep talking."

She sits up, looks at me without looking at me, and forces a smile. "Alcoholosophy," she says. "The act of being profoundly unprofound." The idea of grappling naked with her seeps into my mind. There's something about her smell. I motion to the bartender—another drink for the lady. "I wasn't kidding," I say. "Keep talking. You have a nice voice. I like the sound of your voice."

"A nice voice that has nothing to say." She points to the TV bolted to the corner wall. An old black-and-white movie flashes on the screen. *The Third Man.* "See that?"

Orson Welles fills the screen. Young, still handsome, a mop of thick hair. He and Joseph Cotton are at the top of a Ferris wheel, war-torn Vienna spread out beneath them. A ruined Austria.

"That right there," she says, nodding at the TV. "That's my heart."

On the screen, Welles stares down from the top of the ride at the ravaged city. "Your heart is Orson Welles?" I ask.

"Orson Welles?" She makes a noise that's the approximation of a laugh. Her eyes brim with tears. "God no," she says. "My heart is a divided Vienna."

◆◆◆

We're born with a finite number of opportunities. Attrition, bad choices, misspent goodwill, and fucked-up luck. The opportunities dwindle through a process called living. Our portfolio of prospects turns into a tattered novel of outcomes.

I am twenty-two.

CHAPTER TWO

Windstop, Iowa. My hometown. When I think of it I think of summers, the heat rising in thick waves from the long, flat roads. Never-ending bike rides, tires clinging to the pavement. The rainbow, metallic spray of the garden hose, the calming sway of the cornfields, a sweet, stewing smell. Soil, sunlight, photosynthesis.

When I was a kid, there seemed nothing my folks couldn't do. My father was not only strong and good at sports, he was also an expert with tools; he could build and repair furniture, birdhouses, and nearly anything made of wood. People skills and the power of persuasion were my mother's gifts: gathering signatures for a new speed bump in front of the school, getting volunteers for a bake sale to support my Cub Scout troop, or organizing a drive to collect Green Stamps for the church. Once an idea got lodged in my mother's head, she could corral the whole community into the effort. She could talk anyone into doing anything. What she couldn't do was convince my father to care for her. And unlike one of his projects, my father couldn't hammer the relationship back into shape. They endured each other for me and acted out the role of parents as best they could. Voices rarely got raised when I was around. Arguments were fought in flat, conversational tones, the anger a strong undercurrent.

Still, I had a good childhood, filled with friends, fairly good grades, and teachers and coaches who liked me well enough. Everyone in the tiny town knew everyone else and their business. I never got away with anything. News of the occasional fight or the shoplifted candy made it home before I did. My punishment was rarely severe.

Instead of a sibling, my folks got me a dog, Mackerel, whom I loved like nothing else. Why my folks named her Mackerel, I can't say. The dog hated fish.

Since leaving Windstop, I've traveled the world and killed a few people, though always in self-defense. Always in the interest of self-preservation.

The first time was terrifying. I used to have bad dreams about it.

But that passed. It's the second that really haunts me.

The Greek shouldn't have tried blackmailing me. A marble figurine of Artemis was close at hand. It seems so easy on TV. He made a savage mess as he lurched about the tiny Athens apartment.

By the time he finally dropped, blood sprayed every wall.

People search everywhere for the taproot of their mistakes. They want to blame strict parents, an unsupportive school, a drunk scoutmaster, bullying siblings, or mean friends. They blame anyone but themselves.

I can't blame anyone for where I find myself now. I was taught the difference between right and wrong.

CHAPTER THREE

My ribs crackled with pain when I coughed. Bruises peppered my body. Still, I'd healed enough to be able to walk out. The nurse insisted I exit by wheelchair. Hospital rules. "We wheel you in, we wheel you out," she said, gliding me down Windstop Memorial General's off-white corridors. The odor of urine and pine needles, of desperation masked by cleaning supplies, filled the entire place.

I'd been born in that building and had ventured back numerous times. These were the people who had stitched my head together after the diving board interrupted my backflip, cut out my tonsils, freed my Krazy Glued fingers, and diagnosed the rash speckling my skin as a case of flea bites—courtesy of Mackerel. These were my neighbors, fellow church members, the parents and relatives of my classmates, the people my family and I depended on in times of emergency.

In the lobby, the summer light pounded through the windows, sharp and blinding. Outside, a world I wasn't ready for waited.

I had the nurse stop at the gift shop where I bought a cheap pair of sunglasses and a pack of cigarettes. "Really?" she asked. "I didn't take you as a smoker."

I slid on the sunglasses and gripped the cigarette pack. "I'm not."

A battered ambulette the color of creamed corn waited out front. As she helped hoist me into the passenger's seat, the nurse said, "Don't forget to…" She trailed off, realizing her words—whatever they might be—were useless. I buckled up.

Nodding to the driver, I told him my address. There was no need. He knew me, knew my family. Knew what had happened. He was the father of my old church youth group leader. He used to provide apples and shelled peanuts as snacks for the group. Clamping the steering wheel like it was the last life buoy on a stricken ship, he shuttled me home in silence. Nothing new could be learned through talk.

My father, mother, and best friend Clement. Everyone in Windstop knew what had happened. Just as everyone in Windstop knew of the brutal knocks of life and bad luck my ambulette driver had endured. Within a matter of months, he'd been diagnosed with cirrhosis, lost his wife to skin cancer, and lost his son—my youth group leader—to a meth lab explosion. He'd been stripped of his reasons to live. Still, the magical mechanism propelling life continued to churn deep inside him, pushing him forward.

During one youth group meeting, his son made everyone kiss the blade of a hatchet while he explained that our own birth and death were the only two things we could truly call our own.

But he was wrong. His father was proof. I was proof. Your death is owned by family, friends, and creditors, the people left with the burden created by your absence.

The van pulled to a stop in front of my house. Loneliness cauterized my blood, burning it dry in my veins. I didn't want to be here, but then again I didn't want to be anywhere. I slid out, then turned and offered my hand in thanks. Disdain flashed over his face like the sharp, fleeting shadow of a passing plane. His misery didn't need the company of mine. My tragedy had upstaged his, stolen the town's sympathy, and left him even hollower.

That first night home, I lay in my parents' bed and listened to soft noises work their way through the empty rooms: the drip of the tub's faucet, the rattle of a loose window screen, the scrape of some small animal making its way through the walls. All sounds my father had said he'd get around to taking care of. Now they were mine. Everything that was once my folks was mine.

It'd been my plan to start college in the fall at the University of Iowa. I had my dorm room, my class schedule, and an oversized black-and-gold Hawkeyes hoodie. Forty-five hundred freshmen would swarm the campus. New friends and interests, experimentation and exploration, learning and change awaited me. Or that was the hope.

I'd applied to five schools total, each for reasons other than their programs. My love of the whole grunge era drove my desire to go to the University of Washington in Seattle. I'd applied to Columbia University after reading that Kerouac had studied there. The University of Cincinnati? Because the Bengals were my favorite football team. And Tulane because, well, it was in New Orleans. I was accepted to all of them, but cost and proximity won out. University of Iowa it was.

But plans change. College, it now seemed, was the avoidance of the inevitable. Life was looming, waiting to take hold. *Better to face it head-on*, I thought. *Better to start it now.*

Word got around that I was out of the hospital. Heavy casseroles made with Campbell's soups and topped with fried onions arrived on my doorstep. Food to satiate my grief. I threw them out.

Small, somber cards from my uncles and aunts, from the Hendersons, Joneses, Dices, Wagners, Nees, Reeves, Critlens, Peters, Franks, Lynchs, and Smiths arrived in the mail. I threw them out.

People who had never taken an interest in my parents when they were alive called to offer their condolences, their advice. Everyone knew what I should do. Close out accounts, sign documents, decide on the font for my parent's tombstones. They called to instruct me on decisions I wasn't prepared to make.

Life went on, at least for everyone else.

At first, the money my parents had in the bank seemed like a lot. Then it didn't seem like enough. Mortgage, utilities, taxes, insurance, and the cost of simple upkeep. Why did anyone want to own a house? What kind of dream was that? My dream was to be free of it all, out from under all the things my folks had gathered over time, the debris that defined them. I wanted to shed the load that had been heaped on me and walk away.

I rang a real estate broker. My mind tangled with all the tasks of selling the house: the prepping, the showings, the strangers wandering from room to room, examining my life on display. If an offer actually came in, there'd be haggling, the back-and-forth, and the struggle of closing the deal.

I hung up the phone. There had to be a quicker, simpler way to cash out.

The answer was in the pile of bills—homeowner's insurance.

It seemed an easy way out. But the moment the flames took the kitchen, a crushing sadness gripped me. I'd made a mistake. I was destroying the last bit of my parents, the remnants of what I once was. By the time the fire department rolled up their hoses, there was little left of the house. A flooded, charred frame surrounded by a dark halo of burnt grass. Filled with regret, I held to my story: the lawnmower had somehow set off the blaze.

Insurance investigators don't so much sniff out lies as not believe anything. Cops, though, know a lie. They're fed them daily. They cultivate a palate for what's true and what's not.

Windstop's sheriff visited me at my motel room, my temporary residency. "Shit, really?" he said. "The lawnmower?" It was the ninth time in two days I'd told my story, each time exactly as before. I'd learned that the words inflammable and flammable meant the same thing. It was astounding how many household products were just that. The sheriff sat next to me on the bed. "Listen, I never much liked your father. Me and him never got along. So seeing his house— your house—get burnt down doesn't get me misty in the least. But that doesn't mean you can—" He broke off, stared at me hard.

I couldn't hold his gaze; I had to look away. The only thing worse than fucking up is getting caught fucking up. Needing something to do, I pulled out the pack of cigarettes I'd bought at the hospital. They were still unopened. "Mind if I smoke?"

"Yeah. I do." He stood, hovered over me. "Get up."

Out at his cruiser, I asked, "Want me in the back?"

"I want you to shut up."

He drove me to the next town over. Parking at the bus stop, he said, "You know anything about quantum mechanics?"

I didn't.

"Well, me neither. But I saw this thing on TV about it. Don't know why, but they talked about putting a cat in a bunker with a grenade or bomb or something that had a fifty-fifty chance of blowing up in the next minute. Then they closed the lid tight and waited for the minute to pass." He bit at a hangnail. "Thing is, no one knows if the cat is dead or alive until the lid is opened. So the cat is both *dead* and *alive*, as long as no one opens the lid."

I didn't understand.

"Right now," he said, "you both *did* and *didn't* burn your house down." He pulled out his wallet, tossed seventy dollars on my lap.

I picked up the bills. "What's this?"

"Opportunity." He opened his door and climbed out. "I'm getting a coffee. When I get back, I'm going to have to crack open that lid." He drilled me with a hard stare. "You understand what I'm saying?"

I did.

I bought a bus ticket.

Wedged tight into a window seat, I watched the sheriff slowly make his way back to his cruiser, coffee in hand. He kept his back turned as the bus started up and then lurched westward, kicking off a gray cloud of diesel exhaust.

As the day slipped to night and Iowa disappeared behind me, I tried to sleep, but the woman beside me kept elbowing me awake with her knitting. It was only when dawn found us nearing Sioux Falls, South Dakota, that the worrying thought took hold of me: *Why sell cigarettes at a hospital?*

I USED TO BE BRENDA STARR, REPORTER

BY BETH NEEDEL

SIMPSON LITERARY PROJECT
FOUNDING BOARD MEMBER

I think I have always loved libraries. Early on the library was my heart place, my safe place, my place of peace and exploration.

Growing up in the suburbs just north of Chicago going to the library was a treat, my favorite treat. My library was a modern glass building that was always quiet. It was cool all summer and cozy in the winter. The books smelled of library. There was no yelling or telling, just the anonymity of books that I found sitting on the floor, between the stacks, surrounded by possibilities.

I didn't have a favorite genre but I did have an affinity for biographies. Anne Frank, Wilma Rudolph, and Helen Keller come to mind. And, around the age of eleven, I was welcomed into the adult library where I read first read Herman Wouk's *Marjorie Morningstar*. I can still remember the characters and the juicy bits I didn't quite understand or dare ask my mom about.

I never thought I would work for a library. I planned to be Brenda Starr, Reporter from the Sunday comics and travel the world meeting dashing men and uncovering the truth to right wrongs.

But, when I walked into the Lafayette Library and Learning Center and saw children sitting on the floor surrounded by not one or two books but piles and piles of them, I knew I found my heart place. I could help ensure that children could always have a book in hand and a place of comfort to go.

I recently read an article about the research the Free University of Amsterdam did in preparation of renovating their library. The one request students made was that they wanted books around them. It was not just because of the information that physical books provide, but because of the atmosphere and comfort they provide. So the library kept the books as part of their renovation. A nod to the real future of libraries.

People flock to our library to be around books, to attend story times, book clubs, cultural events, STEAM programs, and more. They seem to prefer to bring their laptop to the library, to be in the company of books and people. So though our library offers one thousand programs a year, from Pulitzer Prize-winning authors to the Simpson Literary Project's prize recipient, and free music, art, and science classes, along with movies, and more—we are still (thankfully) in the very busy business of connecting people with books... How wonderful.

CHINESE OPERA

BY ANNE RAEFF

2019 FINALIST, SIMPSON/JOYCE CAROL OATES PRIZE

(FROM *THE JUNGLE AROUND US*)

The Buchovskys were at the Chinese opera the night Danny McSwene was murdered. The three of them—Simone, her sister Juliet, and their father—had been there all day, from nine in the morning, to be precise, and were not released from the performance until ten that night. The coroner's report said that he had died somewhere between eight and midnight, so his death might not have occurred during the performance but, rather, when they were eating dinner later. The exact time was not crucial. Still, Simone would always think of the actors' endless wailing and excruciatingly slow movements and their white, painted faces whenever she thought of Danny McSwene's last moments.

Their father had a long tradition of dragging them to such events. When they were small, Simone was sure he searched carefully for the most tedious and difficult performances to bring them to. She thought he was trying to teach them something—patience perhaps, or tolerance—but now that she was twelve, her older self realized that he simply had had no idea what torture these outings were for young children, and she was convinced that he thought she and Juliet enjoyed them as much as he did. He liked to refer to the three of them as a trio. Simone always imagined them as a trio of flute, violin, and piano, though she could not say who was which instrument, but as she got older she could not think why her imagination had settled on such shrill and plucky instruments. They were really much more like bassoons and violas—unassuming and hardworking.

It was especially cold the day they went to see the Chinese Opera, the day that Danny McSwene died, and it was cold in the theater too. Simone kept her coat and gloves on the whole time. She imagined, however, that the actors were warm enough. They were heavily clad, and their movements, as slow as they were, seemed to require a lot of effort—each placement of the foot, each slow swoop of the hand, even the eyes labored, prowling slowly, meeting the gaze of the enemy or a lover. At first she enjoyed the performance. She liked the feel of the gong reverberating in her legs and in her heart and was amused by the costumes and the stories, the details of which were outlined in the program. She fell into a sort of trance, concentrating on color, sound, and movement without thinking about the plot or the cacophony, but after the one intermission, during which the three of them ate black bread with butter and honey that their father had prepared at home, she grew increasingly bored.

Their father had promised to take them to their favorite diner after the performance for a late dinner. Their father was able to get them to do just about anything—sit through a lecture about the diary of a foot soldier in Napoleon's army or the uncut version of a movie about the Russian icon painter Andrei Rublev— if he promised that they would have dinner at a diner afterward. Though each had their favorite form of eggs, all three of them always ordered eggs. Eggs and milkshakes.

◆◆◆

During the second half of the opera, it had grown even colder, and all Simone could think about was that she was cold, though she never would have dreamed of excusing herself, of asking permission to take a walk or go to the Coliseum Bookstore, which was just a stone's throw away from Lincoln Center, where the marathon Chinese Opera Festival was being held. So she sat through the rest of the performance, rubbing her hands and dreaming of the oily warmth of the diner. Later, after hearing the awful news about Danny McSwene, Simone felt that she should have been using this time more wisely instead of wasting it, thinking about the cold and wondering whether she should order a mushroom or cheese omelet.

Danny McSwene was their favorite of their neighbors' seven sons. There was quite a difference in age between the oldest sons, who were twins and lived together in South America, where they worked for a philanthropic organization, and the youngest, who had graduated from high school the year before. Danny was right in the middle and the quietest of all the McSwene boys, although Simone did not really know the twins or Alan, who was next in line and had been shot in the lung in Vietnam and then married a Japanese woman he had met when he was on leave. When Alan came home, he and his wife lived with the McSwenes until they could get settled. It was summer, and Simone remembered them lying on lounge chairs in the backyard for hours at a time until they both were very brown. With the two youngest boys, Simone and Juliet played catch, but though both girls were athletically inclined, they were no match for the McSwene boys who included the two of them in their games nonetheless, perhaps, Simone thought, because they secretly longed for sisters.

◆◆◆

But what they really looked forward to were the nights when Danny McSwene babysat. As soon as their father was out the door, the excitement would begin. The first step was to clear the living room, move everything—the couch, the chairs, tables, rugs—through the kitchen and into the family room. They did this efficiently and carefully, making sure not to scrape the walls or scuff the wooden floors.

"You don't know how lucky you are to have wooden floors," Danny McSwene said every time. "Carpeting is the scourge of the modern world. How on earth is anyone supposed to dance on carpeting?"

When all the living room furniture was piled into the family room, they changed into their dance clothes. Danny McSwene wore special shoes and wonderful black pants with pleats. He had a collection of silk shirts—pink and purple and green. Simone and Juliet put on their good school shoes. One night Simone got to wear pants and lead while Juliet wore a dress and followed and the next time they switched roles.

Danny McSwene had a collection of records that he carried in a green, patent leather satchel he had bought in New York specifically for that purpose. They always started with waltzes and ended with the cha-cha, their favorite. His favorite was the tango, which Simone found a little embarrassing, especially when he insisted on more passion. "Where's the passion?" he would call over the music. "More passion, more passion!"

At the end of the dance sessions, they had always put the furniture back exactly right, so their father wouldn't notice, though he would not have minded, would have been happy to know that they were having such a good time with Danny McSwene. Still, Danny had made them promise not to tell anyone, and they never did, not even after he was dead.

◆◆◆

They did not learn about Danny's death until two days after it happened because they were not in the McSwenes' inner circle. Though they were all fond of one another and happy to be neighbors, the Buchovskys kept their distance as good neighbors do, and the McSwenes kept theirs. And so they learned about his death from the local newspaper, *The Suburbanite*. On the front page there was a photo of Danny McSwene in his chef's uniform. He had just graduated from the Culinary Institute of America the spring before and had moved to New York, where he had gotten a job at a restaurant with stars. The newspaper said that he had been found in his apartment in Greenwich Village—shot in the back of the head. *Execution style*, they called it.

They did not go to the funeral. Their father avoided religious ceremonies of any kind, even weddings, and tried to have as little as possible to do with all things religious, though they sometimes went to concerts at Riverside Church in New York because he was a great admirer of liturgical music, especially Russian Orthodox, which he played at full volume while they cleaned the house every Sunday morning. Despite his appreciation for religious music, it was a matter of principle with him to fight against what he called the *forces of unreason* in his own, quiet way, as he did when he was drafted into the army and refused to declare a religion on the official paperwork. Even when the superior officer explained that they needed a religion so that they would know how to dispose of his body if he died, their father was unbending.

"You can just leave me there for the vultures, like the Zoroastrians do," her father had said. Every time he told the story, Simone could not help but imagine her father dead, the vultures pecking at his flesh, his eyes, and when he came to that part she always laughed so as not to let on that she was frightened.

"Like who?" the officer had said.

"The Zoroastrians," her father had answered.

"Is that a religion?"

"Yes," her father had said. "They leave their dead exposed to the elements and the vultures in what they call the tower of silence."

"How do you spell that?" the officer had asked. Her father had spelled it out for him.

The man had grabbed the form, crossed out none, and written *Zoroastrian*. "There, now you have a religion. Now you can die."

Still, even though Simone was afraid to see it, she felt they should be there to watch Danny McSwene's body be let down into the earth, to throw a clump of dirt onto the coffin as she had seen mourners do in movies. "Don't you think we should go?" she asked her father just an hour before the funeral was to begin.

"It's much more important to pay our respects afterward," he explained. "They won't even notice who's at the church."

"But for Danny," Simone said.

"Do you think he was a believer?" he asked.

"I don't know. We never talked about it," Simone said.

"Well, if he wasn't, he would have preferred us not to go," he said.

"But we don't know whether he was or wasn't," she argued.

"No, we don't," he said, leaving her with nothing to argue against, for one cannot argue with incertitude.

"What if it were a Zoroastrian funeral?" Simone asked. "Would we go then?"

"Maybe," he said. "At least then it would be all out in the open."

"What would be out in the open?" she asked.

"Everything," he said.

"Everything we don't want to see."

"Like the wound?" she asked.

"Like the wound," he replied, taking her in his arms, for she had begun to cry.

◆◆◆

When they saw the mourners arriving back at the McSwenes' house after the funeral, Simone, Juliet, and their father went over to pay their respects. They dressed all in black. The girls wore Danskin tops and had made a special visit to the Tenafly Department Store to buy black skirts and tights. Their father wore his funeral suit. They brought a bottle of vodka and baklava because their father said they should bring something not too elaborate. At the McSwenes' house, there were plenty of black scarves and black ties and black shoes, but they were the only ones all in black. They stood awkwardly in front of the picture window that looked out onto the McSwenes' backyard where, just the summer before, Simone and Juliet had played catch and flipped baseball cards.

Their father made his way around the room, shaking hands with Mr. McSwene and all the remaining McSwene boys. When he had finished conveying his condolences to the men of the family, he joined his daughters at the window. "Mrs. McSwene is upstairs in the bedroom," he said. "I think you should go see her."

They climbed the stairs to the second floor slowly. They had never been upstairs before. The McSwene boys had been outdoor companions, and it never would have occurred to them to visit their rooms, look through their books, listen to their records. Mrs. McSwene, all in black also, was lying on top of a cream-colored bedspread like a giant felled chess piece. Surrounding her, on both sides of the bed, were women of all ages, the two oldest seated near her head holding her hands and the younger women closer to Mrs. McSwene's feet, kneeling on the floor, clasping her legs.

No one noticed Simone and Juliet as they stood in the doorway watching. Simone wanted to flee, but she knew they could not simply turn around, descend the stairs, and tell their father that they had not known how to approach Mrs. McSwene. He would not have understood the barrier of women. And they could not have lied and said they had spoken to her when they hadn't. It would have made them sad to lie to their father about such a thing. Juliet pulled on the sleeve of Simone's black shirt, but Simone ignored it. She was focused on Mrs. McSwene's grief. She moved toward Mrs. McSwene and, as if she were Moses and the women the Dead Sea, they parted before her.

"I would like to extend my condolences," she said, but all Mrs. McSwene did was tilt her head without looking in her direction, as if she were blind and trying to hear more clearly. "Of all your boys, Danny was my favorite," Simone said, and Mrs. McSwene began to weep. She twitched on the bed and gasped, and the women ran back to hold her hands and wipe her brow. Someone brought a glass of water, and the older women pulled the weeping Mrs. McSwene up on her pillows and held it to her lips, and when she would not drink, they tried pouring it into her mouth, but the water ran down her chin and onto her black dress.

"She doesn't want to drink anything," Simone said quietly, and all the women turned and stared at her. Juliet ran out of the room.

"Come closer, Simone," Mrs. McSwene demanded in her raspy, smoker's voice that was raspier still from crying. "Sit down."

Simone sat down and closed her eyes. Mrs. McSwene pulled her closer and whispered directly into her ear, "He was my favorite too." Then she turned away and started to weep again.

When Simone returned to the living room, the mourners were looking out the picture window, watching the bright pink winter sun setting. They were standing, holding their drinks as if poised, waiting for that last burst of pink to disappear so that darkness could fall. Her father was not one of the sunset watchers. He was leaning against the wall looking at a large art book, which he was holding up with one hand.

"Simone," he said as if he had been worried that she was lost.

"It's getting dark," Simone said.

"I suppose we should be going. Where's Juliet?"

"I don't know," Simone said.

"We must find her, then," her father said. He returned his book to the shelf. The sun had set and the mourners had dispersed from the window and formed small clusters around the living room, talking quietly; more quietly, it seemed, because it was dark. Someone turned on the overhead light and everyone looked up, as if they had been caught in a searchlight. A woman began weeping.

"Should I turn it off?" the man who had switched it on asked.

"No, it's getting dark," someone answered for all of them.

They walked silently back home. Their father wanted to make scrambled eggs for dinner, but no one was hungry, so they had chamomile tea and zwieback, which is what they ate when they were sick. That night Simone could not sleep. She tried reading, forcing herself to read what she called the *pretty poems*, the ones she usually skipped over—Wordsworth and Cummings, Houseman. She hoped, for some not-very-well-thought-out reason, that flowers and love and small hands would cheer her up, but she could not rid herself of the image of Danny McSwene sitting at his desk with a bullet hole in the back of his head. She tried to imagine what kind of person would feel compelled to *execute* Danny McSwene, who had always been so polite and had a dimple in his left cheek.

Simone closed her eyes and pretended she was sleeping in a house overlooking the ocean. The house was humble—a small, whitewashed cottage with a fireplace and stone floors. She tried listening for the crashing of the surf on rocks and the sound the wind makes on water. But Danny McSwene entered her cottage by the sea, sat in her simple wooden chair in her simple kitchen with cast-iron pans and earthenware pitchers. He sat down and said that he was very, very tired and asked for a glass of water. "Please," he said, and blood was pouring out of his head and onto his shirt, and a puddle of blood formed on the stone floor at his feet.

Simone got up then, walked quietly down the stairs, put on her coat and gloves and scarf. She stood in the backyard looking at the back of McSwenes' house. She had expected it to be dark, but to her surprise, the house was totally illuminated, and she could see clearly into the empty living room and kitchen. She saw the furniture and the bookshelves and the fireplace.

She walked toward the house, and when she reached it, she stood in the flower bed underneath the living room picture window, her breath clouding the glass. She stood there waiting for someone to come down the stairs, but no one appeared, so she stayed put, stood there in the dark and cold until dawn. She wanted, then, to turn around and walk back to her warm house, get under the covers, sleep finally, but she remembered

Danny and how he could feel neither heat nor cold, nor long for sleep, so she stayed.

Finally, just when dawn was turning to day, she saw Mrs. McSwene descending the stairs, pausing on each step as if to make sure it was strong enough to take her weight.

Mrs. McSwene stepped off the last step and walked into the living room. She paused in the middle of the room. Her lips were moving, and then they stopped, as if waiting for a reply. Mrs. McSwene was wearing a robe, and Simone imagined the women helping Mrs. McSwene change out of her black funeral dress. She wondered whether she would have preferred to keep it on. Something seemed to startle Mrs. McSwene, and she swung around, and before Simone could drop to the ground or run, Mrs. McSwene saw her. Because Simone did not know what else to do, she waved. Mrs. McSwene walked to the window and pressed her face to it, and her faced seemed like some separate thing trying to push its way through the glass.

Finally, Mrs. McSwene opened the back door and Simone entered. "Sit," Mrs. McSwene said, pointing to the sofa, and Simone sat down. Immediately, Simone began shaking. "How long have you been standing out in the cold?" Mrs. McSwene asked.

"A long time," Simone said.

"I'll bring some whiskey," Mrs. McSwene said and walked over to the liquor cabinet. She carried two very full glasses of whiskey back to the sofa and sat down next to Simone. Her robe had come undone, and Simone could see Mrs. McSwene's thighs, so she averted her eyes. Mrs. McSwene noticed that her thighs were exposed and stood up to adjust her robe, then sat down again, farther away from Simone. She reached into her pocket for a pack of Newports, tipped a cigarette out, and lit it, inhaling deeply. Simone took a sip of whiskey.

"I need your help," Mrs. McSwene said. Simone leaned in toward Mrs. McSwene. "I want you to tell them to go away," Mrs. McSwene said.

"Tell whom to go away?" Simone asked.

"All of them—my sons and sisters and the cousins and friends and in-laws. I don't even know who they all are, but they seem to know me, know that what I need to do is eat soup and rest and cry. They keep telling me that I should cry, that crying will do me good."

"But, I…" Simone's hands began to tremble, so she put them under her thighs, and pressed down hard upon them. "But I don't know them," she said.

"What?" Mrs. McSwene asked.

"I don't know them," Simone repeated.

"Of course, you can't tell them," Mrs. McSwene agreed. "You're just a child." She pulled out another cigarette and held it gently in the palm of her hand as if it were a baby bird.

"I didn't say I couldn't tell them," Simone said. She thought of Danny and how he would have known how to get them all out of the house without making anyone feel bad.

"So you'll do it?" Mrs. McSwene took her hand.

"Yes," Simone said. "Where are they?"

"They're everywhere. You'll just have to start opening up doors," she said.

Simone climbed the stairs slowly, thinking that the only thing she wanted now was a plate of her father's heavy, hot kasha, thinking that if she ate enough of it, she could finally fall asleep, sleep way into the afternoon until it was dark. She sat down on the stairs and tried to muster the courage to open the doors to the rooms where the sleeping mourners lay. She knew that Danny would have wanted her to help his mother, who had loved him more than she had loved her other six children. But Simone couldn't do it. Back down the stairs she went, softly, so as not to make the floorboards creak. She turned the latch and opened the front door and stepped outside where the sun was now bright and ricocheted off the remaining patches of snow, catching her right in the eye as if she were the killer.

In the days that followed, Simone avoided the McSwenes' house, so she did not know whether the flock of cars that stood in their driveway had thinned slowly or whether they had all disappeared at once like geese from a lake. Once they were all gone, she wondered whether Mrs. McSwene missed having them all there, trying to get her to eat and drink and cry and bathe. She imagined Mrs. McSwene lying on the living room couch and Mr. McSwene standing in front of the fireplace playing the bagpipe that always stood in the corner near the sofa. But maybe he stopped playing the bagpipe after Danny's death. Maybe all they wanted was quiet, but this is something she would never know.

The Buchovskys did not talk to the McSwenes much after Danny's death. They waved at each other from their side of the fence and left them bags of apples from their apple tree on their back porch.

But sometimes at night before she fell asleep, Simone would imagine herself finding Danny McSwene's killer, cornering him in a dark alley, smashing his head against the wall while he begged for mercy and leaving him there, bleeding on the street. It was always raining in her pre-sleep fantasies, and in the distance she could hear cymbals crashing like at the Chinese opera, and she moved in rhythm with them until they ceased completely and all she could hear was Danny's executioner calling out for her help: "Don't leave me here, don't leave me. Have some mercy, for God's sake, have mercy."

LORI OSTLUND & ANNE RAEFF
IN CONVERSATION

BETH NEEDEL (BN), JOE DI PRISCO (JDP), LORI OSTLUND
(LO), ANNE RAEFF (AR)

2017 FINALIST, SIMPSON/JOYCE CAROL OATES PRIZE
(OSTLUND)
2019 FINALIST, SIMPSON/JOYCE CAROL OATES PRIZE
(RAEFF)

Lori Ostlund and Anne Raeff joined Joseph Di Prisco for conversation at the Lafayette Public Library on the evening of February 26, 2019. Their selected remarks are lightly edited for clarity. Beth Needel, Founding Board Member of the Simpson Literary Project, welcomed everyone.

BN: Good evening, I'm Beth Needel, the Executive Director of the Lafayette Library and Learning Center Foundation. On behalf of the Lafayette Library and the Foundation, it's my pleasure to welcome you to our first Distinguished Speaker Series/Simpson event of our tenth anniversary. Yes, we've just begun celebrating the tenth anniversary of this marvelous library.

This brilliant program, like many of the 10,000 programs that we have hosted over the past ten years, which have benefited four million people who have come through our doors, is brought to you through the combined efforts and generosity of donors. From the Friends of the Library, from the Foundation, from the community, and of course, the Contra Costa County Library System. As you might imagine, keeping a library like this running, and open seven days a week, and twenty-three more hours than the county is able to support, takes a lot of additional funding.

So programs like this, and your donations, and purchases of books in our used bookstore, and through our lovely bookseller, really help us. I'll just give you a typical day at the library. Today, for example, we started out with Spanish story time, went into Tai Chi. Then we had African dancing, drumming, and traditions, teen tech help, and homework help. And now we're moving on this great program.

I can't say enough about Joe Di Prisco. We've worked with him for a number of years. He's a prolific writer and memoirist and interesting, funny human being. He's also the founder of the Simpson Project and we've had a great time working with them.

JDP: Well, that was very nice, Beth. Thank you. I don't know how many events I've done at the library, or attended at the library, I still never get over how beautiful it is, and how much love went into creating this fantastic community, which is more than a building. It's a community of people. Congratulations on all you've done.

So here we are tonight, this is a fun event for me. I'm wearing my hat, as you can see, because the authors insisted that I wear the hat. I asked them. I said, "It's up to you. I'll keep the hat on or off. You can tell me what you want."

LO: And I said, "This way, you will be able to differentiate between us and Joe."

JDP: So there. A word about the Simpson Project. We're in our fourth year. We're about to give out our third $50,000 Simpson prize, in about a month or so. We teach workshops at Martinez Juvie, the boys-identified wing, the girls-identified wing, as well as Girls Inc. and Northgate High School. Taught by Simpson Fellows, who are graduate student writers from Cal.

The partnership that is the Simpson Project originated in conversation with the Lafayette Library and Learning Center and University of California at Berkeley. Joyce Carol Oates is our Writer-in-Residence, we do the workshops, we have the prize. We have a terrific publication, called *Simpsonistas*, for that is what we call ourselves, Simpsonistas. Our Project is funded by a couple of dozen altruistic individuals, family foundations, and corporate sponsors. Out of that project comes where we are tonight. With my friends Anne Raeff and Lori Ostlund. Anne is longlisted for the 2019 Simpson Prize. Lori Ostlund was shortlisted, a finalist, for the 2017 prize.

Let me introduce Anne Raeff first. Her new novel, her most recent novel, *Winter Kept Us Warm*, is out in paperback tonight. Speaking of books, we have a Great Good Place for Books in the back. Please frequent your friendly, independent bookstore, tonight, and in the future. It's in Montclair. I've done lots of readings there. You?

LO: No.

JDP: We'll fix that. *Winter Kept Us Warm* was published in February 2018. Anne's collection of short stories, *The Jungle Around Us*, won the 2015 Flannery O'Connor Award for Short Fiction. I could read a lot here, but I think… Let's put it this way: Anne has been honored by many institutions and publications, and we're very fortunate to have her here tonight. Anne Raeff, thank you so much for your presence.

And Anne's wife, Lori Ostlund. I got to know Lori when she and I did a reading together many, many years ago. Maybe it wasn't that long ago. And Lori, as I said, was a finalist for the Simpson Prize in 2017. Her first novel was *After the Parade*, and it met with tremendous critical and commercial success. She also won the Flannery O'Connor prize for short stories, for *The Bigness of the World*.

They both live in San Francisco with their two cats. The names of whom elude me.

LO: Oscar and Prakash. I can't believe you forgot that.

JDP: Oscar and Prakash. Okay. Okay. Sorry about that.

AR: Get their names right.

JDP: I know, I know. I know. Maybe just a little bit of a summary of the fictions that we're going to be talking about to give us some little context. *Winter Kept Us Warm* is a novel of rich details and landscapes; it follows three friends through six decades, from postwar Berlin to Manhattan, 1960s Los Angeles to contemporary Morocco. The twisting narrative of this love triangle reveals their mysteries in fragments, examining their long-ago love triangle and how it changed their lives forever.

Then, Lori's novel, *After the Parade*, is about a sensitive, bighearted, and achingly self-conscious, forty-year-old Aaron Englund, who long ago escaped the confinements of his Midwestern hometown, but he still feels like an outcast. After twenty years under the Pygmalion-like care of his older partner, Walter, Aaron at last decides it is time to take control of his own fate. But soon after establishing himself in San Francisco, Aaron sees that real freedom will not come until he has made peace with his memories of Mortonville, Minnesota: a cramped town whose 400 souls form a constellation of Aaron's childhood heartbreaks and hopes.

I'm going to ask a few questions and raise a few topics. At some point, at some pregnant point, I'll be asking each of you to read from... I don't know what they're going to read, it's a surprise to me. They're only going to read for about an hour apiece.

AR: A little more.

LO: Yeah.

JDP: And so without further ado, please welcome Anne and Lori. I have a question and I think many of your fans out there have a question about this very subject. Since they know your wonderful, wonderful works. I want to ask about furniture.

LO: Okay.

AR: That's a big question. It's part of our lives.

JDP: It's a big part your lives. As I understand it, you had a store in Albuquerque, New Mexico, called Two Serious Ladies.

LO: Okay. Sweet.

JDP: I'm just wondering, did some good stories come about from the store? Were there customers you became friends with? Why Asian furniture? When you go to people's houses, do you analyze their furniture and see them for what they really are?

LO: You covered all of it, I think. It's true, we did have a store for seven years, before we moved to the Bay Area in 2005. And for seven years leading up to that, we had an Asian furniture store, called Two Serious Ladies, which came about because we were teaching in Malaysia for two years. At the end of teaching in Malaysia, I actually wrote a contract, and the contract said we would never ever teach again. But really, it's the only thing I'm equipped to do. I also love teaching. Anne is a wonderful teacher. But we were worn out, so I wrote up this contract.

AR: We were not only worn out, we just were not putting enough effort and time into our writing. And we just wanted to figure out a way that we could do something that we enjoyed, make a living, and really focus more on our writing, because teaching is just so all-encompassing. So Lori, the extremist that she is, which she's not. It's really more…

LO: I'm such a… Yeah.

AR: She created this contract and we signed it. We had a ceremony in our little pad, in Malaysia. Then, we went off and filled a container of furniture with mostly Indonesian furniture and brought it back to Albuquerque. We had no idea how to have a business or what to do, but we had some really cool stuff.

LO: I think my parents were sure that we would be arrested within a month or two. They just thought it was another one of my schemes that would not end well, but it went well. We specialized in Korean and Indonesian furniture and did actually make very good friends through the business. I'm working on two novels right now, and one of them is actually set in an Asian furniture store in Albuquerque and involves two proprietresses. It's called *The Proprietresses*. It's not in any way autobiographical…

JDP: Okay then.

LO: So…

AR: Yeah. It was really interesting. We played around with the name and then Lori, one day, just came up with *Two Serious Ladies*. I don't know if you're familiar with the Jane Bowles novel *Two Serious Ladies*. We both love the Bowleses, as we spent quite a bit of time in Morocco, so Paul and Jane Bowles are just sort of literary heroes of ours. And so we called the store Two Serious Ladies. That whole time that we were open, for seven years, there were maybe what, three people that knew the reference. And so one of our closest friends in the whole entire world we met because she came into the store. She's very eccentric. She had this big hat and a parasol.

LO: And gloves.

AR: And gloves, in Albuquerque, New Mexico. And this sort of fake British accent, but she's great. She's not at all fake, but she has a fake British accent.

LO: She's from Denver.

AR: She's from Denver. She came in, Lori wasn't there, she was doing something else. She came in and she looked around a little, and she said, "Is your store by any chance named after the famous novel by Jane Bowles, *Two Serious Ladies*?" And I said, "Yes." And she said, "All right." Then, we started talking and I said, "So how did you get interested in the Bowleses?" And she said, "I cannot remember a time in my life that they were not part of my life." That started a very long friendship to this day. Actually, Nancy's coming to visit us next weekend.

LO: She is.

AR: She lives in Boston, now.

JDP: So what you're saying is, furniture is a metaphor for everything you do in life?

AR: Yes.

LO: Yes.

AR: Furniture is a metaphor. Our furniture is the opposite of what furniture is, which is where you sit in it or you lie down on it. Because for us furniture is about moving around and traveling and…

LO: And also, kind of coming up with strategic ways to move furniture, which we became very good at.

AR: Mm-hmm [affirmative].

LO: I mean, the interesting thing, I think, was that when we started our business, we did not have any furniture in our house. If you came to our house, we just had a round Moroccan tea table and you sat on the floor. At that time, Anne's grandmother, who was in her nineties, was living with us a lot. She enjoyed sitting on the floor. I mean, less so getting up from the floor. She enjoyed the floor.

AR: She was fine.

LO: Finally, when we opened the store, she came in and bought furniture, for our house. She bought two chairs.

AR: Yes, which we still have.

LO: And that was to begin. Now, we have furniture. It's all highly impractical, but we have furniture, so...

JDP: Well, it's funny you mentioned Jane Bowles, because I have never read *Two Serious Ladies*. As I understand it, it's an insane novel.

AR: It is.

JDP: Okay.

LO: It's a what?

JDP: It's an insane novel.

LO: It's an insane novel?

AR: Yes, it's a...

LO: Actually, that was one of the things that we bonded over, *Two Serious Ladies*. But it was out of print for years, very few people know the book.

AR: Now, it's...

LO: Now, I think, it's kind of... It's had this whole... It's come back. It's in reprints and she's had this whole... There's been a Jane Bowles renaissance...

AR: Oh, let's not exaggerate.

JDP: Yeah, right. Well, maybe... Maybe it'll start tonight, because...

AR: Yes.

JDP: Because...

LO: On my part.

JDP: Because in a letter to Paul Bowles, Jane Bowles wrote, one time… And maybe this will give us a window into some of the fictions we can talk about. Jane Bowles wrote, "Men are all on the outside, not interesting. They have no mystery. Women are profound and mysterious, and obscene."

LO: Oh gosh. We're not meant to comment on that, are we?

AR: That's really…

JDP: Okay, if you don't want to comment on that. I mean, it occurs to me that parallels what Janet Malcolm said: "Writing is a fraud activity for everyone, of course, male or female." I don't think if it was fraud for both of you. "But women writers seem to take stronger measures, make more peculiar psychic arrangements, than men do to activate their imaginations." I'm asking for a friend, over there, if you find that a compelling idea. Because gender explorations in your novels are pretty various. In fact, they're compendious, I mean, if not encyclopedic. I used all my SAT words in a row there.

LO: Yeah, you're done.

AR: Accordingly…

JDP: I brought my accordion.

AR: Of all the first lines.

JDP: So, all right.

AR: No, I would like…

JDP: You don't want to take the bait, huh? All right.

AR: I would like to comment on that. Because Jane Bowles, and Paul Bowles, for those of you who don't know, they're a very interesting couple. They're a sort of classic, old-fashioned, gay couple. So you know, they're both very actively gay, but they were very close friends, and very...

LO: Married.

AR: And married. Married their whole time and very close friends. Also, kind of, in some ways, really supporting each other's writing very, very much. But Paul Bowles was very rational, and kind of together, and Jane Bowles is completely insane, and a total alcoholic. You know, she fell in love in Morocco. They lived in Morocco and she fell in love with an illiterate market woman that they think tried to poison her.

LO: Well, I think they are pretty sure·she did try.

AR: She did poison her. Just lots of crazy stuff. So he was very stable, you know, and she was nuts. So I think maybe, you know, maybe she's thinking more herself and Paul Bowles, not men and women. You know? Because I think that men and women can be equally...

JDP: Obscene.

AR: Obscene.

LO: Yeah.

JDP: Not tonight. Please.

LO: Yeah. I think I would agree. But I mean, you've opened the door, you're asking us to apply it to ourselves, as it might seem appropriate.

JDP: That's what group therapy is all about.

LO: I think that Anne suggested before that I was an extremist, and then quickly said that I wasn't, because I'm so far from that. I think, in fact, the thing that I most enjoy about writing... I grew up in this household where you kind of had to decide whether you were going to be rational or whether you were going to be emotional. It was made pretty clear that things would not go well for you if you were emotional. And so I think early on, I made a decision that I should be rational. I think that fit well, with probably the way I see the world. I was very involved with math. I liked math a lot. I think what I like about writing, or what... You know, and I should also add, I grew up in Minnesota. It was a town of 400 people, my parents had a hardware store. And we didn't leave that place. My parents were very religious. They kind of employed that Protestant work ethic, which involved always being in hardware store, and never leaving town. Truly, we left once a year, we went to the hardware convention and it was a one-day trip. We came home at the end of it; there was no staying overnight. So I lived in this kind of very closed world.

I don't think that writing was something that I ever even entertained, as an idea of what somebody would do. And so, I think that the thing that has always drawn me to writing is that it... Yes, there is room to be rational, but the kind of biggest successes in my writing day have to do with those moments that don't involve the rational. That's always an interesting and difficult position for me to be in, because I resisted it for so many years. I guess, I enjoy it. So maybe that would be my response to that.

JDP: Well, so following up on this. Or pretending to follow up on this.

LO: Okay, yes. Because Anne looked like she had nothing to add, so...

AR: Well I... Yeah.

JDP: That's okay. That's okay. Let's talk about *space*.

LO: Okay.

AR: Okay.

JDP: And we'll leave time for later.

LO: Okay.

JDP: But *space*. So you both won the Flannery O'Connor prize. I know, Lori, you've spoken a lot about Flannery O'Connor, her command of dialogue, her sense of humor, her propensity to represent violence, all that stuff is a turn-on. You like that stuff. But you're kind of, she's great, but didn't really speak to you?

AR: Well, no, I wouldn't say that Flannery O'Connor is one of my sort of literary heroes. I appreciate her work, but she's not going up and when, you know, you kind of… I feel like the people that most influenced me are the people that I read when I was young, and she wasn't one of those. When I was…

LO: Though I think that you are much more likely than I am to address violence.

AR: Oh, yes.

LO: If you want to write about war, and violence, and look at how a woman might write about violence.

JDP: You're no shrinking violet, though.

LO: Well, I'm a little shaken.

AR: No. I'm not *not* interested in violence. It's just that, I think it has to do with when I read Flannery O'Connor, maybe perhaps more than anything else.

JDP: One of the epigraphs to *After the Parade* is by Flannery O'Connor from her novel, *Wise Blood*. Her only novel I believe. "Where you come from is gone," wrote O'Connor. " Where you thought you were going to never was there. And where you are, is no good, unless you can get away from it." If you haven't yet had the pleasure of reading *Winter Kept Us Warm* or *After the Parade* or their books of short stories, I think you're going to find that you're both, in very different ways, trying to represent a world. In small places, in big places, across a large World War canvas, across a hardware store-ish kind of place, even though… There's no hardware store in that?

LO: There is a hardware store in *After the Parade*, but it plays a bit part.

JDP: So my question is, what's the metaphor of searching and traveling for you? Was this a generative kind of motif? Seems like it might be, in both your books, or in both… And maybe, as we begin to talk about that, you might want to reflect on how you see each other's work. Now, because you've lived together for twenty-seven years, right?

LO: Yeah, it will be twenty-eight this year.

JDP: When you look at each other's work, and the searching that you've done in your own career, do you see the same things? Do you help each other tell the stories that you need to tell? Is there friction in that experience? Do you argue in the morning? Do you argue at night?

AR: There's so many questions here.

JDP: I know, because nobody's taking the bait. Anybody want to jump in here?

AR: Okay, I'm…

LO: No, I…

AR: Let me start.

LO: I kept waiting for that…

AR: For your final question. I think, well, to get back to the space thing, I think we can start with that, and that movement and that travel. So both of us, we do feel, we, just as adults, we're very inspired by moving around and by traveling. Definitely. I think that we can get at some core emotion, and some core conflicts in ourselves, and things that we want to explore, when we're very much outside of the familiar. I think we both do really well, when we're outside of the familiar, and we like that kind of challenge.

We like to not really understand what's going on and we like to be uncomfortable. All of that, sort of, I think, helps us with perspective, and helps us to think about what it is that we want to get on the page, so that's one thing. But I think both of us, very much, for us, place is really important, not only in our own lives but in our writing, right. Even though I think we both are very, very influenced about where and how we grew up in the sense of place. Your sense of place was very, very small and very, very rooted, like people in your town were rooted there for a very long time. And my sense of place was the opposite. I grew up with people who are immigrants, so it was all that not being rooted. And I was the first generation that actually was staying in the same place. I grew up in the suburbs of New Jersey. When I come out to Lafayette, I'm reminded of it. That was sort of the opposite of my whole heritage, which was extreme conflict. My parents were refugees their entire youth. So I grew up among people who never had a home, who were constantly fleeing in this very stable, almost innocuous kind of environment, so that sort of conflict is there. So I wanted to kind of go out in the world, and my parents wanted to stay put for once, and be really safe. In your case, I think, you wanted to go out.

LO: I wanted to go out.

AR: So we both wanted to go out in the world.

LO: Yes, I think for different reasons. And we come from very, very different backgrounds. My family, Scandinavian, I grew up in a Scandinavian enclave, they had come in the late 1800s and had always lived in this place. On my mother's side, they arrived, they'd been living above the Arctic Circle. I think there were maybe seven families that were foolish enough to go from Norway, to try to farm up above the Arctic Circle. And so they lived up there. Then, one by one, I think, over the years, realized it was not a good idea and left for the United States. My great-great-grandmother decided the family should go. And when they left, I think there were both parents and maybe nine children. When they arrived in Canada, there was no husband and I think five of the children had died. So they arrived in this place in Minnesota and that was where they settled. It was almost winter, and she and her sons dug a hole in the ground, and they just, you know, slept in that hole during the winter. Then, as soon as spring came, they started farming, so that was the farm... I did not grow up on a farm. But that was the farm that my mother grew up on. That was the farm that was down the road from me, where, you know, the childhood place that we always kind of went to. And so there was very much that feeling that this is where you would stay. I think it struck my family as strange when I resisted that and wanted to go out farther and farther away from that place. I think it struck your family as less strange, I think. They just didn't understand the need to move.

AR: I think they just wanted peace and quiet, and instability, and they did not understand my dislike of the suburbs. My just wanting to just go out and be in places that they found a little bit unseemly.

LO: But I think, in terms of our writing, which is so different, because it's informed by such different experiences, I think that as a couple, we're each other's only readers. I think that when it comes to our writing, if it weren't... I find Anne's family history incredibly interesting and she feels the same way about mine. The few times she's been to where I grew up, she always says that where I grew up, Minnesota is the strangest place she's ever been to without a passport.

AR: Yeah.

LO: That it just feels so... I think the first time I brought her to my parents' place, they hadn't seen me in years. I walked into the house and my father was reading the newspaper in the living room, and he just kind of put it down and called in, "Is that Lori?" My mother was making dinner, didn't stop making dinner.

AR: She was like, "Ooh, Lori?"

LO: "Oh, Lori," you know, in a Minnesota accent. She said, "It's Lori," and kept cooking. My father put the newspaper up and to Anne I said, "They're only this enthusiastic, because they haven't seen me in years." And that was her introduction. She had never seen this sort of thing, where everybody in town greeted me from...

AR: So far away.

LO: Ten feet away. We walked into the cafe in town and my aunt was there. My aunt said, "Oh, Lori Ostlund. Come over here and let me look at you."

AR: "Let me take a look at you."

LO: I went over and she looked at me. She didn't say a word. She looked at me.

AR: And then we went back and sat in the other booth, like she didn't say, "Come sit down, my niece."

LO: She didn't say, "How are you? What brings you to town?" So I think that was an odd thing.

AR: Yeah.

LO: For you. I grew up with it.

JDP: No, it was normal. Totally normal.

AR: Should I tell the story of the one-armed lady at the Jewish cruise ship, where my mother lives?

JDP: Is this the fugitive?

AR: No.

LO: No. So when I go to where Anne's mother lives…

AR: They're called the stationary Jewish cruise ship, because it's like a retirement place. In New Jersey.

LO: I always say it's the best place to spend Christmas.

AR: Yeah.

JDP: Okay, let's talk about the family that you've been representing in your fictions. Your stories take place around families who are unconventional, nontraditional. I'm dangerously speculating there are any other kinds of families than unconventional and strange. I mean, if you think about the kind of families that you guys so beautifully render, such different kind of families. The Minnesota families. Reviewers have talked about your novel, Anne, they say it's European. It has a kinds of European breadth to it. So anyway, so what about the family? What about these families, in your fictions, not in your lives, but in your fictions? What motors your story along from these families? It's a terrible metaphor, I apologize.

AR: Well, it's interesting. I think both of us have written books, where we have these very absent mothers, these mothers that do not rise to the occasion. In Lori's book… This is not a spoiler, the mother kind of abandons her son. In my book, the mother gives her two daughters to her best friend, because she also… There are reasons for it, it's not just like… But I think we're both kind of intrigued by that. Intrigued by women, I think, perhaps we both had that experience, growing up, that our mothers were kind of distant. I was very close to my father and not my mother. Lori is very much like her father, and not at all like her mother. We also find that interesting, because they're stories about absent fathers, they're not so much about absent mothers. And that was kind of interesting for us, I think. But we came to this separately, we didn't talk about like, we're both going to write these books about absent mothers. It's interesting that we have that.

LO: I think that we have, in some ways, very different preoccupations, when it comes to writing, but I think there's a certain overlap. I think we maybe have a slightly different sensibility. If we were to go to a dinner party, and someone would say something, on the ride home, it would be very clear who that story belonged to based on what they'd said. We don't argue about things. Every once in a while, we both want to kind of work with the same anecdote or... But usually, we have very different ideas about where we would take things. But I think one of our overlapping preoccupations is this idea of that absent mother. And in my case, maybe... I think you have a much different approach to fathers, informed by who your father is.

JDP: To whom the book is dedicated.

AR: Mm-hmm [affirmative].

LO: Yes.

JDP: For whom the words *story* and *history* are intimately connected?

LO: Yeah. Anne's father was a Russian historian. He was very kind of calm, and he was a really nice man. He died just before the book came out.

JDP: Well, maybe this would be a good time to do a reading or two?

AR: Sure.

JDP: Does it need a setup?

AR: No, because I'm just going to read right from the first page, just to kind of pull people in.

JDP: No spoiler alert here.

AR: No spoiler alert. Just to pull people in, and it introduces… In the book, there are three protagonists, two men…

A: [Audience] Can you get a little bit closer to the mic?

LO: No, because I'm always telling, her voice doesn't project.

AR: I know that.

LO: Thinks it's just me.

AR: I'm very aware of it, believe me.

JDP: You see, Patti, other married people have this conversation, just like us.

LO: The thing is, I'm the quieter one, but my voice does project more.

AR: Ready? You can hear? Okay. Anyway, there are three protagonists, two men and a woman. And so this is the beginning of the book. I'm not going to say anything more about it.

The Arrival. The journey from Rabat was not easy. On the long train ride Isaac stood in the crowded aisle outside the compartments, leaning his head out of the window to save himself from the cigarette smoke. After the first stop, about thirty minutes in, a young man forcibly dragged him to a nearby compartment. "Asseyez-vous, monsieur," the young man screamed, as if you were telling him to go to hell rather than trying to help him. Isaac explained about his asthma. He would die if you inhaled so much smoke in a closed in compartment. He phrased it that way so his meaning would not be mistaken for politeness, but the young man had ignored him, pulling him into the compartment as he spoke, yelling at the other passengers to move over. Make room for the old man, Isaac imagined he was saying, and he laughed as he fell into the seat they had cleared for him.

As soon as he was seated, Isaac could feel his throat and lungs clamping up. His laughter turned into coughing. The man sitting next to him offered him water, but it was air he needed, so he gathered his strength, pulled himself up and ran back to the corridor, to his space at the window. He reached for his inhaler, but he didn't need it. The sea air was enough.

After that, they left him alone.

The train stopped frequently and lingered at each station. He did not allow himself to look at his watch, knowing that would only make the journey seem longer. And then, finally, they were in Meknes. One minute longer he told himself, as he stepped off the train, and you would have slumped to the floor right there in the aisle.

At the station in Meknes, he engaged a taxi. The driver asked him whether he had a reservation. "The Hotel Atlas is always full," he said.

"There will be room," Isaac assured him.

"But you do not have a reservation," the driver insisted.

Why, Isaac thought, had he had not simply said that he had a reservation. Why had he never learned to lie even when it made things easier?

The taxi smelled of smoke, though the driver wasn't smoking. Still, Isaac rolled the window down just in case. This upset the driver, who explained that the air conditioning was on, despite the fact that it was hotter in the cab than outside, where, Isaac was sure it was already near one hundred degrees.

"Ah," Isaac said, making sure that there was not even a hint of sarcasm and his tone. The last thing he wanted was an argument with a taxi driver. His parents had been in a taxi accident in New York shortly after arriving in the United States from France in 1942, where they had been living in exile. His parents and the driver had been arguing, the driver insisting that the West Side Highway was

faster, but his parents wanted him to take Amsterdam Avenue. "The lights on Amsterdam are timed," they explained.

"I know, I know. Do you think I'm some kind of idiot?" the taxi driver said, turning around to face Isaac's parents and losing control, driving into the divider. Somehow none of them had been seriously injured, but after that, Isaac's parents lost their interest in the outside world. They retreated to the Russian classics and the safety of their dark apartment. Sometimes Isaac caught them speaking Yiddish, which he had never heard them speak before, though as soon as he walked into the room, they reverted quickly to Russian.

After the accident, Isaac's parents rarely went out, and they never got into a car again or left the city, not even to visit their oldest friends in Connecticut. His parents, who had not allowed themselves to be vanquished by Stalin or Hitler, had, in the end, been defeated by an ornery taxi driver. It was as if their brush with death had given them the license to admit defeat, to accept that their exile was now permanent.

But Isaac had been happy to be in New York, far from the old battles of Europe. Still, he had planned to enlist in the army as soon as his parents were settled. He wanted to be part of the fight against fascism. Though he was not particularly optimistic about the world's future, or even sure that war was the best solution, now that it was on, he wanted to do something. But then his parents had been so shaken by the accident, so derailed, that he did not feel he could leave them. He knew it was just a matter of time until he was drafted, so he relaxed for the first time since the war began. He got a job at Florsheim's, fetching shoes from the store room for the salesman, and when he was not working, he explored the city.

His favorite activity was walking from their apartment on 106th Street to Brooklyn, across the Brooklyn Bridge. Once, before he gave up trying to get his parents to embrace their new home, he took them to see the bridge. His father was an engineer, a builder *of bridges. Perhaps, Isaac thought, standing in the wind, looking up at the sky, they would be comforted. They went to see the bridge on a Sunday in spring. His mother had thought there was something not quite right about walking on a bridge just for the sake of walking. "It's not a park," she said.*

"No, it's not a park," Isaac had agreed.

"But that is what is so wonderful. Only in America would people take a leisurely Sunday walk on a bridge."

"And why is that wonderful?" his mother asked. But Isaac could not explain. His father walked slowly, his hands deep in his pockets. They walked from the Manhattan end to the Brooklyn end, and then they turned around and walked back. Isaac pointed out the elaborate spiderweb mesh of the cables and various buildings of the Manhattan skyline. Then, the three of them took the subway back to their dark apartment on 106th Street.

"What did you think?" Isaac asked his father on their way home.

His father had shrugged. "It's just a bridge," he said.

But it was not just a bridge, Isaac thought. It was a bridge about which poems had been written, a bridge that made history. Perhaps he had never dreamed of changing the course of history, but he still wanted to be part of it, to see what would happen, to live. He opened the window wide, breathed in the dry, hot air of Meknes. The driver accelerated and turned on the radio, loud. "C'est merveilleux, cette musique," Isaac said, but the driver did not respond.

When they arrived at the Hotel Atlas, the driver wanted to go in and self to make sure there was a room available.

"There will be a room," Isaac said again.

"But you don't have a reservation."

"How much do I owe you?" Isaac asked, opening the door as he spoke.

"Calm down, monsieur." There's no rush."

"I will pay you now or not at all," Isaac said, getting out of the car with his bag. He walked around to the driver side and the driver rolled the window down halfway.

"Here," Isaac said, holding out the money.

"As you like," the driver said, grabbing the money and speeding off.

Isaac approached the hotel. He took several deep puffs from the inhaler and concentrated on breathing, making sure that the air was flowing smoothly to his lungs so that he would not be gasping for breath as he stepped inside. That was not the entrance he had imagined.

She was at the reception desk. "Ulli," he said, and when he reached the desk, he was out of breath.

"Isaac," Ulli said. "Come, sit down."

And that's where I'll stop.

JDP: And then, amazing things begin to happen for a wonderful length of time. How about you Lori? Do you feel like reading something tonight for fun?

LO: Sure. Well, should I read something that's more for fun than…

JDP: No, I didn't mean it like that. You know what I meant.

LO: Maybe I'll read the one that's in the… Well, I'll read from the one that's in the *Simpsonistas* anthology.

JDP: That's great.

LO: Change the tone a little bit, rather than… I was going to read from my novel, but I was going to read from somewhere in the middle. And rather than do a little setup, I'll just read from the beginning of this story, "Clear as Cake," which is actually the story that I was reading the night that Joe and I read together. So I'll read it for nostalgic reasons.

JDP: It's kind of a homecoming.

LO: It is.

JDP: By the way, Lafayette is not the suburbs. We call it the country.

AR: Okay, sorry, sorry.

LO: Yeah.

AR: The mountains.

LO: "Clear as Cake."

Marvin Helgarson smoked a pipe. When he listened to us, he nipped at the pipe—pah, pah, pah—the way that people who smoke pipes do, and when he told us things about our writing, he jabbed the pipe in the air for emphasis. I liked Marvin Helgarson. He was tall, not just everyday tall but tall even by Minnesota standards, though that's not why I liked him. I'm just trying to give details, what Marvin Helgarson called "salient features."

The class met Tuesday evenings in the Humanities Building library, sixteen of us wedged in around two long wooden tables that came together in a T with Marvin Helgarson at the head. It felt like Thanksgiving the first night, all of us too close together and filled with dread, though later, after Marvin Helgarson explained about perspective, I could see that maybe that was just my perspective.

"Liars and thieves," said Marvin Helgarson to get things going. "That's what you get with a room full of writers." He rose and swept out his arms like Jesus to include us all.

He meant it as an icebreaker, and most of us chuckled, but the woman across from me said, "Oh dear. I didn't know anything about that"—meaning, I guess, that she had a different idea about writers and writing, a different idea about what she had signed up for. Her name was Wanda, and she had large warts on her chin and cheeks, and later these warts would appear on the characters in her stories. We were always nervous about discussing them, worrying, I suppose, that we might read something into the warts that Wanda had not intended and that she would know then what it was that people saw when they looked at her.

"Wanda," said Marvin Helgarson, "I don't mean writers are really thieves." He paused, picked up his pipe, and sucked on it. "It's more like when someone lends you a pen to use, and then you just don't give it back." About lying, he said nothing.

"You're going to be working together intimately," Marvin Helgarson said, "so you need to know who you're dealing with." He asked for a volunteer to begin the introductions, and Fred Erickson, who was wearing a tie with a treble clef on it, jumped right in, describing his family and hobbies and years as the director of a choir in Idaho, from which he was now retired. Idaho seemed far away to me, and I wondered how he had ended up in Moorhead, Minnesota, but I didn't ask because I was intimidated by my classmates, most of whom came to campus once a week for this class but were adults with jobs and families the rest of the time.

I took a lot of notes that semester, tips that Marvin Helgarson shared to help us with our writing, like when he told us that sometimes the things that seemed most compelling to write about should not really be written about at all. They were just anecdotes, he said, odd things that had happened to us that were interesting to discuss in a bar but were not literary, by which he meant that they could not transcend the page. He explained this the first night of class, jabbing the air with his pipe so that we understood it was important, and then he said it again several months later when we discussed the nutty lady's story about a woman who cleaned rest stops along I-94. In the story, the woman and her cleaning partner were finishing the rest area near Fergus Falls when they discovered a body inside one of the trashcans. The story, which was just two pages long, mainly a lot of boring details about cleaning that lent veracity, ended like this: "The woman was dead and she was also naked. We were shocked and scared, and after the police came, we finished the bathrooms and went home."

When Marvin explained to the nutty lady that it wasn't really a short story, that it was more of an anecdote, she stood up. "Anecdote?" she said. "This really happened, you know. It happened to me, right after my ass-wipe husband left, and I had to be at that job every morning at six." She snorted. "Anecdote." Then, she walked out. It was late, nearly nine o'clock, and we could hear her footsteps echoing, not only because the building was empty but aslo because she was wearing ski boots.

We didn't see the crazy lady again, but at the beginning of the next class Marvin showed us what she had left in his mailbox: a manila envelope with our stories for the week, chopped into strips with a paper cutter. You see, she really was crazy. But also, she'd had enough of us I think, enough of us telling her stuff about her writing. Three weeks earlier, she'd submitted a story about a woman whose vagina hurt all the time, except when she was having sex. As a result, her husband, who was a farmer, got very tired of having sex all the time and told her that she needed to go to the doctor to have her vagina checked. "I'm putting my foot down" is what he said, which made me laugh, though I didn't say so because I didn't think the story was supposed to be funny.

The woman and her husband spoke with what seemed like Irish accents, but when they drove into town to see the doctor, they drove to Bemidji, which is in Minnesota. I raised my hand and said they sounded Irish, pointing to things like "lassie" and "thar" because Marvin had told us to back up our comments with examples from the text, but the crazy lady looked pleased when I said they sounded Irish. "Yes," she said. "They're from Ireland. They moved to Minnesota when they were young in order to have an adventure and be farmers and also because something tragic happened to them in Ireland and they needed a fresh start."

"I guess I missed that," I said and began shuffling back through the story.

"No," she said. "It doesn't say it. It's just something I know. I was creating a life for my characters off the page, the way that Marvin said we should."

"That's a lot to have off the page," pointed out Thomas in what I thought was a very nice voice. Thomas was also one of the older students in the class. The first salient feature about Thomas was that his parents met at a nudist colony, where they were not nudists because they worked in the kitchen, chopping vegetables and frying meat. The other salient feature about Thomas was that he was a minister. I knew these things because he sometimes wrote his sermons at Jack's, the bar that I hung out at and one night we drank a pitcher of beer together and talked, but when we saw each other in class the next week, we both felt awkward.

"But the story isn't about them leaving Ireland," said the crazy lady triumphantly. "It's about"—she paused because I guess even a crazy lady feels strange saying "vagina" to a minister—"the pain in her female parts."

None of us knew what to say, so we looked down at the story, at the scene in which the woman and her husband, who was tired from having sex all the time, visited the doctor. When she was in the doctor's office, lying on the table with her feet in the stirrups, the doctor, who was an elderly man, positioned himself between her legs and called out, "Three fingers going."

This was supposed to be a minor detail I think, but Tabatha, who was a feminist, got mad. "That's ridiculous," she yelled at the crazy lady. "What kind of a doctor would say, 'Three fingers going'?"

"Doctors are just regular people," the crazy lady yelled back. "They get tired of saying the same things over and over, day after day. This doctor is like that. He's old, and he's tired. I am showing that he's a regular person who is exhausted and wants to retire. I am developing his character."

"That's not development," Tabatha said. "Then the story becomes about him, about how he's a misogynist and is going to get sued one of these days for saying things like 'three fingers going' to women when they're in a vulnerable position."

I'm going to stop there.

AR: I always laugh at the ski boots. I can be walking around and I think of the ski boots and I just… Every time.

LO: Well, that's the interesting thing about…

JDP: Salient features.

LO: And living with a writer, because when I wrote that, Anne read the story and I took out the ski boots, thinking the ski boots were not funny. Anne reread the story, and she came downstairs and she said, "Where are the ski boots? Why did you take out the ski boots?"

AR: Yeah.

LO: Yeah. I just think that sometimes, you know, I always say that with writing you have to write for one person, one person who really gets your sensibility. And so I always think of Anne as the one and I'm always kind of gauging what she laughs at or what she doesn't understand. But then, even when she does laugh, I still…

AR: You always say, "Oh, you're the only one who's going to think that's funny." If you would take your own advice, you wouldn't have anything funny in there left.

LO: That's good.

JDP: You realize everybody can hear you, right?

LO: Welcome to driving anywhere in the car with us.

AR: Yes.

JDP: This was wonderful. The readings were fantastic. Open up for any questions, comments, anything you want to say? Want to read your own story? No, you can't do that.

LO: There's somebody.

A1: [Audience Member 1] I think you said it was Anne's mother that lived with you for a while when you were in New Mexico?

AR: My grandmother.

A1: [Audience Member 1] My question is, when she went to buy furniture, did she get wholesale?

AR: No, actually, no, she refused. She wanted to help. We were in the beginning of our business, also. She wanted to help us out now, so she paid full price, retail, to buy us furniture.

JDP: *Winter Kept Us Warm* is a title drawn from T. S. Eliot?

AR: Mm-hmm [affirmative].

JDP: And poems seem to matter a lot in these novels?

AR: Mm-hmm [affirmative].

JDP: In *Winter Kept Us Warm*, the narrator quotes from "Dover Beach," "Ah, love, let us be true to one another! For the world, which seems to lie before us, so various and new, hath really neither joy, nor certitude, nor help for pain." And also those famous "Ignorant armies, clashing by night." This, you've spoken about, "Dover Beach" is one of your favorite poems. Also, a driving poem, for you, in your novel, is from Richard Hugo.

LO: "Degrees of Gray"...

JDP: "Degrees of Gray in Philipsburg." "Say you came in here on a whim..."

LO: "Say your life broke down. The last good kiss you had was years ago. You walk these streets laid out by the insane..."

JDP: "Say your life broke down."

LO: Yeah.

JDP: So I'm wondering, what about poetry? First of all, that's a risky proposition and so you're dealing with editors, "You can't quote poetry in fiction." They tend to get very nervous about this stuff. So you did that, it's brazen. It seems to power your stories, these images, these voices.

AR: Well, we kind of courted on poetry.

LO: We got together in Madrid, we were living...

AR: Even before that, when we weren't together, remember, we would sit out in the backyard of my place? When I was sort of dating this woman that I had nothing in common with, and Lori would come over. The woman was in medical school, so she'd be studying her medical books. Lori would come over and we'd read, like T. S. Eliot, out loud to each other.

AR: One of the greatest stories of our courtship was, Lori said, "I bet you can't guess what my favorite line from 'The Wasteland' is." And like I just said, "I know. 'Marie, Marie, hold on tight and down they went.'" And she was like, "Yeah." And so...

LO: It was an innocuous line.

AR: It's not that innocuous, it's a great line. Right from the beginning, we read each other poetry. Then, in Madrid, we would stay up at night...

LO: Yeah. We both had all of our poetry collections along and "Dover Beach" has always been one of my favorite poems. Matthew Arnold is not one of my favorite poets, but I absolutely love "Dover Beach." During that period, those couple of years, we were just reading poetry a lot. Both poets that we both love, like T. S. Eliot, and then poets that Anne didn't know. Richard Hugo, I don't think you really knew "Dover Beach" that well.

AR: We introduced each other to poems that we liked.

LO: We didn't have a telephone, or a television, we were reading.

AR: Just had books. Yeah. And now we started this new thing, where we, just before we go to sleep, we reread... How many collections have we read? We're reading contemporary poets now.

LO: I think we've read eighteen collections.

AR: Of poetry, yeah.

LO: We just pick a poet that we hear about. And so before bed every night, I read. We read Joe's wonderful collection in this way. We read poetry and we work our way through them. I keep a list.

JDP: No ski boots in mine.

LO: No. There were no ski boots. It was very funny though. It was interesting to read yours, before night. We don't usually... I mean, before bed. We don't usually read funny work.

JDP: Sorry about that.

A2: [Audience Member 2] Anne, you refer to some authors that influenced you when you were growing up? You didn't name them.

AR: Okay.

A2: [Audience Member 2] And Lori, would you also talk about who mattered to you?

JDP: Pretty big job.

AR Yes. But I mean, when I was very young, I guess… Poetry, of course, has always been really important for me. And I started out when I was a teenager, writing poetry. But I think the writers that influenced me the most are the Bowles, you know, Paul and Jane Bowles. Malcolm Lowry, *Under the Volcano*, is probably my favorite book.

I like Virginia Woolf. Faulkner. I'll go with Dostoyevsky. *Brothers Karamazov*, I read like five or six times when I was a teenager, so those are the things that kind of… I grew up with. And Salinger, the short stories, the nine stories. I mean, there are others too, but those are the first things that kind of come to my mind.

LO: I read nonstop when I was a child, but they were not the sorts of books that people would have heard of, because they, you know, they were… My father was a reader, but my mother read only the Bible. The Bible was how I learned to read. I read the Bible, out loud, to the family. I read the entire thing when I was in second grade, including all the parts within, so and so begat, so and so begat. I got in a lot of trouble, because about five minutes in, and I asked if we could skip it. And my father was just, you know? And so, no, that could not be skipped. But I think as I got older… You know, I tend to take a writer that I become interested in and then read all of their work. So I did that a couple of years ago with Willa Cather, for example. For a couple of years, we were living in Malaysia, and I think I went through and read all of the Brontë sisters over the course of maybe a month.

AR: You're missing Dickens, who's probably your biggest influence.

LO: I love Dickens. I'm a huge Dickens fan. I've read all of Dickens, numerous times. When I travel, it's always Dickens that I take with me. I think one of the writers that we both loved, Salinger, is somebody we both come back to.

JDP: The stories, or…

AR: The stories I like, *Raise High the Roof Beam*. Not so much *Catcher in the Rye*. Of course, when I was in middle school, I loved it. But…

LO: I think that's changed. But when I think back to the writers that first influenced me. And then, always poetry. I've always loved poetry.

JDP: Well, okay. So, you're both story writers, you're both distinguished novelists, both distinguished short story writers. People have said the form closest to the short story is the poem. Okay, that sticks in my mind a lot, as a truism. But I'm wondering what, when you're, when you have… I don't want to call it an idea for work. But when you begin to work, do you know, "Oh, this is a story. No, this might be a novel." Or, this is a novel, but it really breaks down to stories? I mean, how do you how do you navigate these different tributaries?

LO: I think first of all, maybe just temperamentally, Anne is more a novelist, and I'm more a short story writer. And the novel is just, by its very nature, kind of a messier form, it's more forgiving. And I think Anne is… That works well for you. But I've kind of… I like the short story, because it's very precise and it kind of appeals to my perfectionism. But having said that, I think we both have become very interested in the other form, the form that we didn't maybe gravitate toward, right away.

JDP: Kind of as a challenge, or as a work of discipline, or…

LO: Well, I think that seemed very daunting to me. I'm a big rewriter and the idea… You know, normally, when I sit down to write in the morning, I go back, and I reread from the very beginning of the work. That works with a short story. Then, I move into it that way. But that doesn't work, if you've written… You know, the novel I'm working on right now, I'm 450 pages into it. I have no idea what it's about, but I certainly can't sit down and read from the beginning again. Whereas, I think Anne is much more comfortable with that. I like digression. I'm a digressive writer. I love tangents. But I think you're just naturally more comfortable with that.

AR: Maybe.

LO: Is that true?

AR: Maybe. Yeah. I think, for me, this book started with a short story. So I feel like the characters in this book started in a short story, but that short story didn't seem enough to me, to say what I needed, and so those characters just kept living and then I just kind of kept going with them. I feel like I do that more. Like your short stories are short stories, but I think a lot of my... My next book that I just finished, about Nicaragua, also started with a short story. So I feel like I'm...

LO: Am I allowed to say that you just sold it?

AR: You can say that? Well, you just said it.

JDP: No, it's a secret. You told a secret.

LO: It's like in court, you strike that you heard that. Then, that's stricken from the record.

JDP: Congratulation on your new Counterpoint novel.

AR: Yeah, yeah, thank you.

JDP: But you're both episodic. Am I wrong? But anyway, by the way, this book of short stories, in a way began *Winter Kept Us Warm*.

LO: Mm-hmm [affirmative].

JDP: Yeah, the Bukovsky Family.

LO: Mm-hmm [affirmative].

JDP: It's a wonderful book of short stories. Anne, there's a… Boy, if we had a lot more time. I want to talk about "Chinese Opera" sometime.

AR: Okay.

JDP: I see our time is winding down. But I do want to ask one more question.

AR: Okay.

JDP: Unless somebody has something to say? Okay. So, *Winter Kept Us Warm, After the Parade,* by conscious or unconscious design, would you say these are love stories?

AR: Mm-hmm [affirmative].

LO: You know, it's interesting. This story I'm working on right now… Or the book, the novel, the one that's 450 pages, and I can't figure out what it's about.

AR: I know it's a love story.

LO: Well, maybe not a love story, but I think it's maybe an attempt to figure out what love is.

AR: Yeah, that's a love story.

LO: I say that, because that's an incredibly uncomfortable thing for me. People always ask me, "What is the thing you would never write about?" I always say, "Sex." But I think that even more than that, love seems to me like a very difficult thing to write about. I suppose, it is, in some way. Yours, I think, is much more clearly a love story.

AR: That wasn't the design.

LO: No.

AR: I don't know, I'm going to make a very, sort of a very cliché generalization that all stories are love stories, I guess. I mean, every book, really.

LO: You asked the question earlier, what I like about Anne's work.

AR: Go ahead. Go ahead.

LO: But I do think that one of the things that Anne is very good at… And maybe this is something that as I get older, I'm in my fifties now, that I always thought when I was younger, it would be very nice to have clear answers to things. Or maybe I thought I did have clear answers to things. The older I get, the less clear I am about not really understanding anything very well. Or every time I begin to understand it more, I understand it less, or it shows itself to be far more complicated, and the subtleties and all of these things. I think that's something Anne does so well in her work, is just kind of work within the realm of the subtle, and that's something that really appeals to me. I think even though we come from very different places, I grew up in a place that's all restraints, nothing ever quite gets said. It's all about what doesn't get said. Anne approaches it a different way in her work, I think, but she still gets at those subtleties and kind of the complications of human beings. I think that's the thing maybe I like the most.

JDP: But what I think is amazing about both these authors is that, well, Lori, is that you're not afraid of heartbreak. You're not afraid of the pain and the sorrow of the characters, whom you found in the pages of your stories. I think that takes tremendous courage, because it's so easy to be facile. I mean, that's about love, or about sorrow, or about:… There are solutions that you're saying… I think one would be very hard-pressed reading either of you, to think, well, life is… You guys are still figuring out. You're still emerging writers, you're emerged and still emerging. I really, thank you both, very much, for being here.

AR: Wait, wait. Before you stop, though, I have to be able... Because we have this whole long-standing thing that...

LO: I think we're out of time though.

AR: No, we have this long-standing thing that every time that Lori says what she likes about my writing, then I forget to say what I like about hers. Now she set it up so that there's not enough time.

JDP: No, this is good. Time out. Go ahead, say it.

AR: Okay. I actually like... I think, the same thing. I mean, the subtleties in your writing. For me, it's this, the compassion that's so strong, but there's nothing sentimental about it. But it's just this deep, deep, deep compassion for people's suffering, and for their strengths also. And that the way you use humor, of course. Again, there's nothing surface about it. There's so many layers to your humor. So like, you're laughing out loud. I think humor, comedy, is sometimes much more forceful, and much more emotional than tragedy. I think that you're able to do that. You use humor to really bring out the tragic elements of human existence as well as the joys of it, too. So that's what I would say.

JDP: To quote one of my two favorite authors on stage tonight, "Sometimes you thought you knew what your character wanted, and then you got to the end of your story, and realized that you didn't understand this character you had created at all." That's the wonder, I think, that we both feel in the presence of these two remarkable authors. So please, thank Lori and Anne for being here.

AR: Thank you.

LO: Thank you. And thank you to all of you for coming out.

AR: Thank you.

LO: And Joe, of course.

AR: Joe, thank you.

JDP: Well, it was a pleasure, and everybody, buy books. It is really good to buy books.

LO: Thank you.

AR: Thank you.

POEMS

BY KIM DOWER

INAUGURAL PUBLICIST, SIMPSON LITERARY PROJECT

(FROM *SUNBATHING ON TYRONE POWER'S GRAVE* AND
LAST TRAIN TO THE MISSING PLANET)

UNRULY AURA

The cashier at the health food store
tells me I have a beautiful aura. .
Wait, I tell her, if you want to see
a really beautiful aura, wait until I've taken
my Renew Life, Ultimate Flora, Probiotic.
After that my aura will knock your socks off.
She smiles at me and rings me up. My money
has a beautiful aura, too. My dollar bills
float out of my pink wallet. The man behind me
swells from the heat I generate. Each step I take
brings me closer to God, the final, fabulous aura.
Take my hand, I tell her, squeeze my aura—
it's hungry, and looking for someone to devour.

HE SAID I WROTE ABOUT DEATH,

and I didn't mean to, this was not
my intent. I meant to say how I loved
the birds, how watching them lift off
the branches, hearing their song
helps me get through the gray morning.
When I wrote about how they crash
into the small dark places that only birds
can fit through, layers of night sky, pipes
through drains, how I've seen them splayed
across gutters, piles of feathers stuck
together by dried blood, how once my car
ran over a sparrow, though I swerved,
the road was narrow, the bird not quick
enough, dragged it under my tire as I drove
to forget, bird disappearing part by part,
beak, slender feet, fretful, hot,
I did not mean to write about death,
but rather how when something dies
we remember who we love, and we
die a little too, we who are still breathing,
we who still have the energy to survive.

I WORE THIS DRESS TODAY FOR YOU, MOM,

breezy floral, dancing with color
soft, silky, flows as I walk.
Easter Sunday and you always liked

to get dressed, go for brunch, "maybe
there's a good movie playing somewhere?"
Wrong religion, we were not church-goers,

but New Yorkers who understood the value
of a parade down Fifth Avenue, bonnets
in lavender, powder blues, pinks, hues
of spring, the hope it would bring.
We had no religion but we did have
noodle kugel, grandparents, dads

who could fix fans, reach the china
on the top shelf, carve the turkey.
That time has passed. You were the last

to go, mom, and I still feel bad I never
got dressed up for you like you wanted me to.
I had things, things to do. But today in LA

hot the way you liked it—those little birds
you loved to see flitting from tree to tree—
just saw one, a twig in it's mouth, preparing

a bed for its baby—might still be an egg,
I wish you were here. I've got a closet filled
with dresses I need to show you.

LETTER TO MY SON

Dementia runs in the family, so if I can't think of a name or a place, a moment everyone else can vividly recall, I feel afraid. Useless. Ashamed. You see, I don't want anyone to carry me into another room so I can get a view of a tree or remind me what a tree is or tell me what I'm sipping from is called a straw. I've seen it all before. My grandfather didn't know he was eating a banana—only that someone had to peel it for him, and that thing, that peel had to be thrown away. I'm not saying it's certain I will have dementia, but if I do, please know this: I won't be mad if you don't take care of me. I won't even know that you're not. Tell me everything's okay, and I will believe you. Tell me there's a bird on a branch outside my window, even if there is no window, and I will imagine he's singing to me. Once when a storm was coming my mother looked up at the sky, told me God was punching the clouds to make rain pour out. She never even believed in God. The point is this: I may not know exactly who you are when you come to visit. I may be confused. But when I hold your hand it will all come back in waves: rocking you in my arms when you were a baby, your little seltzer voice, my heart flooding my body with joy every morning you jumped in my bed. I will not be angry like some people with dementia can get. I've never been good at angry. I will not peel the yellow paper off the wall or bite my caregiver. Play a few rounds of Blackjack with me. You deal. I will smile each time I get a picture card. Tell me I've hit twenty-one even if I bust. Use real chips, have party drinks with ice that clinks, a cocktail napkin with which to dab my lips.

THIRST

My father never saw my house
though without his modest savings
we never could have bought it.

My father didn't know his grandson
past the age of ten, but today at twenty-eight
my boy has his eyes

and many of his talents. My father
died thirsty. We couldn't fill
his needs; no one could.

He had a big personality, my mother
would say, sucked the air
out of a room, needed you to pay

attention to his every word, a wall
of talk we wanted to jump over.
My father could tell a good

joke, do the accents, had the timing.
Why wasn't that appreciated.
He could sell anything, untangle a knot

out of the most delicate chain.
His stuff looked nice, his paintings framed.
He'd serve pats of butter on a dish

restaurant style. Our people leave us
and we let them go. They fade
into the tapestry of the dead,

an occasional memory slapping us
in the face tapping us on the shoulder
kissing the breeze by our cheek.

We wait for the wind to blow
these reminders, like it did for me today,
just now, in my garden that he never saw,

but would have loved, even though my roses
are struggling, their white petals dropping
so thirsty they are; so ready for a drink.

"A BIG, BEAUTIFUL WALL": EXCLUSION AND ART ALONG THE US-MEXICAN BORDER

BY GENARO PADILLA

SIMPSON LITERARY PROJECT FOUNDING MEMBER

"On day one, we will begin working on an impenetrable, physical, tall, powerful, beautiful wall."
—Donald Trump

"I hope this will help people see us as differently than what they hear in the media, that they will stop taking us like criminals or rapists... I hope in that image they won't only see my kid. They will see us all."
—Mother of child model of JR border sculpture

"I am alive/or I am dreaming/I am dead they spoke like this/Those figures/Crossing/Deserts across deserts."
—Juan Felipe Herrera, poem "One by One"

Every day in the US, one opens a newspaper or turns on the news to see stories about the supposed crisis at the border between Mexico and the US. Led by President Trump, nativists argue that waves of Mexicans and Central Americans are "invading our borders." For most Americans, there is no crisis. There has been a border between the US and Mexico since 1848, when, in a contrived war, the US incorporated, ate, nearly one-half of Mexico, including Texas, New Mexico, Arizona, and California, those states that front the 2,000-mile southern border.[1]

People in both countries know, have long known, that there is a border, but it has been largely porous, with towns on both sides living in adjacent economic and cultural interdependence. When convenient to its labor needs, the US has as much as thrown open the border, welcoming

Mexicans to work on the railroads and the agricultural fields, in the coal, copper and steel industries, in stockyards and slaughterhouses, and more recently in restaurants, hotels, hospitals, housing construction, and other core infrastructure services. Their labor literally built many of these industries and made American owners wealthy.

Yet, throughout the twentieth century, Mexican immigrants, documented or not, were accused of stealing jobs from *true* American citizens, for taking up space in schools and hospitals, for speaking Spanish in public, for living in neighborhoods where they didn't belong. Now the jingoist script is even worse: Mexican and Central Americans immigrants are figured as criminal aliens "invading our borders." It took no more than Donald Trump's nationalist scream about immigrants in June, 2015, to fuel the launch of his presidential campaign: "They're bringing drugs. They're bringing crime. They're rapists." When he gloated, "I will build a great, great wall on our southern border, and I will make Mexico pay for that wall," what I remember, more than Trump's bloated jingoism, is the derisive pitch of agreement from his audience, especially one woman's guttural "Yeahhh! Yeahhhh!"

Witnessing this nationally televised diatribe, I knew that, yet again, Mexicans, joined now by Central Americans fleeing dire poverty and violence, would play the villains, as we have from the mid-nineteenth century when the US invented a nativist rationale for waging a war designed to expand the country from "sea to shining sea." That imperial goal attained, the same nationalist fear now is that "illegal aliens" will corrupt that bright metaphor of empire. Of course, there have long been markers and barriers along the border, but Trump's unbreachable wall is intended to put an end to border crossing once and for all. Trump bragged in August 2016, that this would be his first priority: "On day one, we will begin working on an impenetrable, physical, tall, powerful, beautiful wall" (see YouTube: https://www.youtube.com/watch?v=2J9y6s_ukBQ). Construction would begin, not with a physical barrier but by making the American heart "impenetrable," his words mounting to a choral voice of assent, "Yeaaah." The materiality of an old anger given voice at every rally, his audiences, growing from this initial fester, began to chant, "Build that wall! Build that wall!"

The Trump chorus is comprised mainly of alienated white voters who trace their own material alienation within a capitalist economy to other workers with whom they share more than they are allowed to understand. Their own spirits mangled by joblessness and shrinking wages, American industries offshored, these blue-collar communities are malleable, gulled by an oligarch who runs his businesses on a principle of labor exploitation inherent in free market capitalism. When it comes to their corporate interests, Trump and his class of one-percenters could not care less about borders; indeed, for them open borders are required in a global market. Reading this alienation, Trump, now the nation's pseudo political leader, assumed a voice of ethnocentric anxiety, stoking fear that hordes of criminals were summarily crossing the border, reducing bigotry to sound bites and tweets on the "crisis on our southern border."

Because the border between Mexico and the US has become a xenophobic rallying point in Trump's presidency, it is also a location (within dislocation) for reclaiming an aesthetics of resistance to the cruelty manifest in this contrived crisis. Against this jingoist rant, artists, poets, filmmakers, novelists, and photographers give witness to the effects of the Wall on human life and, increasingly, on animal and plant life as well. Artists envision the wall as a "big, beautiful" canvas, poets find language in the stark terrain of the border zone, novelists and essayists (re)create the migrant narratives of those who are traversing a searing desert, performance artists mock the very idea of an old-world solution to the reality of people moving across vast geographies merely to survive. This aesthetics of resistance intends to act in the moment as well as to leave a record, a visual trace, an overarching narrative that documents resistance within a wider sequence of provocations.

I offer but a brief survey of these aesthetic encounters with the xenophobe's Wall. These encounters are at once powerfully symbolic, visceral, politically motivating. Whether in unnerving poetry, in hallucinatory prose descriptions of migrant lost in a desert, or in sculptural installations that intend to change people's minds and hearts—the artists and writers whose work I describe all intend their work to inspirit, to anger, to alter the language and landscape of the border, to undo the materialization of border bigotry. While I understand the potential political efficacy of this work, we must remain skeptical of art's capacity for creating social transformation. We liberals tend to applaud the politically symbolic representation of the border zone as inhumane and killing, but we too often chant our slogans at and about the meanness and absurdity of an "impenetrable" wall and then we go off to our private lives, posting selfies of political rallies on Facebook with a few pontificating remarks, "liked" by friends and family.

Let's pursue this concern, opening with the figure of a child, a small body reaching over the wall, an innocent's smile tugging at the viewer's heart.

There is a huge cutout by a French artist who goes by the name JR.[2] He came to the border to understand the devastations of separation and violence we have so recently seen within the US, where migrant families are casually separated, parents detained as criminals for crossing the border, their children not only detained in border zone warehouses but delivered into "foster" care, often hundreds of miles away from mothers who are not told where they have been relocated. Installed just prior to the 2018 zero tolerance policy that allowed breaking families apart, JR's sculptural piece places the figure of a child, placidly smiling as his fingers, made giant, gently touch the fence as he peeks over into the US.

Scaling sixty-five feet, JR's sculptural piece is at once monumental, a powerful and sentimental performative piece. A child's giant image softens the steel fence, transforming it into a playpen. The piece was viewed at the border close to San Diego by thousands of people, with border agents themselves warming to this vision of innocence. The image lingers in the viewer's heart as well as in the political imagination, for it invites the viewer from the American side to conceptualize Trump's border as absurd, a child's play crib. However, we know that the border is no plaything. It is a gash in and across the land. As Gloria Anzaldúa writes in *Borderland/La Frontera*, "The US-Mexican border *es una herida abierta* where the Third World grates against the first and bleeds."[3] The child looking over the border in JR's installation inspirits, but, I want to say, dispirits, because we know that, should we apply Anzaldúa's metaphor, the metal fence will lacerate these child's hands, will cut and bleed him. In the months that followed JR's installation, Trump's administration took action that would negate the very idea of a child's innocence and potential for a life fully lived. Some 3,000 children were separated from their parents as families sought to cross the border and were put into warehouses where they slept on mats, their blankets Mylar sheets. Children were not smiling. They cried, calling for their mothers; their mothers were desperate, heartbroken, afraid they'd never see their children again. The security we imagine parents providing their babies gone from one moment to the next at some nameless facility.[4]

This is all the more anguishing when we learn that the child rendered in the sculptural cut is based upon a boy living on the Mexican side, whose mother allowed JR to use the backyard of their home, nestled right at the fence, because she believed in the conciliatory potential of the piece. As JR reports, "I did a rendering in my studio in Paris, and then we went back to see the mother again. She approved it. She said, 'I hope this will help people see us differently than what they hear in the media, that they will stop taking us like criminals or rapists.' I could feel—wow. It was very strong from her. She told me, 'I hope in that image they won't only see my kid. They will see us all.'"[5] But, *do* they see us all as other than criminal? Will the Trump base have their hearts and minds changed by seeing this astonishing photo sculpture of a young child, so full of possibility, so curious? I doubt it. Yet, I know that JR's work is intended to remind us of our common love for children. Perhaps he can do no more than remind us. Perhaps this visual narrative will embed itself in the American social imaginary to see their own children living in common with Mexican children, their families living in community. Perhaps.

In 2011, artist Ana Teresa Fernandez set up a ladder on the Tijuana–San Diego border wall, constructed here of steel slats, and started painting it a powdery blue so that with each broad stroke it gradually disappeared. The "*Borrando la frontera* / Erasing the Border" project is a minimalist work and an incredibly powerful political statement on the absurdity of border walls. The beach on the Mexican side of the border is a popular spot for families, who are forced to face the looming, threatening metal structure as they picnic at the ocean. Fernández's mural offers a vision of a geography before, or long after, the border was erected, suggesting a return to a world without walls, without nations. Utopian aesthetic desire in a dystopian landscape.

Fernández's revisualizing, or erasing, of the very concept of border, imagines restoring the sightlines of land and sky, an azure palette of light, a blue that erases the man-made barrier between the clear and cloudless sky and the desert horizon line at the Pacific. Fernandez's installation is a hopeful call for reclaiming a common humanity, even when distinct human cultures are maintained; "Two cultures, different cultures under the same sky," Fernandez herself notes. As one viewer comments: "This is beautiful, moving, breathtaking, gracious, clever... Love it." and another writes, "This is so cool and at such a right time. Art can move the emotions that we are unable to express any other way."[6] Indeed, other activists were moved to follow Fernandez's strategy by taking brushes and blue house paint to the fence, extending its erasure. If only the border could be made to disappear.

My own unsettled heart, not unmoved but wary, skeptical, recalls the long xenophobic history of the US-Mexican divide and refuses to be moved by art, or narrative, or poetry that, however powerful and politically capacious, has not led to the removal of the historical barrier between two countries. Both JR's and Fernández's art offer a representational vision, or illusion, of a common humanity along this and all borders. Each artist offers figural gestures that "can move the emotions," that well of sentiment and sensibility that tricks us again and again into something we call hope. I don't want that kind of hope. I won't accept—at least not here, now—the artifice of transformation when it seems to me we are stuck in the historical vortex of an old xenophobia that continues to damage the soul of both countries. What I do want is to be reminded of that which appalls and to be made responsible for every breach of that "common humanity." This is where we come to a sociopolitical cul-de-sac that art alone cannot erase. Yes, art must arouse the emotions, but here at this border, as at all borders where vitriol and violence meet the people who are escaping to possibility, it must also shame us. We must have an art and film and poetry that appalls so deeply that we must move to action in community against the inhumane treatment of the stranger.

One such installation does appall with its unremitting reminder that the border zone is treacherous, a long stretch where hundreds of migrants die every year.

Alberto Caro's "Border Coffins," an installation on the sheet metal fence between Tijuana and San Diego, offers a stark memorial to those immigrants who have died along the vast reach of desert between the two countries. The caskets, each painted in bright colors with the lettering *Muertes / The Dead* and the number of (unnecessary) mortalities in a given year, are attached to the Mexican side of the fence. One must imagine that as migrants who have journeyed hundreds of miles from the deep interior are all at once starkly confronted at this spot with the specter, and reality, of death. Indeed, the border patrol has documented more than 8,000 deaths since the 1990s, as reported by *The New York Times*.[7] This is surely an undercount since so much of the southern border is desert, a no-man's-land where isolated small groups of migrants have died and melted into sand and rock and wind, or who have drowned in the Rio Grande, hundreds of children, mothers, young men floating into oblivion.

Caro's "Border Coffins" finds its corollary in poetry and narrative that surveys the human misery along the border, where sojourners moving north on the vague promise of a new life often die in the gamble. These migrant souls will have to venture on in the afterlife without the ritual celebration of death their family members and friends ordinarily offer, adorning small altars with bright flowers, their favorite dishes and fruits, candles, coffee, and incense, all the necessities a spirit will need on his or her journey through the underworld. The "Border Coffins" installation celebrates these spirits with brightly colored wooden coffins, festooned with designs of roses, doves, serpents; yet, what mars this gesture of affection is the very abstraction of death, the tallying of those anonymous individuals who, day after day and year after year, have died crossing the border: "2004. 373. *Muertes*." Caro's coffins represent a mass burial site for thousands of nameless people, who, without the ritual practices of remembrance, are now spirits that shall remain in the desert or watery reaches where they expired.

In 2004, Luis Alberto Urrea, novelist, poet, and journalist, published *The Devil's Highway: A True Story*, an account of a group of twenty-one men who crossed the border into the Arizona desert during one of the hottest times of the year. This is a harrowing and deeply anguishing story of the hapless journey these migrants took to make a better way of life, only to end up swirling aimlessly in the desert, dehydrated, lost in the scorching horizon of sand and rock. Listen to Urrea's opening passage:

Five men stumbled out of the mountain pass so sun struck they didn't know their own names, couldn't remember where they'd come from, had forgotten how long they'd been lost. One of them wandered back up a peak. One of them was barefoot. They were burned nearly black, their lips huge and cracking, what paltry drool still available to them spuming from their mouths in a salty foam as they walked. Their eyes were cloudy with dust, almost too dry to blink up a tear. Their hair was hard and stiffened by old sweat, standing in crowns from their scalps, old sweat because their bodies were no longer sweating. They were drunk from having their brains baked in the pan, they were seeing God and the devils, and they were dizzy from drinking their own urine, the poisons clogging their systems.[8]

Urrea is among those journalists and documentary film makers who make the trek north themselves, following the migrant trails through desert or across river and, only after absorbing the jarring experience, reporting their findings, in piercing language or astonishing film footage. In the Oscar-nominated documentary, *Which Way Home* (2009), Rebecca Cammisa followed the route taken by thousands of Central Americans, many of them youngsters, trying to make their way to reunite with parents or siblings already in the US. The freight trains they glom to are called *La Bestia* (The Beast), rightly named because people commonly fall to their deaths beneath the tracks, suffer amputated limbs, lose their way along the nebulous route, and are commonly assaulted and robbed by equally desperate groups trying to survive degrading conditions. The film exposes us to the poverty, family breakage, and the desperation that leads so many young people to brave the long and treacherous journey to what, for them, is the utopia of the United States, a place imagined as perfect. Very few of those who travel on El Bestia make it into the country of their illusions and this film unsparingly shows the devastation that ensues in the lives of young migrants.

In the poem "One by One," Juan Felipe Herrera,[9] recent poet laureate of the United States, also writes of the long journey to *el Norte* from mountain villages and destitute *ranchitos*. Herrera's nameless speaker, following migrants as they huddle together in pairs or small groups, allied in loneliness, want, and confusion, records their common sentiments. The poem is hallucinatory, a jangle of voices, dream notes, bodies moving through vast spaces of disintegration, boarding buses, as it turns out, with ghosts who speak to the living. Some of these travelers drown crossing the Rio Grande: "transparent fleeting you rise and fall/appear and dissolve among the others/like you/like me." Urrea's figures are lost in an estranging geography of sand, "that rectangle of nothingness/that bone oven." This rectangle of nothingness is a furnace in summer, "a desert that never ended," a land with only dew for water, brittle shade, directionless in every direction.

> this is how their dreams arrived
> walking
> dragging themselves hugging each other
> through the tunnels the canyons this is how they lived
> …
> without sun without earth or house without anything
> no sky nor floor

This figuring of migrants as delirious, sunstroked, "dragging themselves" across perilous terrain instantiates dislocation so pronounced as to lose any mooring in time and space. They float outside of our, or any, solar system, the body wilting, the mind dissolving. These migrant souls are lost not only to hometowns or villages but also to the earth itself, to its spin through the day, its cycles: "legs/without a planet or a season." Herrera gives language to a condition of privation denuding of flesh and skin, the migrant body desiccating so quickly as to be turned to leather and bone before the mind understands its collapse:

> I am alive
> or I am dreaming
> I am dead they spoke like this
> Those figures
> Crossing
> Deserts across deserts

These now planet-less, season-less people are transformed into eternal desert inhabitants, a diaspora of the dead, the living evaporating into "shadows." This netherworld is prefigured in the poem when the speaker remembers himself as one among a "busload of shadows and nightriders." The border zone is terrain where the dead and the living dissolve into the same dream, all crossing and crossing. If their bodies are retrieved they will figuratively inhabit Caro's "Border Coffins," as one among hundreds of *los muertes*,　.

> *their hands as if almost playing guitars*
> *crossed over the breast*
> *in a box without a name ...*
> > *their lips half open as if about to drink water*
> > *their hair thin brilliant waving*
> > *in the winds*

The poet refuses illusory compensation. It is as though the poet's imaginative capacity has dissolved, become another shadow, the poem itself a "rectangle of nothingness." Herrera's is a poetics of the irretrievable. The poem is a coroner's report, a forensics of death in enjambment, lines spilling over their own walls, a "cage of voices." The poet speaks to and through the living and the dead. For both Urrea and Herrera, the border zone, *la frontera*, is its own wall against human habitation, an ecology deployed against all intruders—no need here for wire when heat will shear one's clothes, no need for Trump's, or anyone else's "great wall," when sheer granite outcroppings, sandstone cliffs, the vast rectangle of sand will suffice to bring feet and hands, lungs and heart to a stop—"the throat shut."[10]

This story of people crossing the desert in this region is as old as the border. What makes Herrera's and Urrea's accounts all the more lyrically searing is the knowledge that, because of the US's criminalization of southern immigrants, these and untold thousands of men, women, and children have perished trying to reach a land they have been told opens to material possibility, to safety from desperate poverty, assault, and state-sponsored violence. These immigrants, whose spirits remain fastened to their bones, bespeak a history of desire for human dignity come to its broken end.

I close with a lingering sense of alienation and anger over the humiliations, the unnecessary suffering and death, the sheer cruelty and meanness of spirit experienced by Mexican and Central American migrants as they reach for the slightest possibility of possibility in their flight to *el Norte*.

I want to believe that art and sculpture along the border will make visual and visceral the absurdity of all such walls, whether built of stone, concrete, metal, or human hate. I want to believe that poetry, documentary film, and journalistic narrative, true and truly imagined, will make a difference in law and policy that tempers and transforms. But we must keep pressure on ourselves to think through, to puzzle over, to resolutely refuse the embrace of illusory resistance and resolution. The hopeful, utopian vision offered by JR and Hernandez must gather in us, embed an idea that, in action, may not erase concrete and steel, but lead us to make as widely and unquietly public our opposition to Trump's "big, beautiful wall." This art premises transformation, but it must be measured against the realities, the daily nightmare of border crossing so unsparingly represented in the work of Herrera, Caro, Cammisa, and Urrea. What we must ask ourselves is this: What is it that art and literature can do and what is it that can they not do? Border art compels us to believe that minds and hearts can be changed, and that these aesthetic gestures and voices can shore up our common humanity, can bring us into a community of accruing force for mass action on the ground, at the border itself. Even when we are uncertain how much we can accomplish in the everyday, we must still commit our art and literature to leave a trace, a historical record of an aesthetic response to a killing xenophobia at this and all borders.

CODA: AN AESTHETICS OF DESPAIR

I worried while writing the earlier sections of this piece that sculpture and stories and poetry and documentary film could not stop the meanness of spirit being enacted at the border. I kept writing as a way of keeping hope. But nearly every phrase that conveyed hope evaporated when confronted with the latest news of the Trump administration's next measure of "border control" and then the next and the next: children yanked from their parents, unwanted human beings penned in warehouses, tired bodies huddled on concrete floors, the wretched refuse just refuse. Day by day, I could feel my heart withering.

The gladdening JR sculpture of a Mexican toddler leaning over the border fence, a child's curious, joyous face, his baby fingers made giant by an artist whose vision of possibility was billboard size, withered. JR's sculptural response to the absurdity of nations and borders produced both a sense of aesthetic precision—JR's visual calculation is perfect—such that the monumental figure of a child looking over the border into the US produced a sense of wonder and hope. Who wouldn't smile at such a child's innocence, a smile that obviates xenophobia? How could anyone fear such a little stranger? Still I knew, I knew that JR's brilliant sociopolitical imbrication of artistic practice put to political critique could not hold against the deep hatred of a government bent on destroying our capacity for human embrace.

Now there is a piece of art that rolls a boulder over my heart. A photograph by Julia Le Duc (Associated Press) that appeared on the front page of *The New York Times*, June 25, 2019. A moment caught by lens. Click. Death stilled. Two bodies at a river's edge. Both bodies staring down into silted water. Five or six Bud Light cans, trademark blue, tossed casually the previous evening by guys fishing, as I imagine, decorate the frame. A child napping across her father's back. Papi's sweet daughter throws her arm across his shoulder, tucking her head into his dark hair, safe under his black T-shirt. Her mother changed her diaper and pulled up her red cotton shorts this warm morning. They would change to dry clothes once on the other side. They would.

Now, the father and the child entwined, floating, facedown in the Rio Grande, the watery border. The photographer did not need to structure the scene. This is real, not staged to produce its effect. I imagine the last struggling moment, the sudden weariness that overcomes the girl's father, his legs kicking their last, his cupped hands reaching and reaching, his nose and tongue lost in a confusion of water and sky. Tiny fingers holding tight and tighter still. Then, still. Hope is pulled into the drowning pool. Force of river water, vortices scooping sand, branches, debris carried from Colorado where it sources, across 1,896 miles through the middle of New Mexico, across Texas from El Paso to the Gulf of Mexico. This river carries their trace into eternity.

ENDNOTES

1   The US-Mexican War, which began in 1846 and ended in 1848 with the Treaty of Guadalupe. In the terms of the peace treaty, Mexico lost more than 2,500,000 square kilometers (970,000 sq mi) of land, 55% of its territory, including what today are the states California, Arizona, New Mexico, Texas, Utah, Colorado, Nevada and stretches of Wyoming, Kansas and Oklahoma.

2   See Wikipedia for profile of JR and a chronology of his work: https://en.wikipedia.org/wiki/JR_(artist).

3   Anzaldúa, Gloria, *Borderlands/La Frontera: The New Mestiza*, 1987, Spinsters/Aunt Lute Press, p. 2.

4   It is likely that several thousand more children than reported were separated from their parents. Why was this human tragedy not reported by the government itself? See Jordan, Miriam, "Many Families Split at Border Went Untallied," *New York Times*, Jan. 17, 2019, Section A, p.1, p.12. *"The federal government has reported that nearly 3,000 children were forcibly separated from their parents under last year's "zero tolerance" immigration policy, under which nearly all adults entering the country illegally were prosecuted, and any children accompanying them were put into shelter or foster care." The article then goes on to report that even before the "zero tolerance" policy was publicly announced/enacted (and reversed by federal court order in June 2018) thousands more children had already been separated at the border, "Thus, the total number of children separated from a parent or guardian by immigration authorities is 'unknown,' because of the lack of a coordinated formal tracking system ..." (p. 1) One official from the Health and Human Services Department acknowledged that "The total number is unknown…. It is certainly more than 2,737 (the number given for separations after the zero tolerance policy was enforced), but how many more, precisely, is unknown." (p. 12)*

5   Schwartz, Alexandra, "The Artist JR Lifts A Mexican Child Over The Border Wall," *The New Yorker*, Sept. 11, 2017, see link [https://www.newyorker.com/news/as-told-to/the-artist-jr-lifts-a-mexican-child-over-the-border-wall]

6   Woodman, Stephen, "Meet the 5 Artists Redefining the US-Mexico Border," *The Culture Trip*, March 1, 2018 (updated), see link [https://theculturetrip.com/north-america/mexico/articles/meet-the-5-artists-redefining-the-us-mexico-border/]

7   Romero, Simon and Dickerson Caitlin, "'Desperation of Thousands' Pushes Migrantes Into Ever Remote Terrain," *The New York Times*, Jan. 29, 2018, see link   [https://www.nytimes.com/2019/01/29/us/border-wall-crossings.html] *"The grim cost of United States immigration policies is hardly new. Law enforcement authorities have found the remains of about 8,000 migrants who have died while crossing the border with Mexico since the 1990s... . At least 413 migrants were found dead along the border in 2018, according to a preliminary count by the International Organization for Migration, up from 412 in 2017 and 399 in 2016."*

8   Urrea, Luis Alberto, *The Devil's Highway: A True Story*, 2004, Little, Brown & Company, Boston. 2004, p. 5

9   More information about Juan Felipe Herrera can be found on the *Poetry Foundation* website, see link [https://www.poetryfoundation.org/poets/juan-felipe-herrera].

10   Herrera, Juan Felipe, "One by One," *187 Reasons Mexicanos Can't Cross the Border*, 2007, City Lights Books:, p. 89-103.

For the full essay, with images and links, visit simpsonliteraryproject.org.

SIMPSON LITERARY PROJECT
WRITING WORKSHOPS

WINTER/SPRING 2019
WORKSHOP SELECTIONS

MEMOIR WORKSHOP:
LAFAYETTE LIBRARY AND LEARNING CENTER

JANINE NOËL, FRANCIE LOW

MEMBERS OF THE SIMPSON PROJECT MEMOIR
WORKSHOP

VOICEOVER

MEMOIR

BY JANINE NOËL

1.

January 2006. San Francisco Bay Area.

Back from Sundance, driving home. I feel close, industry again. A siren, a cop car behind me, I pull to the side of the road. I could punch tears on command, but I don't. I am thirty-one. My boyfriend's church programs are on the passenger's seat. I spin them so they're in plain view. *I'm a good girl, officer.*

The officer returns with my license and registration. "Do you know you come up as a missing person?"

"No," I say. I'm in some system? I wasn't even gone for a day.

"Someone reported you down in LA. You live up here now?"

"Off Magnolia."

"Everything okay?" He shines his flashlight into my car, an edge of light cuts through my lap, onto the church pamphlets. "Not in any trouble? Medication's handled?"

"It was a while ago." Who did they make me out to be?

"Drive safe tonight," he says. "Thirty-five around here."

"Yes, thank you, officer."

I didn't know it was official, that I was in an incident log. Official codes, official history.

My sister reported me missing on Highway 101. She never told them I was found.

LIGHTS UP.

JANINE. I've got a great ass.
What makes a great ass? Roundness, firmness, moon-like silkiness, bounciness, grab-ability?
The Coppertone commercials where the little girl gets her panties chewed by a puppy—that was me. By high school I reached all-ass glory. Crowned homecoming queen, lassoed in the studly swimmer boyfriend. On the football field bleachers, carved next to my initials, is the outline of my ass.

After college, we found yoga. Always in the front row, we'd sit back into an imaginary chair longer than anyone else. An illustrious career as the fit model for butt-lifting jeans. Queen of the boy shorts.

One night, after some passionate lovin' and spankin', my boyfriend says, "Damn, girl, your ass is on fire."

"Thank you," I say.

"No, I mean it. Your ass is burning up." I look into his eyes, excited. He insists I touch it and see for myself. "Your entire right butt cheek is red, ablaze!"

I touch it. There's a raised welt covering my cheek. My ass, my great, wonderful ass…malfunctioned.

I wait in an exam room, in walks the doctor. A very young, cute resident. Someone I'd definitely let see my ass under other circumstances. He demands the full history. I tell him that my ass has always served me very well, thank you. Beyond well. He returns with two real doctors.

I'm on the table, down on all fours. The
doctors stare into my ass and speak softly, matter-of-fact.
Then a pause, concern in their voices, now intrigue. "See,
if you look at the rectum at the ten o'clock position."

Oh my god. My ass is no longer sexy or
ripe—it is a scientific teaching tool used to demonstrate
a defunct ass.

"Janine, do you partake in anal sex? If so,
we highly recommend that you stop."

Are they accusing me of bringing this on
myself?

After the scoping, it is confirmed. I have
an ailment of the ass. There, on the insurance form, in
bold letters, diagnostic code: BUMR. Officially known as
Crohn's Disease: a chronic inflammatory gastrointestinal
or bowel disease causing ulceration of the GI tract
presumably triggered by an overactive immune system.

A crone is a shriveled old woman. That I
am not. If only I had developed a cute disease, a sexy
disease—laryngitis or narcolepsy. Oh no. I get a disease
of the ass.

My friends know the terror in my eyes. I
take deep breaths, devise a quick plan of attack, hunt for a
bathroom where I won't need a key with a coffee pot tied
to the end. I'll flash my "Disabled Asses Card" when they
say, "No, miss, employees only." Not quite the VIP
treatment this ass is used to. Mutiny on the Butt-ny.

Do I tell a guy on the first date? Put it right
on the table that I have an angry ass?

Each and every one of you has a better ass
than me. You, sir, with your flat man-butt, you have a
better ass than I do. You want this ass? Let's trade.

It's what's on the inside that matters. Tell
me about it. But it used to shimmer and glow. God I want
that back. I want to be fearless and free, with all my sexy
ripeness radiating from behind. Ladies, never deny

your ass the chance to take you far in life, you never know when it may run out of steam. I got a compliment the other day. This guy said, *Honey, your ass is smoking.*

Oh, he has no idea.

LIGHTS OUT

2.

February 2004.

My audition is at Raleigh Studios in North Hollywood. *Pieces (of Ass)* is running on a soundstage that's been converted into a theatre. The show is getting press, the casting search has been publicized on the radio, on the morning news. "Seeking beautiful, dynamic, talented actresses to write and perform original monologues in a groundbreaking Hollywood theatrical event," my friend Steve had said, reading the casting notice over the phone.

"Like *The Vagina Monologues?*" I had asked.

"Attractive women reveal what goes on in their pretty little heads. You need to submit."

"I don't know. I don't have a car." Am I pretty enough? I had been taking a break from acting, hiding out at my mom's, getting healthy, teaching yoga at Bikram East Bay.

"Well," Steve said, stretching out the word, his voice going up. I could see him shrugging his shoulders, thinking, *How hard is it to get to LA? It's your life, it's your career.*

Midway down I-5, on the way to LA, I start seeing stars. Quick flashes of light in the corner of my left eye. Low iron. Shit, I'm anemic again. I open a Gatorade, sip some electrolytes, pop a few Vitamin B. My health has been holding. I need it to hold. I have an audition.

I like the idea of hitting Melrose and Sunset in the gold Toyota minivan I've borrowed from my sister. The graham cracker crumbs lodged into the bucket seats comfort me, anchor me in reality as I take on Hollywood. This could be my minivan, I could have a couple of kids. I am old, twenty-nine. I hope the producer thinks I'm younger. I'll drive this clunker onto set. I'm edgy, I'm real. I'm not just another blonde in a black SUV.

I drive down Melrose, follow a white Porsche, find the studio entrance to my left. There's a guard shack, security. The Porsche makes a left into the lot, a woman extends her hand through the driver's side window, gives the guard a quick wave, the gate arm swings up. I can't follow the girl in the Porsche. I've lost my chutzpah. I drive the beast down the block, park under a tree, next to a school. I walk up to the guard shack.

"Audition?" the guard asks. "Last name?"

I begin to spell out my name, three letters in, he says, "Stage ten—make a left—loop around—you'll see ten—main stage—back of the lot." His tone is calm, protective. I'm one of the dozens of girls he directs safely to set. I squeeze through a gap between the guard shack and the orange-and-white gate arm—no need for him to lift it for me. I walk through security, like I'm walking to school. Who walks onto a film set?

I cut through parked cars, past the soundstages—giant, beige, windowless warehouses. The girl gets out of the white Porsche. She is in pink velour sweats, fresh out of the shower, she rolls onto set, it is her home. The weekly table reads, the production assistants making coffee runs, the makeup girls giving actors skinny straws to sip waters through between takes so they don't mess up their lipstick—these are the rituals.

In New York, I was home, where I needed to be, in the kitchen backstage at *All My Children*. Susan Lucci at the microwave, body so miniature, joy in her eyes. She said, Welcome, hello, enjoy your day. I was just an extra in mint-green scrubs, a nurse with brassy blond hair, a stethoscope looped over my shoulders. She saw my hope, the possibility in my eyes, took her coffee mug out of the microwave, smiled and waved goodbye. During taping, the heartthrob actor made a joke and Susan Lucci squealed. The crew laughed, even though they'd have to redo the shot. It was a family.

The stage ten door opens with force, a brunette, older than me, uses her body weight to push through. She's six feet tall, curves held in by a tight gray Lycra dress, pretty in a maintained way, lip liner too dark. I should have shown some leg, worn a skirt, showed off my toned calves.

A guy in a white baseball cap grabs the door before it slams shut. "Sorry," he says. "I'm running behind." We shake hands, his hands young, knuckles pudgy. He wears flip-flops, his frayed jeans drag on the floor. Feels less like a Hollywood film lot, more like a campus quad. I follow him in, stop picking my thumb's cuticle, breathe, try to listen.

The soundstage is cavernous. The producer weaves through an aisle of white pod-like chairs, waves me along. The stage is made of metal pipes; blue and pink lights hang from scaffolding. Urban, industrial, raw. He presses himself up onto the stage with a hoist, a hop—he's done it a hundred times. He extends his hand, I use my other hand to lift myself and scoot my hips over the edge of the stage. We sit, legs dangling over the ledge, we turn knee to knee.

"You look like a soccer player," the producer says, scanning my black-and-white headshot. A tight crewneck T-shirt, jean shorts, my hands on my waist, a big eyes-alive smile. I do look athletic, strong, healthy. I took that picture four years ago, before I got sick.

"New York credits," he says, reading my résumé. "An Ivy girl." He asks me if I know a few guys with Irish names from school. I don't know many people from Dartmouth. I was hardly there.

"Where'd you go?" I ask.

"Holy Cross," he says.

A Catholic boy with freckles. We're two friends at a bar. Is this how real Hollywood works? A quick chat and I'm in?

"This show needs some weight, something smart," he says.

"A monologue about illness," I say. "An attractive woman with an un-sexy disease."

His phone buzzes, he answers, I can hear a woman's voice. "I'll call you back," he says, his tone low, professional. "I'll call you right back." He turns to me, whispers, "Sorry."

I'm more important than the woman on the phone.

"What about illness?" he asks. "We've done cancer, dyslexia, eating disorders."

"A disease of the ass," I say.

"Send me a draft, come see the show." He walks me to the door, pushes it open for me. A good guy hiding out in Hollywood, he knows talent when he sees it. A quick interview, no lines to read, no emotions to push. My résumé, my New York credits prove I can act, that I'm smart. Hollywood wants me because I am smart.

3.

Before She Was Famous! Actress Crashed on College Friend's Couch! I won't mention my friend Kelcey's couch is oversized, brown, feathery, chocolaty—once you sink into it, it's hard to get up. I won't mention her cream organic cotton sheets. I won't mention my friend's pad is prime Santa Monica, a beachfront luxury condo, subsidized by her mother.

Kelcey is an LA girl, all sinew and slim hips, forever thin from beach volleyball carving out the muscles in her legs, sucking up fat stores before they deposit. She hands me a Diet Coke—an LA dinner—I crack it open, take a sip, the bubbles attack my empty stomach. I'm too self-conscious to say I'm hungry after a long day, so I show control and starve.

"The producer comped me tickets," I say.

"The Produce-saaaah," Kelcey sings. As if I've dreamed him up. "Sounds so big-time."

It's a bit of a jab, stretching his name out all sexy as if I'm enamored, but I laugh. "Want to see The Produce-saaaah's show?"

"No," she says. She's busy with her other friends. Her green eyes are always hard to read, she has this glare, and whether she means it or not, her look says I am so far from cool.

Doesn't everyone get excited to see a play! To sit in the audience, to feel the tension if actors will get their lines right, hit the notes in a song, make you believe in their world? Doesn't everyone want to run up on stage for a minute or two, say a few words that aren't your own, take a few breaths and forget?

◆◆◆

My mom tells my *Annie* story. I was seven. She took my older sister and me to see the musical in San Francisco. They both remember sitting in the back row of the balcony. I was on the edge of my seat, watching tiny girls with big voices jump in and out of barrels, dance with brooms, voices so strong I couldn't take my eyes off them. I knew I could do that, be a pint-sized orphan with a Broadway belt. I'd be allowed to dance and sing and be bigger than myself, allowed to have attention. I could grow up and be an actress. I would play on a stage. That would be the best job in the world. Don't all little girls grow up wanting to be actresses? Don't we all want to be famous?

◆◆◆

There's a hot pink banner hanging on stage door ten. *Piece(s) of Ass ~ Enlightening for men. Empowering for women.* A red carpet swept to the side of the door. A vinyl backdrop leaning against the wall. You've seen them before, those backdrops with film logos that celebs stand in front of on opening night. This one is shiny white, hot pink and black. *Pieces (of Ass), Sky Vodka, The Palms Casino, Pieces (of Ass), Sky Vodka, The Palms Casino.* A real red carpet backdrop where girls twist, place one hand on a hip, tilt their heads, demand sex into their eyes as the cameras flash. A "step and repeat" or "repeat." That's what they're called. I know the lingo but I've never walked the red carpet before. Will the show use this red carpet again?

I flip through a thick, glossy, professional program. Looks as good as a *Playbill.* I dream of Playbills, the program for all Broadway and Off-Broadway shows. If I am cast, I'll have a professional LA credit. Will it be recorded? Archived? Where do LA credits go? The cast is introduced as "The Pieces." Each woman is cast in the role of *Piece.* One *Piece* was formerly a guest host on *Regis and Kelly*; another *Piece* was a "Barker's Beauty" on *The Price Is Right*; another *Piece* is on *LA Mag*'s up-and-coming list. Paris Hilton has been a "CenterPiece," a guest star, for a few shows. I have fewer credits than each *Piece.* I'm a replacement *Piece* for burnt-out *Pieces.* I want to be a *Piece.*

Lights down. The DJ blasts Kelly Clarkson, a woman in a black leather miniskirt and black bustier walks on stage, big steps, a model strut, her hips sway, then she swivels to the audience center stage, the music is cut, she pops her knee, thrusts out her butt. Video monitors flank stage left and right and flash one word, "Icing," in hot pink, flash, flash, blink, then off.

Lights up. The woman in black is a peroxide blonde. She extends her hand to the audience, shows off a giant diamond ring, winks. "My secret weapon," she says. "I couldn't walk out of the house without it." She has a shrill laugh and gummy smile, a turned-up nose—a look that matches her playful lines—but her timing, her nods to the audience, the way she moves on stage, how she cocks her hips and points her toes, how she lets the audience laugh, then picks up the next beat—this woman's a pro.

One monologue after the next, the women walk on stage, strike poses, move in platform shoes, wedges, stilettos, a few in bare feet. Their monologues are diverse.

A blonde. *Women can never be friends with men.*

A brunette. *Dear Diary: Dyslexia made me feel dumb until I found modeling.*

A black woman. *White boys say the stupidest things.*

A blonde. *Warning! Never get caught in granny panties during an impromptu striptease.*

A brunette: *Beauty rituals are exhausting but the alone time is satisfying.*

A blonde. *Men always fall for a woman who speaks French.*

A black woman. *My fan mail comes from prison.*

A brunette. *Being gay in high school...*Wait, the butch brunette in her red-and-white cheerleading costume just forgot her line? "Shit," she says. "It's my first night." She shakes her pompoms overhead, sticks out her tongue. "I wasn't a cheerleader, but I nailed the head cheerleader on the Ping-Pong table in my high school gym." She laughs at her own joke, the audience loves her, she trots off stage, bowlegged and stiff. But it's the confidence, she moves with it, too. I would never go up on a line; in New York you can't, even in an Off-Off-Off Broadway show you know your lines.

Lights up, another blonde, me. Can I move like them for ten minutes on stage? How did they learn, where is it written? The poses, one arm up, then shimmy down some fake pole. Do they copy their friends, sisters, moms? With their rhythm and hips they punctuate their beauty.

Act from your pussy, an acting teacher once said. *Carry a secret in your pussy.* Can I lead with my body, with sex? *Pull the scene up from my pussy.*

4.

Kelcey's up at seven for her nanny job, or mother's helper job, or whatever the trendy way to say babysitter is. She is babysitting for a power producing duo that runs Reaction Films. *Sophisticated storytelling that provokes and challenges audiences of all ages.* Where the betterment of mankind and Hollywood intersect. She's doing script coverage, too, helping the producers find the next hot screenplay, getting her foot in the door while bouncing their toddler on her hip. She's more connected than I'll ever be.

"Good luck with The Produce-saaaah," Kelcey says on her way out the door.

"Thanks," I say. She doesn't think I will get this. There's that look in her eyes again, like if I turn away, she'll whisper into the next person's ear: *Look who's back in town, look who thinks she's an actress.*

I sit at Kelcey's dining room table with my laptop. A table of substance. Distressed wood, chairs with crisp linen slip covers. A grand table—too big for the condo—too mature for the setup. An email from The Producer. *Nice start, Janine. I marked a few places. Get me a final draft. Let me know who your rep is.*

He's added two lines to my monologue: "Why do dogs lick their butts? Because they can."

I'll say anything. I have booked. I am a *Piece*. He wants to talk to my "rep." He likes how I write. I'm pretty enough to be in the show.

.

My "rep" is Sheila Weintraub of Maximum Talent Management, but Sheila doesn't exist. Stella Stevenson, a thirty-something actress/filmmaker created Maximum Talent Management with the alias Sheila Weintraub. Under a fake company name and fake manager name, Stella has signed up for network television and studio film casting notices that only registered talent agents and managers can access. "It's smart, not subversive," Stella says. "Why wait for the invitation to get your face in front of the networks and studios?"

I had been sending out my headshot and résumé for a year and still hadn't landed an agent or manager when my friend Evan introduced me to Stella. I trust Evan, a working screenwriter. I joined Stella's membership group and paid $200 a month for her to submit me for castings. Now that I've booked the show, The Producer needs to know I'm legit, that I have a rep. I have to sign back up with Stella. She's all I've got.

Stella means well, she thinks of herself as a mentor, emails audition tips and inspirational quotes. *At Maximum, we build your persona, your backstory. Your career is now!* Stella had a short film at Sundance, but the behind the scenes photos posted on IMDb made it look like a big-budget film with a set photographer. She posed next to the camera in a baseball cap and tank top and looked through a viewfinder. *Director surveys scene for next shot.*

"It's a big deal," Stella says when I tell her about *Piece (of Ass)*. "Have him call Sheila." I can see her now, lounging on her sofa, feet on a pillow. Part actress, part manager, part dreamer. "Really, Janine, this is big, the press alone."

◆◆◆

A memory. A composite memory—my memory, an old photo, my mom telling it to me as a story. I'm four years old, we're in the French Quarter, on vacation. A man is dancing in front of a fountain, a big crowd, a semi-circle, people clapping along to the beat, he's dancing so fast, a tap dance without tap shoes, and he dances up to the audience, invites one person after the next with an outstretched hand. Families smile but step back, kids, even older than me, shake their heads as he moves through the crowd and he's coming up to me, going to ask me to dance, I know it, I'm next, if he reaches his hand out, I'll take it, say yes, I'll go into the circle and smile and dance, his dark hand grabs mine, and I'm in, I shuffle ball change shuffle ball change hop, hop, fast, fast, as I can, he takes my hand, twirls me, the crowd claps and cheers. I hop and shuffle and smile and know it's better to say yes to a dance, to jump in, the crowd wants a dance, they want to smile and clap to the beat, they like how I dance with the man, they take my picture, more pictures, flashes go off, me and this man. Mom and Dad smile, the man twirls me, lets go of my hand. Dad pats my back.

◆◆◆

The Producer emails back. *Wardrobe fitting and rehearsal early next week. We'll start you Thursday. Monologue's pretty good now. Made a few edits, now it's tight, tight like your ass.*

5.

Stella@MaximumTalent emails: *Thought of the Day: Can you say with confidence that you are an actor without apologizing or looking away?*

Yes, Stella, I've been calling myself an actor for six years. In New York, Ray, my acting coach, said, "Call yourself an actor," on our first day of class. "Sitting in this playhouse, learning to act, rehearsing, auditioning. This is your career."

I call myself an actor. But I'm careful. Not with family or old friends. They will listen, act polite, but will not hear my dream again.

The Cedars Sinai Infusion Center is packed with patients and their partners. Dr. V squeezed me in when I told him I moved back to LA, that I needed an infusion before my show. I follow the nurse to the only empty chair. She sweeps saltine cracker wrappers off the armrest and asks if I'd like a hot cocoa.

"How'd you do this week, Bill?" she asks the old guy next to me. "Any pain, bleeding with your BMs?"

"Better," he says. His wife pops open a bento box and they start going at it with chopsticks.

I can't stomach these people, this place. I'm shitting blood, too, but don't need to hear it from the next guy over. All these different-colored IV bags dripping into our arms. Saline, chemotherapies, deep red packs of blood cells. The nurse gives me Benadryl so I don't go into shock when I'm infused with this new drug. Dr. V hoped the drug would put me into remission, but my symptoms quiet down for a few weeks and then rev back up.

When Steve told me to seize the day, to drive down and audition, I didn't tell him it was bad timing, that I had moved home because I was sick, that I was afraid to pick up and go back so soon. I'm not a girl who can throw a pair of panties in her purse, leave town on a whim. Injections, infusions, procedures. It's too hard to explain, so I keep things vague, come off as a flake.

The nurse chats with the patient across from me. She's about my age, wears a USC baseball cap over long brown hair. She must be a regular here. I can tell by her eyes that she has a good husband, lots of friends, a full life—even when sick. I want life in my eyes, a body that works for me, a body that can make it through the show.

I watch a minute of TV, *All My Children*, close my eyes, sleep.

◆◆◆

I ask my mom and sister if we can wait in line for Annie's autograph after the play. The stage door finally opens and the girl who plays Annie waves to the crowd. She is pale and frail, wears a thin lavender sweatshirt, faded blue pants. Her hair has been dyed orange to match the wig. It blows in thin wisps. I've never seen a child so pale and skinny, so different from me and my sister and brother. We brown right up from the sun. My mom will make a comment later. She didn't like seeing a child so scrawny. *Too many days rehearsing in the basement of a performing arts school.* Thirteen years old and bones like chalk. I want to be her. The ghost girl gets to dance and sing.

◆◆◆

I hand The Producer a Ziploc of baby photos my mom sent. He wants to project them on the screens at the top of my monologue. *The Rise and*

Fall of a Great Ass. From my perfect baby ass to my hot ass to my diseased adult ass.

He takes my pictures up to the projection booth, turns on the screens, clicks through each photo, my childhood lighting up the stage. Me, baby on my belly with a pink bum, then as a towheaded toddler. He pauses, leaves one picture up on the screens. I'm two, naked, standing in our kitchen windowsill. I remember climbing up there, it was a wide countertop that I could stand and play on. I'm holding onto a white pole in the corner of the window. The photo is of my backside, tan, fine gold locks of hair, my nose in soft profile. A potted ivy hangs from the ceiling and my mom's reflection is in the photo, muted, she wears a burgundy top, has flowing brown hair. The Producer has angled the photo so you can't see her reflection.

As he walks back to the stage, I wait for him to say, "You were a gorgeous kid, no wonder you're a knockout." Isn't that what we all want to hear? That we were beautiful babies—a Gerber baby or baby commercial star? "Ah, beautiful," I wait for him to say with a smile.

"That's the one," he says.

Like a baptism into the biz, my childhood made public, destiny.

◆◆◆

"You would pound on your highchair at dinnertime until we all turned to look at you," my mom says. "You loved attention."

"I was more attention-seeking than other babies?" I ask my mom.

"You just knew how to get attention," she says.

I grew up with this story, my dinnertime game. Give me attention. A manipulative infant.

◆◆◆

The Producer has been talking on the phone my entire rehearsal. He is the *director* of the show, too. He paces around the empty audience, rests a hand on the back of a pod chair, nods, paces some more. He's so hands-off it gives me confidence. New York trained, I can self-direct.

I get down on my hands and knees center stage. I stick out my butt, twist my face into a pained pout. *My most memorable rectal exam: a reenactment.* Four years ago, a huddle of Columbia-Presbyterian physicians and residents were staring at my anus, counting rectal fissures—small tears in my asshole. I was acting in New York, bleeding, afraid I'd lose the boy I wanted to marry if he knew I was in pain. I would line up at urgent care clinics, slip into gastroenterology appointments, and not tell a soul.

The Producer has asked me to tell my body's story. Make theatre out of it. The disease feels distant, less shameful. Still on all fours, I turn my head to the audience. "See, if you look at the rectum at the ten o'clock position," I say with a stuffy-nose-scientific-sounding voice.

"Maybe not," The Producer says. His first note he's given me all afternoon. He wants me to say the line again in my own voice.

"See, if you look at the rectum at the ten o'clock position," I say in my voice. Serious, just stating the facts.

The Producer nods, keeps talking on the phone, sits on the edge of the stage. Just one adjustment and her monologue is ready. She's ready for Thursday night. He hangs up, throws down his phone, lies down on his back, hands behind head.

"I can't take it," he says. He means how the women call to complain about hair and makeup and tickets and something bitchy one said to the next.

"Please tell me you're not crazy."

I lie down, too, turn on my side, prop my head up with a hand. It would be flirtatious, but there's half a stage between us.

"Maybe a little," I say.

"A little crazy is interesting," he says. "Not scary actress crazy."

"I'm interesting." I've shaken off the crazy. LA can't see it on me. "You don't have any more notes?"

"You're golden," he says.

Young, beautiful, stable—I'm ready for his show.

In New York, Ray would stop us line by line as we went through a scene. "I don't believe," he would say, stretching out the word *believe*, taking a drag from his cigarette. You couldn't get one word out unless Ray believed what you were saying on his stage.

I was doing a scene from *Boys' Life* with Victor, a Greek god model/ construction worker. We were husband and wife. I would yell at Victor, then he would grab me, wrap his arms around me. I'd wrap mine around him, hold his head, then we'd go in for a deep smooch. I'd smile at the quiver of his lip. We'd let our nerves work for us. We were in scene: present, listening, responding, kissing.

"No," Ray yelled in his drawn-out way, like he just smelled something rancid. He put out his cigarette, hopped up on stage, stepped into my place, grabbed Victor's neck, leaned in for a mock kiss, then stuck his butt out, way out. "Get your ass in the scene, J. Can't act from the waist up."

I didn't know I was sticking my butt out. I stepped back into my spot, Ray slapped my ass, his way of roughing us up, teaching us our bodies don't belong to us on the stage, but to our character. You have to be able to stand it, to get touched, to act with your body.

We started the scene again. I pressed my hips into Victor, he put a hand on the small of my back. We kissed. It was awkward. I had a boyfriend, he had a girlfriend. I could feel his dick. I was not ready to act with all of my body.

"Believable," Ray said. "Believable."

For the rest of the year, Ray called me "Get your ass in the scene, Janine." I was healthy then, a few symptoms, not yet diagnosed, happy. I called myself an actor.

.

6.
.

The manicurist starts to buff my hand, stops when she gets to my thumbs. "You been sick," she says. She runs her index finger over the ridges in my nails, examines the deep groove where my nail beds should be.

"I was," I say.

"I hope better," she says. "I can fill in, to look nice." She dabs powder with a small paintbrush, presses it into my nails. She massages my hands. I close my eyes, she weaves her fingers though mine, shakes out my wrist. I let my head lean forward, my neck releases, shoulders relax. Touch, connection, I have to pay for it. How did it come to this? Who will get close to a body like mine?

The aesthetician at Pure Beauty wears a white smock, her hair an artificial orange. A Beauty School girl. I don't know that world, where trade school's enough, where you're free to exist without going to college.

"My arms are so furry," I say. "If I wax, how long before I can spray tan?"

"Give it a day," she says. "For your pores to close up."

I've wanted this. To be paid to maintain my appearance. I've watched backstage interviews, actresses complaining about days spent at the salon, getting hair extensions every few weeks. I'll let it take up some of my time, this demand to be hairless and smooth. A smooth girl dipping into the pool, slipping into auditions, gliding, easy.

It's tough to stay in the easy, with beauty, with beauty being okay, not damaging one's self or others with screwy ideals. Stop. Just give the girl your arm. Let her do her craft, let her slide the wax on with a popsicle stick, rip it off with a swatch of cloth. Let the makeup artists, the hair stylists, this chain of artists, women linked by their livelihoods for centuries, indispensible, let them do their work. Women's bodies sustaining women. Give her your arm, don't apologize for what needs to be done.

The stylist doesn't ask my name. "I think he wants red," she says. I follow her around a boutique in a strip mall off of Sunset. It's not high-end, but she's there just for me. She pulls tops off a rack, spreads out hangers over the dressing room door. She hands me a red cotton halter top with a built-in scarf. It's retro, so Farrah Fawcett. She hangs a pair of faded jeans inside the fitting room, sets a shoebox on the bench. I slip into the jeans, the top, wrap the scarf around my neck. I force my feet into a pair of stilettos that are a half size too small. I don't speak up. I'll only wear these a few minutes each night. I've never seen a shoe like this. Black-and-white patent leather, like men's saddle shoes propped up on bright red spiked heels. Bad girl shoes, just a little classier than those platforms girls bring to pole-dancing class.

The Producer whistles, I hobble out. He glances up from his text conversation. I do a twirl, he nods, looks back down at his phone.

"We're good to go," the stylist says.

It's a wrap. Jeans. They've put me in jeans, not even a skirt, but it's fine. The Producer is so hot and cold. Today he looks through me. I don't know what he sees, but I feel low on his list, like he's given the real girl a sympathy spot on his varsity team.

Bella Bronze Tanning Salon has me on their books. The show has its own account. Honey. Toffee. After Dark. I choose Cocoa Starr. The Producer has them spray us down, then picks up the tab.

The more beautiful we are, the more our audience will listen. Beauty as sugar, to help get a woman's story down an audience's throat. Smoother, tanner, sexier—they lend us an ear.

Lexi, our makeup artist, is prettier than all of us. Red jeans, skinny, tight, gold retro zippers down to her calves, emptying into black pumps. She intimidates me, like the wardrobe girl; they're too confident to be actors. They have this backstage vibe, this production vibe, like they're above the bullshit, or at least out of its way.

I sit in a black canvas director's chair, little light bulbs frame the makeup mirror. It feels so official. Opening night, I'm early, it calms my nerves.

Lexi runs her hands through my hair. B wants it bigger, she says. She means The Producer—he's just an initial to her. She wraps my hair around giant pink curlers, bobby pins them to my head.

"My hair's a little thin from a medication," I say. Why did I say that, why am I talking about the illness? She has bobby pins stuck between her teeth, doesn't reply. Enough. Don't draw attention, don't make excuses, enough with the illness.

When she gets my curlers in, she puts her hands on my shoulders, says, "Don't be nervous, you'll be fine."

A half hour to curtain and the girls roll into hair and makeup. I've only met Holly, the blonde who wards off throngs of men with her faux wedding band. She's dropped by the soundstage to see The Producer during my rehearsals. She slips into a black leather miniskirt, spins it so the zipper is in the back. Her waist is thick, still a little baby fat, college girl puffy. Imperfect, but how she smacks her lip gloss, smiles through the tiny gap in her teeth, runs her hands through her thick blond hair, she doesn't notice flaws, doesn't care, doesn't carry shame—she's perfectly cast as YB, *Young & Beautiful*, the agents say.

The butch-brunette and the model-brunette show up with Sonic Burger bags. They hop up on the makeup counter, eat their burgers and fries, so chill, no nerves, they've got the ritual down. The girls pass around shots of Skyy vodka, but don't offer me one. A black girl walks in her thong, rubs glitter lotion over her tiny waist and hips full of stretch marks, waits till the last minute to put on her costume, what a drag these things called clothes, she'd rather hang out naked, in this body, her body. Another girl looks like a black Niki Taylor, eyebrows arched high, thin nose, hair straightened. She reads off two blue notecards, trying to recall lines. "Shit, shit," she says. I can tell she's one of those girls with a phone always ringing. *I have one for you*, her agent says to one casting director after the next. She's got a great look, so her career grows even if she bobbles on camera, doesn't nail the first take. Moderate talent, permission to grow because it's her look that they want.

Through the giggles and glances, the women talk about The Producer, how he makes his way through the cast. It's Holly right now and her boyfriend's on his way to the show. The Producer is cute, has sincere moments—is on a cabbage soup diet. But how can an eye roll make this OK?

My bowels rumble. I'm nervous. I find my bathroom. Art Deco, Old Hollywood, pink tiles, miniature toilets. I massage my guts with two fists, distract myself from the bloating and pain, talk to my bowels, ask them to simmer down for three hours. I bend forward, whip my hair back, it's big—almost eighties metal band big. I let the spots, the flashes of light in my anemic mind settle. My eye makeup is dark blue with silver highlights, almost garish. The false eyelashes take over my face, tickling my brow with each blink. My collarbones angular, softly sparkling with glitter, my red halter top sexy, the only strapless top I've ever worn. I look thin. I could be a model. A shorter model, but height's not in my control. I place a hand on my hip, look over my shoulder into the mirror.

Here, on this film lot, so many actresses before me. Mary Pickford, Bette Davis, Lillian Gish. I don't know much about Old Hollywood, but tonight, I'm a studio actress.

"Ladies, let's go," The Producer yells from the stage door. "Tonight's a big deal." There's authority in his voice, not the guy who chewed gum during my rehearsal, eyes on his phone. "George Lopez, Danny Bondaduce, Lance Bass. The cast of *Survivor* is in the front row. Deliver to the front row."

My palms sweat. A New York director would never make it about the audience. He'd help keep us calm, focused.

"We need the reviews to kick off Vegas," he says. A New York director would never scare us with the threat of reviews.

"Last night felt like a dress rehearsal," he says. These aren't notes. Directors give specific adjustments. Try to be a director and not a prick. I bet The Producer's mom is cold and bitchy. She just gave up on scolding her son for running his mouth. I'm pretty sure prick sons have bitch moms. Why do I keep thinking about his mom? Why do I keep thinking about him?

His phone buzzes. "I need to take that," he says. "Janine, lighten up, this isn't *Medea*." He half smiles, half looks at his phone. A cooler version of me smiles back. Stay in the zone. *You need the reviews, the exposure. Sounds like we're picking up and going to Vegas.* I'm as light as I can be.

I step over long rolls of carpet backstage, find a corner to get quiet in. I clasp my hands behind my back, release them wide, open my palms to the sky, arch my back, open my chest. Lead with your chest. Find the arch in the small of your back. I twist my hips, reach my hands up high over my head, stand on my toes, make myself as big as possible. *Take up space, command the space, Janine, this is your stage.*

LIGHTS DOWN.

The audience claps, Holly slips through the curtains, scuttles past me. I send up a prayer, look down at my come-fuck-me pumps, Katy Perry blasts, I step through the curtains, one toe in front of the next, shoulders back swinging my red scarf like a lasso. I stop center stage, hand on a hip.

LIGHTS UP.

I look right, then left, hands on knees, butt out, Betty Boop. "I've got a great ass."

A whistle from the back row. I stand center, cock a knee, shift my weight, swing my hips to the right. "What makes a great ass?" Two bald guys elbow each other in the front row. "Smoothness, roundness."

"Owww," yells another guy from way back.

I have them, they're listening, the pinch and the ouch, the give and take, we're playing back and forth. I'm fast, laughing back, the power, the energy, the same as a scene in a play. Self-consciousness gone, it's not you anymore, just a girl sharing a private moment in a public space.

7.

Lexi unpacks her stainless steel makeup case, stacks pallets of blushes and bronzers on the counter, lines up her brushes on a paper towel. We're in a routine, a rhythm. I'm still the first girl on set, the first into her makeup chair.

"Your lashes are too long," she says. "And stick straight like my son's. The fake ones have nowhere to sit." This woman knows me, my eyelashes, the cowlick in my bangs that gives her grief each night. I can relax in this chair, let someone take care of me for a change.

The trailer steps squeak with heavy footsteps. Flip-floppy footsteps. The Producer's footsteps. He knocks and cracks open the door.

"Everyone decent?" The Producer asks.

"We're decent." She gives me a wink.

The Producer maneuvers around a large drying rack of Spanx tummy control biker shorts and camisoles, shakes his head like he didn't need to see the help we get with our bodies. He pulls out his wallet and starts flipping through a thick stack of twenties, counting them out loud. "Here's eight, J9, for the week." J9, a childhood nickname from my brother. It calms me.

Eight hundred dollars. It feels so legit, my first week of work, this big wad of cash.

◆◆◆

A self-portrait. First grade. Mounted on lavender construction paper. Hair in ponytails. My face is a bright shade of peach. On thick-ruled cream paper: *When I grow up I want to be an actress and singer. I will sing on a stage. My mom and dad will clap if I am good and boo if I am bad.*

◆◆◆

The Producer expects us to stay after the show, to schmooze at the bar, to talk to the audience. I ask the bartender for a vodka cranberry. "That'll be ten," he says.

"I'm in the show," I say.

"My bad," he says. A week in the show and he doesn't recognize me. I haven't chatted him up, told him my favorite drink, requested a cocktail pre-show. I don't get to know bartenders, it isn't my thing. He hasn't once glanced up at me onstage.

I need this drink as a prop in my hands, I am naked without lines, without character, without the division between audience and stage.

Holly's family gathers around her at the bar. Her boyfriend has flown in from back east, her mom and sister, too. The Producer makes Holly's mom laugh. One of his comments about how exhausting it is to deal with a bunch of broads. He's probably using his go-to line: *I should have called the show Pains in the Ass. The hotter the woman, the crazier.* He chews a toothpick, baby hands holding a drink.

Holly's eyes twinkle, she laughs, holds the hand of poor college boyfriend who doesn't know she's fucking The Producer like it's the next step in a master's program, how to be up-and-coming, move to LA, screw a producer, your college boyfriend won't mind. Even her mom looks supportive, knows her daughter is gifted with talent and looks. She just needs to get seen by the right people, get into the right hands.

◆◆◆

Dad and I wait in a line that wraps around a big theatre. Mom is working. I am eight. I am going to audition for *Annie*. I think I can get the part. I'm wearing my soft blue plaid dress with a light brown sailor collar.

Understated. Young. An Orphan's dress. Some girls are wearing *Annie* dresses. But why would you wear the red dress if you haven't got the part?

They let us into the theatre, we sit high up, toward the back of the house, a theatre packed with girls. I watch as they step up on stage, sing, one by one. Some girls are afraid to sing with the accompanist, so they sing along to their tape players. You can't even hear them.

Maybe, Tomorrow. I've got this down. When they call my number, Dad pats my back, says, "Sing as loud as you can." The man at the piano starts to play "Tomorrow." It's hard to know how to start. He nods, but I don't start, he plays the same notes again, nods again, oh, my cue, I begin. *The sun'll come out, tomorrow, bet your bottom dollar that tomorrow, they'll be sun.* I stretch out notes, make my voice jiggle. I look at the back row, puff my chest, sing, *When I'm stuck with a day, that's gray and lonely, I just stick out my chin and grin, and say Tomorrow, tomorrow, I love you tomorrow, you're only a day a—*my big finale, just like the Annie I saw in the city, I extend my right arm to the side, fan out my hand, and say—*waaaaay*, sweeping my arm slowly up to the ceiling as I stretch the note out until there's no breath left.

"How'd it go?" Mom asks.

"Loud," Dad says.

I get a callback. I am one of the best, but I don't get called back for Annie. I get called back to be an orphan. We stand on stage, four girls in a row, taking turns, waiting for the singing teacher to point at us, widen his eyes, nod, our cue. The notes are higher than I'm used to, so high my voice turns soft to keep on key. The other girls know what the singing teacher's hand signs mean, how to raise and quiet their voices. The teacher nods and points with one hand, while moving his other hand to-and-fro, keeping the song going for the rest. He stops giving me cues and the three girls sing on. How did they learn? Why didn't I?

◆◆◆

I put my sister Danielle's car keys in the bunny bowl by her front door. I thank her for letting me drive her car down south, tell her without her I wouldn't have gotten cast in the show. I never know if I should sit down for a minute and talk or if she'd rather I leave. She's always in action, moving fast. She's making the kids' lunches for the morning, scraping peanut putter out of a near empty jar.

"So all the women talk about their asses?" my sister asks.

"Well, mine's the most literal," I say. My sister is a third-grade teacher, her life is literal, her kitchen is yellow with cow and barn paintings; she has a golden retriever who always gnaws a stuffed beaver; her boys run and squeal in blue footy pajamas; my three-year-old niece won't stay in bed. Theatre, film—anything creative requires an explanation.

"Have you told Mom?"

"Vaguely," I say. "She's never supportive."

"We're all supportive. But you can't get sick, Mom can't come down and pack you up like before."

I stay the night at my mom's, so I can pick up my repaired car, then head back to LA. As I drive up to her house, I take deep yoga breaths. *Stay in the zone, calm, preparing for a show.*

"Your coloring's off," Mom says when I walk through her door. She thinks I look gray. *I just got cast in a show as a hot babe, can you lay off it for once?* I'm a permanent patient in my family's eyes. Not even an adult. No husband, no home, no career, just poor health.

I want to tell my mom about the play, I want her to say, "That's great." I want to invite her to the show. But in New York, the one show she saw, the one where I sat on a washing machine and did a monologue about being aroused, she sat stone-faced in the center row, looked like she was in pain. She broke my concentration. I had to look away. After the show, in the lobby, she was stiff, didn't speak. I learned not to speak about roles or shows but to give updates on my health.

Back in Mom's guest room. She has framed my ugliest headshot. My hair too short. I chopped it all, a pixie-cut dyed black, for an indie film that got called off. There have been so many headshots.

There is a dream catcher that hangs from the headboard of this guest bed. Blue leather stretched into a web, yellow beads with white feathers. Go catch your dreams. Mom loves the ballet, loves the symphony, supports the arts, but not her daughter.

I can't come back to this room. I can never move back to this house.

8.

September 2004. Santa Barbara County.

A policeman walks up to my table. Clean-shaven, handsome, thick biceps, the man's on my team.

"Deputy Esparza," he says. He looks me in the eye, hands me his card. I am safe, on the good side, just a blonde, a *rubia*, a girl in red shoes.

"Can you tell me where you're coming from, what brought you here?" he asks.

"I need to be here," I say.

"What do you mean?" He takes out a small notepad and pen. "Why this golf course, this country club?"

"I'm ready." I smooth my bangs, tuck my hair behind my ear, pause, inhale, exhale. "Things have aligned."

"Anyone harming you? Do you feel safe?"

"It's just been hard." Let him in. Let him in. He takes me in. Someone's sister, a cheerleader, a story behind her eyes. "My family can't see, they don't know that it's good—the show, the article. I'm getting there, we're getting there."

"Families are rough." He smiles like we've both had long days. "We're going to get you some help. You have my card. If you need anything at all, just call me. Really, call me anytime."

"Thank you," I say. His golden card. Deputy, Santa Barbara Sheriff's Office, his cell phone number handwritten on the back. He doesn't give anyone his card. The cop, the police station babe, the partnerships we make.

Esparza stands, shakes a tall man's hand. The tall man sets a red binder down on our table, pulls up a chair. A man with a binder, a man on set, a script supervisor, a stage manager, flipping through pages, where he'll put me, which soundstage, which lunch break—where we'll shoot tomorrow. He checks his watch, asks for my address, starts filling out a form.

"Can you tell me the cross streets where you live?"

"There aren't any close," I say. "I'm on Montana, near Brentwood." I've lived there six months, but cross streets?

"Can you tell me what year it is, who the president is?"

"Two thousand and four. Bush."

"What's the boiling point?"

"I don't know." I don't cook. It's been years since chemistry class. Why is he grilling me? Esparza watches with kind eyes. Has confidence in me, my life not reduced to some pop quiz.

The man closes the binder, stands, Esparza stands, they tell me to stand. I'm flanked by two strangers. They tell me to walk toward the ambulance.

"I don't need to," I say. "I'm ok. I can call my sister."

They each grab an arm, push me toward the ambulance. A young paramedic has opened the back doors.

"Step up," the binder man says.

"You can't do this," I say. "You can't make me."

"Step up," the binder man says.

I look at Esparza. "Can't you do something?"

The binder man pushes my shoulder forward. I step up. The young paramedic tells me to lie down. Fake medical equipment, fake bandages, fake tubing, all fake out of some fake fucking plastic doctor's kit. I close my eyes. I'll play the role. Patient. Lights down.

The doors slam shut. The binder man and Esparza shake hands, say, Thanks, man, thanks, head home for the night.

·

·

·

·

ALIVE AND FIXABLE:
A ROAD TO LOVE AND RECOVERY

MEMOIR

BY FRANCIE LOW

Francie and Tony had it down: A happy family life in a vibrant community with two fine young boys. Then she got "the call." Tony had been in a terrible cycling accident that brought their summer to a screeching halt. For fifteen months, Francie protected Tony on his bumpy road to recovery and he protected his family from knowing just how much he hurt.

Excerpted from Alive and Fixable.

Getting the Call
The Day of the Accident, Friday, July 30

My cell phone rang. I pulled over. I never stopped for calls, and to this day I have no idea why I did this time. I was almost out of our neighborhood, barely in the car three minutes.

The caller ID read "Tony." *I just saw him thirty minutes ago! He's in trouble already? I bet he got a flat and didn't have a spare tube. That's unusual.* I began planning in my mind. *I can rescue him since I don't have any kids to pick up for at least an hour.* I answered the call.

"Hello, Francie?" an unfamiliar female voice asked hesitantly, as if the woman wasn't sure who I was or she was scared to talk to me. My heart dropped. I knew instantly. Something was wrong.

"Oh no," I answered back, fear beginning to bubble in my gut.

"I'm going to pass the phone to someone," the woman said slowly and softly.

A man spoke, his tone restrained. "Francie. It's Damon."

Damon is a family friend and a fireman. *Why is Damon calling me on Tony's phone? Why is he calling me at all?* He had coached my younger son, Alex, in Little League—taught him how to pitch. Our boys hung out sometimes, so it felt strange talking to him as a professional now. He told me Tony had crashed, near Starbucks in Alamo, thirty minutes away. I thought I heard him say a bike had hit Tony, but my mind was reeling. Nothing was making sense.

"Um, Tony is OK. He says his scapula hurts. Um, let's see. His eye is cut." Damon was trying his best to tell me what was wrong, but I could tell he was choosing his words carefully. "I wrapped Tony up good," he said. He would take him to the ER. *Ugh. I hate the ER. All that waiting and wondering.* The last time I was there with Tony, TJ was a baby. Tony's lungs had swelled up from some virus; ibuprofen was the solution.

"What do I do?" I asked evenly. It didn't feel real. Nobody in our family had ever been taken to the hospital in an ambulance. *Do I go to the hospital or go home and wait for a call? Do I cancel our dinner later tonight? My friends will be disappointed if our plans change.*

"Meet us at the hospital. You'll probably beat us there." Damon was gentle and calm. He also told me he had Tony's bike and his shoes.

"OK," I answered. My mind was foggy. Nothing seemed to stick.

I pulled away from the curb, slowly driving the same route Tony had just ridden. My brain started swirling. *Where do I begin? Hit by a bike? It can't be bad. He'll be fine. It's his collarbone, I bet. Breaking a collarbone is common for cyclists.* We'd seen it happen many times to cyclists who crashed on a casual ride or in a race. *The ER will take a long time. It's one thirty. We might make dinner. What about the kids? I will be gone all afternoon.* I kept thinking of all the things I had to arrange, hoping we would be home later that night.

The battery was low on my phone. Shoot. I plugged the phone into the car charger and called my eldest son, TJ, first. He was alone at home, waiting for a tennis clinic.

"Hey, TJ."

"Yeah," he said with annoyance. I'd probably interrupted another episode of *Psych*.

"Dad was hit by a bike. He will be OK, but he has to go to the ER. I'm sure it will take hours so I won't get home until about six p.m. Ride your bike to tennis at three. OK?" I informed him with slight irritation because I didn't know very much about Tony's condition yet and the day was in shambles.

"OK." TJ's mood was flat. It was always flat. He was almost thirteen.

I called my friend Carol. "Tony crashed." I knew she'd understand because her husband was also a cyclist.

"Oh, those bikers," she said, half kidding. We knew someone who'd been killed recently while riding their bike, so we had a certain amount of trepidation about our husbands riding. Carol agreed to get Alex for me. My ten-year-old played tennis with her son at our neighborhood club, two minutes from our homes. He could stay at her house until I could pick him up later. *Oh good. One less thing for me to worry about.*

I kept driving. I called another friend. I left a message: "Tony crashed on his bike. I think dinner is off. I suspect Tony won't feel up to it. Sorry to ask, but if you have a minute, could you bring me a phone charger? I'll be in the ER. Oh, can you tell Mandy my phone is about to die?" I couldn't spare my battery for another call, but I dreaded telling Mandy dinner was canceled as well. We had planned dinner months ago for a new restaurant in Berkeley. All three couples loved dining out, looking for the next foodie haven.

I found my way to Ygnacio Valley Road, just off the freeway, fifteen minutes from my house. I drove this busy six-lane road often, mostly to Target. I saw the red bull's-eye from the first stoplight. A deep red medical truck was just ahead and to the left of me. I knew it was my husband. The lights were flashing and if the sirens were sounding, I couldn't hear them. Everything around me was so eerily quiet and slow, as if I were in a dream. The truck drove through the intersection smoothly when the light turned green. I followed. I could almost talk to the passengers; I was so close. I strained to see Damon, but I needed to watch the road. The paramedics pulled ahead, farther and farther from me. *They will arrive first*, I thought. There were so many cars and so many traffic lights slowing me down. My hands tightened around the steering wheel. My eyes were scanning the lanes for a quicker path. *Darn it! This road is always jammed.*

I saw the hospital and an emergency sign. I pulled in to park, only to find the ER lot full. I didn't know where to go, so I drove around the hospital perimeter until I spotted an attendant.

"I don't know where to park," I called out to him. He stood outside a tall white box with windows, similar to a telephone booth. He looked out of place in his sharp white dress shirt and black pants, too much for the hot July sun. His dark skin sparkled with perspiration.

"Where are you going?" he inquired.

"The ER."

"How long?" he asked. I winced. *I don't know. Who can predict what happens in the ER?*

"Four hours?" I offered. He didn't really listen; he was getting it now.

"Don't you worry, miss. You can take as long as you need. Parking is free too," he said in a soothing voice as I handed him my keys. "ER is on the other side of the campus. I'll call a courtesy van to take you there."

"Thanks." *Good. I won't get lost trying to find my way.*

Within minutes, I arrived at the ER entrance, welcomed by a small trail of people in front of a desk. *Do I wait in line? This is a serious emergency. It doesn't seem like I should have to wait to see my husband.* A guy in front of me was coughing. I cringed, hoping I wouldn't get sick. I turned my head to avoid breathing in germ-infested air. As I waited, I looked around at the glass walls. I could see out to the hills a blanket of long grass bronzed from months of sun and heat. Shadows of scrub oak, craggy and massive, dotted the landscape, all marks of a typical Northern California summer. The street below the hillside was bustling with cars. Chairs lined the perimeter of the waiting room, and a chattering TV had been placed high in the corner where anyone could watch it.

It was my turn now.

Do I sit at the admittance desk at all? Maybe I just give my name. A large, young lady with wavy, dark blonde hair appeared a few feet away. She was dressed for an office, black pants and a beige blouse.

"Francie?" She called my name in a soft, friendly voice. I had no idea who she was, but somehow, I knew she would help me.

We stood by two big swinging doors to the ER. It was like she was expecting me. *Did Damon tell her about me?* She smiled slightly, taking my hands and asked, "Can I get you some water?"

"Sure." As I held the small paper cup, she told me I'd need to wait a little longer until my name was called again. She kept tilting her head, looking closely at my face, searching for something. Nobody gave me any information about my husband. I did what I was told. I didn't want to be rude since I felt more like a guest in somebody's house.

I sat in the chair facing the window out to the dry, grassy hillside. The TV was blabbering on and on. I didn't care to watch. I stared straight ahead, looking at nothing really. My phone rang. It was Carol's husband, Mike.

"Do you want me to come?" he tentatively asked.

"Sure. I guess. Company is good," I replied flatly, not convinced I knew the right answer. *I don't know what to do. Who do I call? Do I need anyone?* All I could think of was the TV show *Melrose Place*. Somebody was hurt once, and everyone from the apartment complex came to the hospital. *Who were my apartment complex people?* I didn't want to call my family. My mom was gone and my dad was eighty-four and hard of hearing. I didn't want to scream into the phone so he could hear. *I need to wait until I know more. Family is stressful, and they are mostly in Colorado anyway. Tony's family will have to wait too. I don't want anyone to fret.*

I wasn't worried; at least I tried not to worry. *I'm sure it's a simple break.* I didn't cry or panic because I didn't really know what was wrong. *He's alive. He isn't like the other cyclist I knew—the one that died.* My mind wandered, avoiding the tragic what-ifs. I was glad I had showered and dressed in comfy, cute clothes: gray cotton chinos and a fitted black, long-sleeved tee with pale-pink stitching around the seams. Usually I wore a sweaty tennis skirt.

It wasn't long before the young lady was back. She was with an ER doc in bright blue scrubs, matching surgeon cap, and wire-rimmed glasses. He was my age, fortyish. He took both my hands. It felt awkward. He walked slowly with me, our hands still entwined. The girl followed. We found an empty room. It was cold and dim. The doctor sat close to me while the woman settled in across from both of us. She kept looking at me with supposedly sad eyes, like a bad actress. The doctor started to talk. His voice was gentle and slow. My eyes darted between the two of them, back and forth. *Can't they just spit out what's happening? Why aren't we in the ER with Tony?*

The ER doctor wasn't sure what happened, stating Tony was probably walking his bike because Tony's legs were fine. An SUV had hit him, he guessed, going on to list off the injuries. Tony had lacerated his eyelid.

He'd dislocated his shoulder. He'd broken three ribs. I didn't cry. Instead, I soaked in the information. What he was telling me seemed bad, but they were all commonplace injuries that would heal. *An SUV? A mom hit him. She was in a rush, drinking a latte, I bet. That could be me. How awful for her.* I looked at the woman. She turned on her "sad" eyes again. She still wasn't saying anything, and I wondered why she was in the room.

The doctor raised his left arm. He showed me his black sports watch with a silver ID plate wrapped along the plastic wristband. "Your husband needs to wear an ID bracelet or watch. So we know who to call."

I looked at him, a bit confused by his comment. "He does; it's on his ankle." The doctor was flustered. He hadn't seen the ID. *Why tell me this now?* I wondered.

"We are still working on him. You can come in soon. He will repeat himself because he hurt his head," he continued, returning to telling me about my husband's condition. My body felt chilled and stiff despite their attempts to comfort me.

The woman was still quiet, tilting her head to one side again. She was trying so hard to look concerned. Her brow furrowed. Her mouth was downturned and closed. I felt like they were not telling me something. They seemed nervous. Hesitant. The doctor gave me Tony's wallet, phone, and a yellow plastic bag. I didn't want to look inside that bag. I dreaded seeing Tony's bloodstained clothes, even though I wanted to know about the injuries. It was hard enough for me to look at his phone, knowing he always kept it in his jersey pocket. A spiderweb of cracks spread across the screen, and it made me wonder. *How the heck did this happen? How is it even possible it still works?*

I sat in the waiting room with a clipboard of hospital forms. A policeman in a tan, sharply pressed uniform squatted down beside me and introduced himself. I don't remember his name. He apologized for the bad timing of his visit, but he needed to ask me some questions.

Could I talk about my husband's injuries with the officer? I repeated what the ER doctor had told me. "What was he wearing?" he asked. I told him a green-and-white jersey. He seemed to think the colors were dark and unsafe. I opened the bag to show him the brightness of Tony's racing jersey. Seeing splotches of dried blood, I didn't pull it out. I held the bag out for the officer to inspect, turning my head like I would during a gruesome scene of a movie. Next, the officer examined the crushed, bloody helmet. After each inspection and response, he scribbled notes into his small black notebook.

Could he call me on Sunday, two days from now? I guess. *When was a good time for these things?* He would call at 10:00 a.m. OK. What could I say to him? I didn't want to say the wrong thing. Would I get Tony in trouble? I didn't know what to do. The policeman seemed nice, but I didn't know why he was asking so many questions and taking notes.

I was alone again. I called my friend Carol to give her the update.

"It wasn't a bike. They think an SUV hit Tony. I'll be here awhile," I said unemotionally. "I don't think I can work my volunteer job at the swim meet tomorrow."

"Hit by an SUV? Boy. You'll do anything to get out of your job," she joked, knowing I drove an SUV. I tried to laugh. I had been whining about my swim meet commitment all week.

"Can Alex go to the pasta feed with you?" Our swim team hosted a pasta dinner the night before a big swim meet. Carol would handle it all for me. Another worry checked off my growing list: Alex would get dinner and be with his friends.

My phone rang again as I tried to complete the intake forms. A girlfriend told me our friend Jules was coming to the ER since she was already at the hospital, visiting a sick friend. "OK," I said, and we hung up. I stared out the glass doors. I saw my friends Sharon and Steve walking from the parking lot. I spotted a white string. *Phone cord! My dinner friends have come!* I was so happy to see them. I immediately plugged my phone in by the TV, the only outlet I could find. I filled them in on what I knew about Tony's injuries, not getting very far on the forms. They both took in the injury update like I did, calmly. I don't think they could believe their ears either.

My phone rang again. The TV was too loud to hear, so I unplugged my cell and stepped outside. It was HR from my husband's company. A lady gave me so much information I couldn't absorb the words. *Tony has just been injured. How did she know to call?* She talked about forms. *Leave of absence? Does Tony need it?* I wrote down phone numbers and names. I tried to press what she was saying into my memory.

Friends called nonstop. More friends dropped by the ER. I called a few moms I could depend on. Left messages. TJ needed a place to stay; this was taking too long. Insurance forms went unfinished—too many interruptions. *How is the word getting out so fast?*

"Francie Low?" I heard my name called. I jumped from my chair to walk back with the doctor. Sharon grabbed the clipboard. She would finish filling in the forms for me, as much as she could.

I was scared to see Tony. Surprisingly, he was very clean, and there wasn't any blood. He was lying on a gurney, wrapped up tight in crisp white sheets, as if he were a human burrito. His right eye was sealed shut like a boxer's, black and blue and puffy. A white rectangle bandage rested on his cheekbone, a wide dash. I was afraid to touch him.

"Thanks for coming," he said right away. He looked up at me with his left eye. *What? Of course I would come.* "I'm sorry I'm messing things up. You go to Portland without me." *I can't believe he's thinking this way.* We were supposed to go on vacation in a week. Then over and over he said in a raspy whisper, "I don't know what happened. I just don't know what happened."

"An SUV hit you," I answered. I looked hard at him to see if my words registered. I was scared to tell him too much.

"Well, that's fricking obvious." He was alert and feisty. Apparently, he knew more than I thought; he knew he was in an accident and could not remember how he was hit. He was so careful when he rode. Desperately, he tried to recall every detail. Find the flaw—his engineer mentality.

A doctor came in, blonde with a thick mustache, wire-rimmed glasses, and jeans. He talked to me as if we were neighbors, standing over a diseased tree instead of my mummy-wrapped, banged-up husband.

"His brain is fine. Spinal cord is OK. He cracked three neck vertebrae, but they are all perfectly aligned," he said, pointing to the X-ray. My mouth dropped. My eyes popped. This was so much worse than I thought.

"Do you not know?" the doctor asked, looking at me now. He must have seen the look on my face.

No, I didn't. He went on to say Tony had broken the hooks on the spine, a clay-digger's fracture he called it and explained the term. Useless fragments of bone that can snap off while shoveling dirt. He might need surgery. I was stunned.

Another doctor entered. He wore a white coat. I stared at the navy embroidered stitching of his name. *Spanish*, I thought. He was friendly. His accent sounded like Ricky Ricardo, his tongue thick around English words. I glanced up at his face, framed by dark, slightly graying, slicked-back hair. We looked over at Tony in his dazed state. He told me Tony's lung was punctured, so he needed to insert a tube to let out the pus building up in his lung drain. Tony would move to ICU—a precaution. ICU? *He is not going home tonight.* Everything was stated matter-of-factly. He obviously said these words often.

"I guess we will be working together a lot," I tried to joke with him. I wasn't sure how long Tony might stay in the hospital, but I knew his care was up to this doctor and me. Each mention of an additional injury slid off my brain, like I had a protective shield to deflect any feeling.

"When can he ride again?" I asked, trying to think of normal things. He told me Tony should be back on a bike in three months, maybe more. *Three months isn't too bad. We can get through this.*

ER to ICU
The Day of the Accident, Six Hours Later

"What's next?" someone asked. All eyes were on me. I stood in the waiting room, my friends hovering around me, anxiously anticipating news of Tony's condition after my visit with him in the ER.

"Tony will go to the ICU, just for observation. When he's ready to move, someone will come for me," I reported, looking off into the distance more than at any individual. I didn't want anyone to get too close or the compassion in their eyes might trigger a flood of tears. I needed to stay strong. Sort out the details.

Tony was assigned a bed in the NICU department. *What did that mean?* I tried to imprint NICU into my brain, repeating the letters over and over. Did I remember the order of the letters? My brain was numb. I didn't pick out, I-C-U, **I**ntensive **C**are **U**nit. The N confused me. I had to let it go.

My friends sat on either side of me in a quiet row. Nobody knew what to say. All the colors in the room seemed dull, gray, and black, including my friends' clothing. My phone interrupted the silence.

"Hi. It's Denise. Can I do anything to help?" she chirped.

I paused. Denise was a spiritually minded friend. She could help me get God in on this one. I hated asking for prayers, a sign of vulnerability to me. I'd rather divulge my weight, but I wanted to cover every base, whatever it took to get Tony better.

"Can you call my church? Is that OK?" I asked.

"I'm opening up the Yellow Pages right now," she assured me.

It was something I should do, but I didn't want to admit it or ask myself. Within minutes, a minister called me. I told him what I knew. He said a prayer over the phone with me. Even though I'd asked Denise to call the church, and no one could hear, I squirmed and stared at the ground.

My friends were watching me as we waited. No tears slid down my cheeks. No cloud of gloom enveloped me. "You are taking this really well," one said.

I didn't really know how to respond. If I were hysterical, they would tell me to get a grip. I was not hysterical, and somehow this felt wrong too. I knew Tony would be OK. I was happy my kids were being taken care of by friends. I was happy to have other friends with me. I was happy so many wanted to help.

I confessed something on my mind. "Ya know, when Tony rides, I say a prayer. Today I didn't." I wasn't blaming myself. It was just that the thought stuck in my mind and made me wonder.

It was getting late, so Sharon and Steve invited me to have dinner at their place. I couldn't eat in public. I couldn't face anyone. *What would I say to people?* A couple of friends would meet me in NICU. *Did I remember the correct letters?*

I found the right place, the one labeled, "NICU." The doors were locked to screen for family members only. I pushed the buzzer. I told the voice that answered that I was there to see my husband, Tony Low, and magically, the double doors opened. I walked into a room with beds arranged in a half-moon shape, each one with small machines wired to the wall and the patient. The nurses' desk faced the patients. Midway was my husband's bed. I exchanged hellos with the nurse. She seemed spunky and cool. I didn't know if I could even talk to Tony. *Is he in a drug-induced sleep?*

Raspy, Tony piped up, "Take a picture. Take a picture. The boys. They'll be curious." I snapped a few shots. I had no intention of ever showing the boys the gory photos. I didn't want to look at them either.

Tony had sleep apnea, so he asked for his sleep machine. *How did he think of these things in his state?*

And as if on cue, a lung doctor sauntered into the room. He had a graying beard and a set of wire-rimmed glasses. It was like a uniform, those glasses. The lung doctor said he could fashion a mask for him to help him sleep like the machine he had at home. He went on to tell me Tony had broken nine ribs, on one side, not the three I was told about in ER. Humans have eleven on each side. Tony's punctured lung prompted the doctor's visit.

"Your husband is very, very fit. If he weren't, he'd be on a respirator right now." That gave me pause.

"OK." I didn't know what else to say. I should have been relieved he didn't need a respirator, that he was so strong, but I couldn't feel. *Is anything really sinking into my brain?* The lung doc wandered out as quietly as he arrived.

The nurse gave me permission to go home, assuring me Tony would be fine. With so much medication, he wouldn't remember whether I stayed or not. Funny, I thought, because he sure acted like he knew the score, bossing everyone around. "Take a picture. Get my sleep machine."

"I like your nurse. I think you will be in good hands," I assured Tony. I didn't want him to worry if I didn't stay. I kissed him on the cheek. I couldn't say much because the nurse was standing right there, and it felt weird to say anything mushy, like I was undressing in front of her or asking for another prayer. In any case, I needed to leave so I could tend to the boys. I needed to eat; my energy was fading.

From the hospital I drove straight to Sharon and Steve's home. Before I went inside, I checked on TJ. *Did TJ need a toothbrush or pillow from home?* I called the friend's dad caring for my son.

"What? Unless he has favorite jammies, we are fine," the dad laughed. Dads were so different than moms. I asked to talk to TJ.

"Dad is worse than we thought, but he'll be fine. He's in ICU." I dropped the *N*. I didn't know what to do with it.

"Is he on life support?" TJ demanded to know. No, I told him. *How does he think to ask that? What are you watching on TV?* He took the news well.

My phone rang and rang as I ate with Sharon and Steve, spaghetti with meatballs, and a much-needed glass of red wine. I was tired and anxious. I didn't want to answer. Two calls were the same number, so I picked up. It was a mom calling me back about TJ; I had asked her if he could stay with her. She was cool, as in not pressuring me for information or weepy on my behalf.

I explained the situation for the tenth time in six hours.

By eight o'clock, I picked up Alex from Carol's house. I was upbeat and thankful for her help.

"You sure are taking this well," her husband commented on my calm demeanor. *Is there something wrong with me? This is the second time I've heard this in one day.*

"He's alive. I'm sort of going with that one," I stated flatly.

Before we slept, I filled Alex in a little more, but I didn't make a big deal out of it. One of my many friends who'd flocked to my side at the hospital had channeled her therapist mother: "Tell the truth without a trace of worry. Listen and nod so they feel heard."

"Do I send Alex to the swim meet?" I didn't know where to send him otherwise. He was ten and the NICU only allowed children twelve and up to visit.

"Yes. Go about your life as normally as possible," she said reassuringly.

I tried out her suggestion on Alex. Earlier in the day, he'd broken down at the tennis courts when he was told his dad was OK even though he got into a bike accident. I braced myself. We settled into my king-sized bed, him taking Tony's spot. I needed someone close by, and Alex slept better with someone anyway.

Before I turned out the light, I matter-of-factly told Alex, "Dad will be OK. He just needs to stay at the hospital awhile to get better." I didn't go into details. He seemed to take me at my word. If I wasn't worried, he didn't need to worry either.

With that, I turned out the light. As I lay there, I wondered if I could sleep. Emergencies kept people awake, a fact I remembered from a TV show or a movie. I ended the night with a prayer for Tony and the mom who hit my husband in her SUV.

GIRLS INC. WRITING WORKSHOP

OAKLAND, CALIFORNIA

LAURA RITLAND
SIMPSON FELLOW

VOLLEYBALL HAIKU

BY AILANI BRAVO

on the court
with 5 other players
protecting the ball

trying to get one pass
right to the setter
to get one kill

protecting the back
trying not to crack
and falling straight on back

back to service
and get an ace
and win the point

back row attack
straight to my hands
to pass it right back up

doing it all over again
trying to get to 25 points
and win the match

WHERE DO WE GO?

BY ALEXIS GUZMAN

tell me do you know where the wild things go?
do they stay hidden beneath the sea
or do they climb trees that kiss the stars' feet
they're always out of reach both the stars and the wild things
they sing and scream songs of poetry
where the words drip out slowly like tar
melting everything leaving nothing but black
ruining every good thing we once had
they dance around the fire and fall straight through the heat
the wild things grow only to remain unseen
similar to flowers yet they resemble the trees
so high i can barely see
perhaps the wild things are more than i can believe
have you ever seen the wild things?
they haven't shown themselves to me
but they're chasing other children in their dreams
are they hunting you in your sleep?
my love have you been searching for the wild things?
they got me hung up on a tree
nailed to the branches with my bones breaking silently
can you find the wild things?
they've taken me and placed me far out of reach
next to stars that the trees barely reach
there is no place to be except among the wild things

SHE'S PERFECT / ELLA ES PERFECTA

BY ALEXANDRA MALDONADO

Huge heart, amazing soul, caring human,
Beyond perfect for her kids, she's perfect,
Fighting through her struggles alone, she's all in,
Brave but scared, she only wants to protect.
"She failed, she failed," she can't believe she's sick,
She's blind, she doesn't notice her talents,
She wants to be perfect, and not a tick.
She's hurt, finally breaking her silence,
She's perfect through my eyes, doesn't she notice?
She has been to war and won the battle,
Walking in the hands of god, she's hopeless,
She's gone through a lot, she needs to travel.
She's not alone, she has me, I love her.
She's just perfect. I wish that I was her.

ELLA ES PERFECTA

Corazón enorme, alma increíble, humana cariñosa,
Más allá de perfecta para sus hijos, ella es perfecta,
Luchando a través de sus luchas, sola está adentro,
Valiente pero asustada, ella solo quiere proteger.
"Falló, falló," no puede creer que su hija esta enferma,
Ella es ciega, no nota sus talentos,
Ella quiere ser perfecta y no una molestia.
Ella está herida, finalmente rompiendo su silencio,
Ella es perfecta a través de mis ojos, ¿no se da cuenta?
Ella ha ido a la guerra y ha ganado la batalla,
Caminando en las manos de Dios, sin esperanza,
Ella ha pasado por mucho, necesita viajar.
Ella no está sola, me tiene a mí, la amo.
Ella es simplemente perfecta. Me gustaría ser como ella.

(Author expresses thankful acknowledgment to Bernardo Hinojosa for editing the Spanish version.)

HAIKU AFTER REMEDIOS VARO'S "THE CREATION OF BIRDS"

BY ALEXIS PETERS

Spirit and body
Endowed by my Creator
Free to fly the skies

Surge of vibrancy
Fusion of light and song
One stroke at a time

Piercing eyes swallow
All enticed by my Creator
But no harm implied

I spread your wisdom
Far through the universe
My Creator, I am Free

ACCIDENTALLY MEANT TO BE

BY VANESSA SMITH

Lost under the brush of the sky
I never lose you
you are by my side always
every breeze holds your scent
and every turn is your smile
we are together because
the world needs us to be
just to spin, you are my
flight, my winds and the wind
that makes me soar
through the storms of life and without
you I would be
lost

MORE THAN ENOUGH:
TEACHING WITH THE SIMPSON LITERARY PROJECT

BY LAURA RITLAND

SIMPSON FELLOW (2018 & 2019)

I began the Simpson Literary Project writing workshops by asking my students at Girls Inc. if they thought they were "good" at writing or not. All of my students were young women from Alameda County and high school seniors. They were also all women of color. In response to my question, most of them shook their heads. A few others modestly twisted their hands "so-so." It strikes me that the conviction that one does or does not have the ability to be creative starts at an unfairly young age—before, even, one has the opportunity to test the reality of those beliefs. Luckily, beliefs can change. Though many of my students had never formally enrolled in a writing workshop or written creative work beyond what had been required for their high school English class, it didn't take anything but the gentlest of nudges to let them see themselves not just as readers, but as writers more than worthy of the pen.

In thinking how best to empower the students I worked with in these writing workshops, I often reflected on my own beginnings as a writer. I remember the desire to create, the longing to be heard, and the incomparable excitement of putting your thoughts down onto paper and out into sound. That one could have effect on the world in that way—to bring what is within out—was a power and invaluable freedom unlike anything else I knew as a young adult. And yet, of course, I was terrified. (I still, sometimes, am!) To be laughed at, ignored, and criticized for baring your creative soul to others is an excruciating pain, all the more acute when everything is new. For women of color, I believe, the stakes of such pains are often higher. Economic and social barriers wrought from an all-too-continuous history of exclusion confront black, Latina, and Asian women in disparate ways, yet with a common, sinister message: "you are not enough." To write while also expending the constant mental energy necessary to resist this message involves enormous bravery.

All my students were enough. Far more than enough. It was important to me to repeatedly prove their abilities to them: through praise, yes, but also through realistic and measured judgments that would, in turn, allow them to recognize their agency over their writing. *Here* is why this plot or character you imagined sounds compelling. *This* is why this adjective brings this noun to life. The more specificity in my response, the better. Part of learning to appreciate one's craft is by understanding, with precision, how one uses it. Mentors and teachers have the crucial task of helping students learn this technical knowledge. Even more importantly, they are the mirrors by which students see themselves. The fears and terrors of my sixteen-year-old self simply do not exist as they used to over a decade later because trial and error, a healthy amount of failure, inspiring mentors, and years of writing have proven them wrong. Yet of course I did not know this when I was sixteen. Time and experience allow us to live out this knowledge and internalize it as a belief. In the meantime, until my students get to this place, I can reflect back to them the truth: that they are—have always been—worthy of writing. They are more than enough. They may not *believe* this yet, but they can *know* it.

Besides, literacy and the literary belong to everyone. Language is power, a tool of perception, and the more people can use it, the better. In the first sessions of both years I've run these workshops, the first activity I assigned my students was an exercise in description: they were asked to edit and fill in the blanks of a short paragraph about their environment—in this case, the Girls Inc. building in downtown Oakland where they attended the workshop. The activity is very simple yet for some students offers a "break through" moment. Altering a single word can change the meaning of a whole sentence. Adjectives create mood and tone, like shades of color. The humble simile has enormous elastic range depending on what the writer decides to base their comparison. For students who are unfamiliar with seeing themselves as writers, they become excited by the realization that *they* can be the agent of these changes—and, furthermore, that these changes have effect on others. It comes down to intention: what they see in the world and what they want others to see of it. And this, I think, is a power of choice that should be available to all of us.

The road to calling oneself a "writer" without self-doubt and with a measured understanding of one's abilities is a long one. For students of these workshops, this is the beginning of what might be a much longer journey. However, wherever writing takes them, I hope that they find something in it that liberates the mind, body, spirit, and perception. For ultimately, writing is a way of attending to our environment and our places within it, of bringing consciousness and empowerment to our choices. With practice, attention, and kindness to ourselves, it *can* make us free.

CONTRA COSTA COUNTY JUVENILE HALL STUDENT WRITING WORKSHOP

MT. MCKINLEY HIGH SCHOOL
MARTINEZ, CALIFORNIA

ISMAIL MUHAMMAD, SIMPSON FELLOW,
PINE UNIT

ROSETTA YOUNG, SIMPSON FELLOW,
SHASTA AND TAHOE UNITS

APARTMENT #1 ON LJ STREET

BY A.M.C.

This apartment was honestly supposed to be my sweet sanctuary. It was a step away from my emotional struggle. It was a step toward something better than the simple life that I had lived every day. I envisioned this small home to have baby pink and shimmery white flowers in the windowsills. I expected the smell of fresh carpets and new paint when walking through the wooden door with a thick glass pane that shone like crystal. I wanted to feel that when nothing else felt safe in the world, this place was safe. Well, this apartment turned out to be the only place in my life that wasn't safe.

Honestly, this place *was* very clean and extremely safe before the Larue family of eight moved in. Only God and I know who these people are. This isn't exactly important compared to the importance of the events that took place in Apartment #1 on LJ Street. When these people entered my life, they shattered my perfect vision of what the sanctuary should have looked like. There were dried flowers in every windowsill and the small space certainly didn't smell clean in the slightest way. Nobody could ever relax because there was always some sort of loud music that included old-school rap or heavy metal. I had to learn to love both those genres of music because that was the only option. There was a poorly painted shade of blue molding that aligned the crumbly popcorn sealing and stained carpets.

The little girl in the house was the only bit of light that this awful place held. She was so innocent yet she was experiencing something that could damage a grown man emotionally. Every day she'd ask the older children to play dolls or ride scooters outside, but they would always say no, because they were getting high just like the only "adults" in the house. The hardened carpet was brown to begin with, but began to turn almost black because of the spilled drinks from the night before. Since everyone was already broke from spending what change they had on their fix, we had no furniture until the young adults would go out and find stuff that others threw away on the side of the road. I guess that's the reason that the definition of Larue is "on the side of the road." The creaky cracked wooden bed was one of those few ugly pieces of furniture that we owned. We were so broke that we all tried to figure out a way to collect enough coins to buy a comforter for the winter since it began to get extremely cold in the room. Especially since with all the smoke, we had to leave the windows cracked. The one bedroom that we had was really small, but at least the adults were coherent enough to let the four children have the bed. Let me tell you about how we had to take turns sleeping on it because it was only a single twin-sized bed.

The suffocating cigarette smoke lingered in the air while the children and adults got high on whatever they could. Some of the children began to have lung problems. For example, I got bronchitis and developed asthma over a period of a few short months. Since there was so much trash, there was a nasty dumpster aroma that was filled with bacteria and it really began to deteriorate every one's immune system. The closet used to be filled with dirty clothes that hadn't been washed in about five months. Some of these clothes weren't even washed when we moved in. The kids used to climb on it and call it the Mountain of Larue. Mt. Larue for short. We came up with that one night while we were all high on speed. There was no TV so there was nothing to do but get high in the front of the window since it used to rain a lot and nobody ever went outside.

I guess you could say that this apartment was like a nightmare except it was my reality just a few short months ago. Sometimes things don't always turn out the way you expect them to. I definitely wanted this place to be something special. But I guess it wasn't meant to be. There isn't any excuse for what happened at this house. As far as this story goes, I shouldn't have gone along with the things that were going on in the home. Especially being one of the older children in there, I really should have been responsible enough to stop more traumas being inflicted on the younger kids. I had a hard childhood so the way I saw the situation was that it didn't matter because I survived so they will too. It's sad but it's the truth. All I can do is move forward now with all of the knowledge that I've gained over time. One of those points being "treat others the way you want to be treated." I didn't want to be treated that way when I was little, so why would they? Why would I complain about my childhood so much when I am not doing anything to stop it from happening to someone else?

I know that I need to forgive myself for what happened, because the main reason for my behavior was the need to feel accepted from everyone in the environment. I wanted to feel loved since no one was caring or loving in any way. I won't really say what happened in the end except that everyone ended up where they were supposed to be. I am currently sober and Apartment #1 is just a figure in the past. My future holds something greater and God was just telling me to be patient. I wasn't meant to have that type of sanctuary in my life yet. That will come but only when I'm ready for it in my personal journey. For now, I need to be a kid and enjoy school and enjoy living a simple and comfortable life that my loving grandparents and now currently sober mother provide for me. It took her seven years but as they say in AA, it's never too late to make amends. I'll leave you with this: never trust those you just met, and approval and popularity aren't important. What's important is reassuring your own success in life as well as taking care of you! Don't worry about others because they should be doing the same. Pay attention to the red lights and pay attention to the warning signs because if they are ignored, there can be devastating consequences.

CHINESE FOOD

BY N.M.

Where the smell reminds me of my childhood home—
I can see her ordering
the same meal for the hundredth time.
the sweet smell of the chicken,
the great taste of the meal,
the great feeling of being at home,
my mother watching television,
the best feeling of that sentimental meal and family.

PIZZA IS THE WAY

BY H.S.

I love pizza
I love this food because it's so so
good.
Smells like heaven and I like
To eat it with my parents.
I love pineapple and pepperoni.
It makes everything better when
I eat with my parents.

UGLY GREEN BEANS

BY A.C.

I dislike green beans
  I don't know what they taste like
but they smell like driving down
  I5 to LA

In the Hall it is easy to get 2
  times in a week!

Every time that they serve it
  On my plate, I'm like, hell no
    No green beans again

LEMON BARS

BY A.M.C.

The sweet smell of
lemon fills my nana's
kitchen.

The smell is warm
and comforting and a little tart too.
Around every year at
Christmas time I
hear the mixture mixing.

This always means she's making
her famous lemon bars
since she knows they're my
favorite.

No one knows how to make
these bars besides my nana.
They say they do, but theirs
just don't taste quite right.

I love my nana's lemon bars
when we sit around the table, all
it takes is one bite. It usually
takes a minute but soon
they'll all be gone. Till next time.

UNTITLED

BY J.G.

I like the Unlimited Feast.
Red Lobster is significant to me,
Because it has everything
I love on one plate.
Smells like heaven, tastes so
islandly. The chef does
a great job on my sea food
platter—all in butter goodness.
I feel delightful at Red Lobster.

NORTHGATE HIGH SCHOOL WRITING WORKSHOP

WALNUT CREEK, CALIFORNIA

JOHN JAMES, SIMPSON FELLOW

PARASITES

BY OLIVIA LOSCAVIO

Parasites suck the blood from fauna that serve a purpose.

Sucking and sucking,

Draining and draining,

Until all that's left is the carcass.

A body void of the life that once ran through it

Life,

Ingurgitated,

By the parasite.

But what if a parasite were to latch onto another?

Would it know,

That it had, in vain,

Latched onto something as worthless as itself?

The two parasites,

Holding on so tightly to the very thing that will kill it.

A vortex of blood, greedily imbibed by both at once.

Sucking and sucking,

Draining and draining,

Until they are fattened with the infected insides of the other.

And eradicated by their own greed,

The parasites will turn to carcasses,

And the carcasses to nothing.

HOW TO FALL OUT OF LOVE

BY OLIVIA LOSCAVIO

I think the hill knew she wasn't the one.
We had to continuously adjust ourselves so as not to fall off.
And maybe the daisies knew too.
They must have.
For why else would they,
This one time,
Refuse to bend and tie in my hands?
They protected me, from creating a crown for someone who didn't
deserve to wear it.
The light was also in on the secret.
Deathly white and ashen, beneath the knowing silver sky.
And somewhere in my soul, I had known it too.

FIVE STEPS OF FORGETTING

BY GRACE DECKER

1. It's like this: One day you open your eyes and look right into the sun and don't realize that you're going blind and even if you did you wouldn't care and you don't notice yourself burning while everything around you turns to ice and you're too busy looking at the sun that you don't see the expanse of the sky or the stars falling down and everyone always says to never look right at the sun but you can't stop yourself from staring too much, too long and when you finally look away everything is dark and dull and turned around and your eyes hurt and you can't see things the way you once did. But you don't care.

2. On the fifteenth day of the beginning of your new life you aren't thinking about anything at all and then suddenly you remember lying in bed when it's past your bedtime but all you can do is look out the window at the darkness and the moon glistening against the water until the sound of the waves crashing against the rocks lulls you to sleep. And when you think about it now you don't even know how you remember that moment of lying in the bed that doesn't belong to you but you spend a long time wondering if the moon hits the water the same or if the oceans still collapses into the world or if tiny cracks of familiarity are still there or if everything is different now and what you remember wasn't ever really there at all.

3. The answer to every story in the entire world is clear: There is no resolve in loving something that much. Every morning the fog seeps through the choppy water and every night the sun drips down the sky. The moon always chases the sun but never reaches it and the stars look close enough to touch yet too far, and yet

nothing is the same. You love them, and that's it. There is no clear resolution in yearning or dreaming.

4. One day you will look right into the world you once knew and shout, "Does it get easier?" And the waves will crash into each other and the moon will disappear into the sky and rain will fall relentlessly into the grey water and disappear after a few seconds. You will watch the whole world fold into itself, over and over; and you will know the answer.

5. But maybe one day you'll be sitting in the back of your sister's car and the window will be down and you'll be speeding through the back roads of some far away town with a scattering of run down houses every few miles and there will be endless redwoods and the sunlight will be filtering through the trees and you'll stick your hand out to feel the cold wind press onto your skin, and nothing will matter. Nothing at all. In a day or two you won't be able to pinpoint the exact freeing feeling of the sun warming your cheeks or the trees going on forever or the sight of the rolling green hills that will dry up in a few months, but it doesn't matter.

IF

BY ELIANA GOLDSTEIN

The wind is different here.

Its chilling tendrils swirl gently through soft grass, lifting my hair so it floats delicately in the misty air. I can feel the breeze swaying the blanket of flora as it brushes against my bare feet. It calms me, washing away any fears I might have had, cleansing me of any stresses that may have been weighing me down. I suddenly feel much lighter; my posture straightens, and I let out a breath that I didn't realize I was holding.

I look up at the sky, lifting my head to see the stars twinkling in the darkness. The crescent moon glows brighter than I've ever seen it before. I notice that the grass, the benches, and the trees all reflect its light so that they're silverish in color. It's beautiful, I think, and the stars as well. Especially the stars. I could get used to this.

But I blink, a little split-second blink, and it all changes. All of a sudden there are billions more stars than there were before, arranged differently in constellations that I don't recognize. They're all different sizes and shapes and colors. Some are so close that they're massive; probably ten times as big as the moon.

Bewildered and confused, I look around, and am startled to see an old man wearing gray trousers and a blue coat sitting on a crooked wooden bench, accessorized with a short tie and a hat that remind me strongly of the forties. His circular glasses are tilted toward the sky, his eyes full of serenity.

Before I can ask him if he's noticed the change, he speaks, without looking away from the stars.

"This is what the universe really looks like," he tells me.

"Oh," I say.

I pause.

"… Can you put it back?"

He smiles and nods, and when I look up, the sky has returned to normal.

We sit in silence for a few seconds.

"Listen," he says.

"To what?" I ask.

"Just listen."

"I can't hear anything. What am I listening for?"

"Close your eyes. Concentrate."

I shut my eyes and breathe in deeply. A few moments later, I hear them. Faint echoes of children's voices, so distant I almost missed it. I can hear them laughing and playing. I can almost see the smiles on their faces, their eyes twinkling with absolute glee.

The old man smiles, content. He knows I've found them.

"What… what do I do?" I ask, turning to the man again. "With this information, I mean."

He turns to look at me, clearly troubled, and says, "Be careful."

When I blink next, he's gone.

The children aren't there anymore, either, and the stars and moon aren't as bright as they were before.

I am suddenly exhausted. I give in to the urge to lie down, and I fold my hands and legs under me. The cool, delicate grass tickles my skin and my fears once again seep away, leaving behind a beautiful and sweet tranquility.

Before long, I am asleep and alone, the wind whispering in my ear.

TEACHING VOICE

ESSAY

BY DAVID WOOD

Simpson Literary Project Board Member
& Northgate High School Teacher

I have been teaching high school English for a long time. I think I know what I am doing.

That is, perhaps, the art of teaching English, particularly in high school: to think you know what you are doing. But you must never be too sure. You are teaching literature and writing to young adults ("Aye there's the rub!") so you must never be too sure. Just when you think you have it down and you know where you are taking them, they will surprise you. An unexpected voice comes from somewhere in the room, like Esther Chou's one day, asking, "Hey, if *Hamlet* is set in Denmark, why are these characters named Bernardo, Francisco, and Horatio?" And better yet, later she asks, "What is Horatio doing there anyway?" I am stumped—I had taught *Hamlet* how many times and these questions, obvious though they may be, had never been asked. I never thought it would occur to them. I know I could babble some nonsense about iambic pentameter and the mellifluous sound of Italian names. ("How could they possibly be named Gunther or Wilhelm? It just wouldn't sound right.") but I stop short—and give that question the answer that no methods and material textbook ever recommends: "I don't know," I respond. "Whaddayathink?"

But that was the shot that crossed the net and got the back-and-forth volley of the teaching game going: it put the ball in their court, something we try to do as often as we can, but at which we so seldom actually succeed. Many times it takes an Esther Chou to make it work.

Or there was the time about ten years ago in a class of very bright talented seniors. We had just finished reading aloud "The Love Song of J. Alfred Prufrock" when Laura Melton raises her hand.

"I don't have any idea what it means, but I sure like the way it sounds. 'I grow old, I grow old, I shall wear the bottoms of my trousers rolled.'" I sit back and wait for the usual silence to roll in. But it does not. Others have things to say. We get at the meaning of "Prufrock" their way, piecing it together talking about sound, about voice, then what it means to them. At least that is the goal. Did we reach it? Hard to tell. We can never be overly sure, but we have given it an honest effort.

What I do know is that this is a messy process that takes time and many blunders and listening to many voices along the way, some of which are tangential, and others that say nothing at all. But in the process the students learn that I listen to them, and we all learn to listen to each other. Therein lies the heartbeat, the essential life force, of a high school English classroom. Before one can teach, one has to learn to listen. We need to be able to listen to each other, to the literature we read, to the words we write. All important learning stems from our ability to hear each person's voice and to take that voice seriously. If we cannot do this, nothing else really matters.

But at least one problem arises from this view of what makes a vital English classroom. It not only seems messy and inefficient, it in actuality is messy and inefficient, and its effectiveness cannot be measured nor calibrated, all things that the powers that be in education find anathema. Every reform effort that has taken hold, from No Child Left Behind to the instituting of the Common Core, has emphasized increased rigor and standardization in English curriculum and instruction, and runs counter to my vision of teaching English. In order for the people who instituted these programs to see if these programs have indeed increased student learning and achieved their stated goals, they must be able to measure student achievement, leading to a barrage of standardized tests and quantifiable data. If it cannot be measured, it cannot be evaluated and therefore it is dismissed. One cannot quantify the effectiveness of finding voice in an English classroom—it has to be observed firsthand, and it has to be felt, which cannot be translated into hard data.

This need to collect measurable data also leads to a so-called objectifying of the English classroom, calling for an equity of instruction, the goal being to make each classroom the same in curriculum, in instruction, in tone. As more than one administrator has said to me in so many words, "We want to make sure that a student is getting the same quality of instruction in each classroom, and that if a student is transferred from one classroom and one teacher to another, the transition should be seamless and the student should be able to pick up right where he or she left off." Some skeptics refer to this as "teacher-proofing" the curriculum so that it remains the same no matter who is teaching it. The many arguments against this idea I will not go into here, but for the purposes of this piece, let me say it immediately eliminates consideration of the individual student perspective, the interaction of teacher and student, the importance of the authentic voice of both the teacher and the student from the discussion.

I believe all these factors coalesce to lead English Language instruction into forced mediocrity. The drive toward the uniform classroom mandates the use of uniform texts and reading material. The Common Core English curriculum emphasizes primarily short nonfiction works to the exclusion of other forms of literature. Longer fictional works most times are dismissed as independent reading with little in-depth study of structure, or discussion of the importance of imagination and storytelling. Poetry is almost disregarded altogether. Students are exposed to voice only as it is used to form an argument, for its utilitarian purposes, and student-written responses emphasize summary and analysis, short précis-like responses that objectify their learning and can be used easily to measure student achievement. Granted, successful students must master this skill, but for teachers to focus on this skill to the exclusion of other affective aspects of the literature and writing experience diminishes what an English classroom can and should accomplish. In these classrooms, the idea that students may respond to the beauty of language, that they may like it and be drawn to it even if they do not understand it, that they can use language to expand their current worlds or invent new ones, is beyond alien.

This mediocrity becomes even more pronounced in writing instruction and how it limits what students see as good writing and how they learn to use voice. Writing instruction many times reduces the idea of form to formula. Let me count the ways: the thesis sentence must appear at the end of your introductory paragraph; the thesis sentence must contain in it three points of proof that the writer will then examine throughout the rest of the paper, each in its own separate paragraph; each body paragraph must have two quotes (and no more) from the sources the writer is using; the word "I" should not appear in the paper as it should be written in academic voice. All the nonsense that we thought we had done away with in the seventies and eighties has reared its ugly head in the pursuit of rigor. The most insidious part of all of this is it is almost impossible to get these rules out of students' heads. Because they are formulaic, they are easy. Students do not have to think about how to tackle a writing problem or how to formulate an essay because they can fall back on the formula that allows them to fill in the blanks with whatever it is they are writing about. There is no thought about purpose, or impact, or oftentimes most importantly, the voice of the writer because it has been eliminated from consideration. When I tell my students they do not have to write a paper in a five-paragraph essay format, or they can use first person in their papers, many struggle or fall back into the formulas that have served them in the past; others, though, relish the opportunity to try new forms to play with the material and their voices, and though they oftentimes fail to achieve what they might have set out to do, I tell them it is a noble failure, that they have tried to write something authentic, and next time it will be easier. Sometimes that is a lie, sometimes, gratefully, it is not. But I know they are better, more thoughtful writers for it.

The main casualty in this formalization of writing instruction has been student imagination and voice. Their use of language has become almost totally utilitarian, so students have little idea how to tell a story or even that they have story to tell that matters, and a voice that is theirs in which they can tell it. Each year I ask seniors to write a reflective essay on an experience that says something about the writer and who they are, a paper that can be used for college applications. It is the worst piece of writing I receive all year because they cannot come up with a meaningful subject, small as it may be, or the authentic voice to make it theirs and make it come alive.

This is where the Simpson Literary Project workshops come in. For the fifteen or twenty students at Northgate who have partaken over the past two years, they have been a godsend. The project has a mantra: "Storytelling is the foundation of a literate society." These workshops have reinjected the importance of storytelling into these students' lives by convincing them that each of them has a story to tell. The evidence of the success is in the student writing published in *Simpsonistas Volumes 1* and *2*. Each of these writers has discovered their unique voice and worked with each other to hone that voice to give their stories some universal power.

So I want to append the mantra for the Project like this: "Learning to listen and care about each other's stories is the foundation of a humane society." In these workshops over the past two years I have observed young writers come alive with each other by listening to what each of them has to say. Students time and again ventured sophisticated comments and took chances they would almost never take in a regular classroom because they knew they could, that the comment would be listened to, valued, and many times expanded upon by others in the room. In short, these students whose voices are not always treasured in the day-to-day mill of school found a room of their own, where they felt safe, and they came alive. That, along with their writings, I believe we should treasure.

Now let's hear from some of the participants who can speak to the success of the Project much more personally and eloquently than I can. Olivia Loscavio writes about her experience: "I enjoyed the workshops immensely. I decided to participate because I had been writing poems and pieces of stories for several months, but I wasn't sure that if anything I had written had any merit. I came to the workshops and my peers and facilitators assured me that they did; and even better I found a community of people who wanted to share their stories and make their stories more engaging. Every week I gained more confidence in my stories, and I became more inventive as I felt freed from the need that my writing had to be perfect so that others wouldn't judge me. I knew that whatever writing was in my head, those around me knew what I was trying to say and would help me get my ideas on paper the way I envisioned them. Readers were always honest about what could be better in a piece without being cruel, and their genuine compliments about a piece encouraged me to go home and write something that they would like even more. This workshop not only improved my writing and editing skills, but also gave me more confidence in my writing and myself." That is the kind of response that should make any teacher proud, for it is what we should be striving to achieve.

Grace Decker's comment speaks directly to the humane aspect of the Project: "In high school," she writes, "it is difficult to think of your peers, some whom are essentially strangers, as people who have complex lives that are almost unfathomable to anyone else. This view changed entirely in these workshops. I read poems about what it was like to be a woman, historical fiction, and stories about being in outer space. These pieces helped me understand the people who wrote them and gave me a new perspective." Study after study has shown that reading literature has one indisputable affect: it increases students' feelings of empathy, their ability to walk around in another's shoes, to feel how life and experiences impacts others. Reading each other's work, knowing each other's stories and imaginings, also increases their abilities to see the world from lens larger than their own and value the perspective.

The work of the Simpson Fellows in the classroom has been a joy for me to watch. They presented the writers with difficult texts by accomplished modern writers and allowed them to respond to them. They have drawn out unusual responses from the students and pushed the students to ask different kinds of questions from what they are used to exploring, not "What does the work mean?" But what has the writer done to tell his story, to make reader express surprise and delight over her poem, how has she used words to create new and vibrant worlds? They made language come alive and showed students what it means to love language for the worlds and beauty that it can create—and then set them loose to do it themselves. The professional writers—Simpson/Joyce Carol Oates Prize winners—who visited the classrooms not only shared their work but also gave the students living proof that writers do these things and they have succeeded. When Prize winner Anthony Marra visited the workshops this year, he shared some of his high school poetry, which he would be the first to admit was sentimental dreck, as if saying to them: "Look where I started. YOU CAN DO THIS, TOO!"

And many of them did just that. Please look at Grace Decker's piece in this volume as one example of a writer developing her writer's voice. I will quote her third step in her "Five Steps for Forgetting":

The answer to every story in the world is clear: there is no resolve in loving something that much. Every morning the fog seeps through the choppy water and every night the suns drip enough to touch yet are too far, and yet nothing is the same. You love them and that is it. There is no clear resolution in yearning or dreaming.

Or look to Olivia Loscavio's poem "How to fall out of Love":

I think the hill knew she wasn't the one.
We had to continuously adjust ourselves so as not to fall off.
And maybe the daisies knew too.
They must have.
For why else would they,
This one time,
Refuse to bend and tie in my hands?

In these pieces I hear talented writers' voices emerging. It is our job to encourage them to grow and develop and become what they can be, to express the joys and sorrows that they are meant to express. John James, Simpson Fellow who worked at Northgate High School this spring, wrote of his experience that "I was pleasantly surprised by the enthusiasm and talent of the students. Our group was small, but intimate, and the work—stories and poems—was remarkably polished. Mostly, though, we had a lot of fun."

Nothing is more fun in an English classroom than hearing authentic voices come alive and expand. That is what the Simpson Literary Project gives to these young writers, a room of their own to express themselves. And so they did. What could be more indicative of the success of the Project than the vision that one of these young writers will be published in *Simpsonistas* again down the line, only this time in the company of some of the finest writers in the country, as one of them? I hope I am here to see it.

POSTSCRIPT
THE LAST/NOT LAST WORD

BY DIANE DEL SIGNORE

EXECUTIVE DIRECTOR

We hope you enjoyed sampling the riches gathered in *Simpsonistas: Vol. 2*. If you're like me, you will return again and again to these stories, conversations, essays, and poems, and you will find yourself enticed to read more of the work of authors you discover in these pages. We also warmly invite you to track the Simpson Project at our website (https://www.simpsonliteraryproject.org/) and take advantage of attending our exciting upcoming events.

When it comes to reading and writing, there is no such thing as the last word. Just the next word. And the one after that. All in the ardent pursuit of the most beautiful, powerful, resonant words and stories. This point strikes home for us with force as we embark on a new year (2019–2020) and all that it promises: offering writing workshops free of charge to younger, underserved writers; considering candidates for the 2020 Simpson/Joyce Carol Oates Prize; hosting readings and talks at the Lafayette Public Library, the University of California, Berkeley, and elsewhere; coordinating with the Berkeley English Department on the selection of new Simpson Fellows, and so much more.

Long before I accepted the executive director position in April 2019, I was already captivated by all that the Board has accomplished in such a short period of time, since the founders originally explored the idea of the Project in the Summer 2015. It has been my pleasure every day to collaborate with our Project Board, with the impassioned, dedicated, visionary people who created, and who continue to recreate, the Project. I would like to highlight again and applaud the collaboration between the

Lafayette Library and Learning Center and the University of California, Berkeley, English Department, who are the institutional bulwarks of the Project. With each day I come to understand more deeply, and appreciate with increasing urgency, our mantra: *Storytelling is the foundation of a literate society.*

When I consider the hundreds of high school and college students we have taught, the hundreds of avid participants in our events and workshops, the many authors who have benefited from our recognition, I see our future is bright indeed.

After beginning my professional career working in the private sector at Hewlett-Packard, twenty years ago I turned to nonprofits, in executive leadership roles and in serving on boards. Working with altruistic, far thinking people, I experienced the joy that comes with dedication to causes larger than oneself. In Robert M. Sapolsky's groundbreaking work on neurobiology, *Behave: The Biology of Humans at our Best and Worst*, he writes provocatively about humans' capacity to delay gratification, to pursue rewards in the short term, certainly, but also pursue those rewards only attainable for and by *others* long into the future: "[I]t's unknown how we humans do this. We may merely be a type of animal, mammal, primate, and ape, but we're a profoundly unique one."

In this spirit, the Project is fully committed both to the immediate needs of the community—underserved younger people who develop talent and confidence and personal strength in our workshops—as well as to the longer term, bigger picture: because yes, storytelling is indeed the foundation of the society we wish to sustain, and it is a literate society. The Simpson Literary Project will strive to serve in the years to come all our diverse communities—writers, students, teachers, libraries, readers, and storytellers everywhere. We are grateful for those of you who have become involved in our work over the past several years and welcome our future friends to learn more. If you wish to discuss our work, or to share any suggestions, I warmly, eagerly invite you to reach out to me: diane@simpsonliteraryproject.org

I look forward to hearing from you, my current and prospective fellow Simpsonistas.

CONTRIBUTORS

Ailani Bravo is a rising senior attending Holy Names High School (Oakland, California). Her passion is volleyball and she hopes to pursue this in college as well. She wants to major in developmental psychology and minor in immigration law. Her parents, family, and sisters are her biggest motivation to keep doing big things. She hopes to help her family as well as her community.

Grace Decker is a rising senior at Northgate High School.

Diane Del Signore is the inaugural executive director of the Simpson Literary Project. She has had extensive experience leading both nonprofit and corporate teams. She directed for over ten years global partnerships for Hewlett-Packard, managing a worldwide team of sales, marketing, and technical personnel. Then for ten years she served as executive director of a statewide nonprofit dedicated to sustainable agriculture. Over her entire professional career, she has been actively involved with nonprofit boards devoted to arts, education, and community health. Beyond that, Diane is an urban farmer, raising goats, chickens, rabbits; she also teaches cooking classes with her local 4-H club. She is a Stanford University MBA, and throughout her life she has cultivated love and admiration of writers and writing, teachers and teaching. diane@simpsonliteraryproject.org

Joseph Di Prisco is Founding Chair of the Simpson Literary Project and author of fifteen books, including novels, poetry, memoir, and nonfiction. His most recent works include *Sightlines from the Cheap Seats* (poetry; 2017), *The Pope of Brooklyn* (a memoir; 2017), and *Sibella & Sibella* (a novel; 2018). He grew up in Brooklyn and Berkeley, and now lives in Lafayette, California. He received his PhD from UC Berkeley, and has taught English and creative writing, from middle school through college and beyond. He has also served as Trustee or Chair of several nonprofit boards devoted to education, the arts, theater, and children's mental health. Forthcoming in Spring 2020 is his sixth novel, *The Good Family Fitzgerald*. www.diprisco.com

Kim Dower was formerly the publicist for the Simpson Literary Project. She grew up in New York City and received a BFA in Creative Writing from Emerson College, where she also taught. Former City Poet Laureate of West Hollywood, Kim has published four collections of poetry, all with Red Hen Press: *Air Kissing on Mars*, which was on the Poetry Foundation's Contemporary Best Sellers list and described by the Los Angeles Times as, "sensual and evocative…seamlessly combining humor and heartache"; *Slice of Moon*, called "unexpected and sublime," by *O Magazine*; *Last Train to the Missing Planet*, "poems that speak about the grey space between tragedy and tenderness, memory and loss, fragility and perseverance," said Richard Blanco; and her new *Sunbathing on Tyrone Power's Grave*, which Chris Kraus, author of *I Love Dick*, calls "exuberant, sexy and sobering." Nominated for three Pushcart Prizes, Kim's work has been featured in Garrison Keillor's "The Writer's Almanac," and Ted Kooser's "American Life in Poetry," as well as in *Ploughshares, Barrow Street*, and *Rattle*. Her poems are included in several anthologies, notably, *Wide Awake: Poets of Los Angeles and Beyond*, (Beyond Baroque Books/ Pacific Coast Poetry Series) and *Coiled Serpent: Poets Arising from the Cultural Quakes & Shifts of Los Angeles* (Tia Chucha Press.) She teaches *Poetry and Memory* in the BA Program of Antioch University and *Wake Up Your Prose* for UCLA Extension. She is also the proud founder of Kim-from-LA, a well-known literary marketing and publicity company that helps writers get their beautiful words out into the world. http:// kimdowerpoetry.com/

Eliana Goldstein is a rising senior at Northgate High School.

Alexis Guzman, a rising senior at San Leandro High School (San Leandro, California), has spent the last five years scribbling down lines in hopes of expressing more than what is on the surface. Inspired by countless forms of media such as books, music and cartoons, she has developed an increasing interest in poetry. In the upcoming year she hopes to be able to pursue and further her education in literature or writing.

John James was a Simpson Fellow in 2019. He is the author of *The Milk Hours*, selected by Henri Cole for the Max Ritvo Poetry Prize (Milkweed, 2019). His poems appear in *Boston Review, Kenyon Review, Gulf Coast, Poetry Northwest, Best American Poetry 2017*, and elsewhere, and his work has been supported by fellowships and awards from the Bread

Loaf Environmental Writers' Conference, the Academy of American Poets, and Columbia University's School of the Arts, where he completed his MFA. He is pursuing a PhD in English and Critical Theory at UC Berkeley. https://milkweed.org/author/john-james

T. Geronimo Johnson was the 2017 Simpson/Joyce Carol Oates Prize Recipient. He was born in New Orleans, is a graduate of the Iowa Writers' Workshop. A former Stegner Fellow, Johnson has taught at UC Berkeley, Stanford, the Writers' Workshop, the Prague Summer Program, OSU, TSU, San Quentin, and elsewhere. He has worked on, at, or in brokerages, kitchens, construction sites, phone rooms, education nonprofits, writing centers, summer camps, ladies shoe stores, nightclubs, law firms, offset print shops, and a political campaign that shall remain unnamed. He also wrote a couple of novels that have—between the two—been selected by the Wall Street Journal Book Club, named a 2013 PEN/Faulkner Award finalist, shortlisted for the 2016 Hurston Wright Legacy Award, longlisted for the National Book Award, longlisted for the Andrew Carnegie Medal for Excellence in Fiction, a finalist for The Bridge Book Award, a finalist for the Mark Twain American Voice in Literature Award, included on Time Magazine's list of the top ten books of 2015, awarded the Saroyan International Prize for Writing, named the winner of the 2015 Ernest J Gaines Award for Literary Excellence, and the inaugural Simpson Family Literary Prize (now known as The Simpson/Joyce Carol Oates Prize). Johnson was a 2016 National Book Award judge. He is a Fellow of the American Academy in Rome, and currently resides in the Eternal City. http://www.geronimo1.com/

Laila Lalami is the 2019 Simpson/Joyce Carol Oates Prize Recipient. She was born in Rabat and educated in Morocco, Great Britain, and the United States. She is the author of the novels *Hope and Other Dangerous Pursuits*, which was a finalist for the Oregon Book Award; *Secret Son*, which was on the Orange Prize longlist; and *The Moor's Account*, which won the American Book Award, the Arab American Book Award, and the Hurston/Wright Legacy Award. It was on the Man Booker Prize longlist and was a finalist for the Pulitzer Prize. Her essays and opinion pieces have appeared in the *Los Angeles Times*, the *Washington Post*, *The Nation*, *Harper's*, the *Guardian*, and the *New York Times*. She writes the "Between the Lines" column for *The Nation* magazine and is a critic-at-large for the *Los Angeles Times*. The recipient of a British Council Fellowship, a Fulbright Fellowship, and a Guggenheim Fellowship, she is currently a professor of creative writing at the University of California at Riverside. Her latest novel, *The Other Americans*, was published by Pantheon in March 2019. lailalalami.com

Douglas Light was Longlisted for the 2019 Simpson/Joyce Carol Oates Prize. He is the author of *Girls in Trouble*, which won the 2010 Grace Paley Prize in Short Fiction. He cowrote *The Trouble with Bliss*, the screen adaptation of his debut novel *East Fifth Bliss*. His work has appeared in the *O. Henry Prize Stories* and *Best American Nonrequired Reading* anthologies. http://www.douglaslight.com/

Olivia Loscavio is a rising senior at Northgate High School.

Francie Low was a student in the Simpson Project Memoir Workshop at Lafayette Library and Learning Center in Spring 2019. She has published personal essays, written award-winning blog posts, and published her first book: *Alive And Fixable*. Some of her work is on *HuffPo*, *Literary Mama*, *Retrospect* and featured posts on *BlogHer*. She's aired on the San Francisco Bay Area NPR station for their listener commentary *With A Perspective*, and performed in *Listen To Your Mother*, a live-storytelling event. Francie is a former marketing and sales professional turned full-time mom and career volunteer. While her two boys are at university, most of her days are dedicated to book talks, writing, blogging, and enjoying time with her husband. https://www.francielow.com/

Alexandra Maldonado is a rising senior who attends San Leandro High School in San Leandro, California. She has been in Girls Inc. for eight years. She has been writing poetry since she was in ninth grade. English and Science are her favorite subjects. She wants to become a pediatric oncologist, as well as major in English.

Anthony Marra was the recipient of the 2018 Simpson/Joyce Carol Oates Prize. He is the author of *The Tsar of Love and Techno*, a finalist for the National Book Critics Circle Award, and *A Constellation of Vital Phenomena*, longlisted for the National Book Award and winner of the

NBCC's John Leonard Prize, the Anisfield-Wolf Book Award, the Barnes and Noble Discover Award, and Greece's Athens Prize for Literature. He has received the Guggenheim Fellowship, the Whiting Award, the National Magazine Award, the Berlin Prize Fellowship, and his work has been translated into seventeen languages. In 2017, Granta included Marra on its decennial Best Young American Novelists list. He has taught at Stanford University, and currently lives in Cambridge, MA. http://anthonymarra.net/

Beth Needel is a founding member of the Simpson Literary Project. She is currently the Executive Director of the Lafayette Library and Learning Center Foundation, a job that for the past six years has kept her deliciously surrounded by books. She has spent much of her career working on other passion projects, creating programs and raising funds for organizations like Tony La Russa's Animal Rescue Foundation and the Oakland Zoo. Beth is from the Chicago area, holds a degree from Southern Illinois University, and lives in Walnut Creek, CA, with her husband, Aaron; dog, Mia (who also thinks she works at the Library); and cats, Timmy, Kay1 and Kay2. Her son Michael and daughter-in-law Kelsey live too far away in Boston.

Janine Noël is a graduate of the Saint Mary's College of California MFA program, where she was awarded the Jim Townsend Scholarship for Excellence in Creative Writing. She holds a bachelor's degree from Dartmouth College and is completing her first book, a memoir. Janine is interested in what we aspire to, the power of our dreams, how they motivate us, fail us, and how they keep us alive. She is cofounder of Diablo Writers' Workshop where she teaches *Writing from Life Experience* courses. As a bookseller at Orinda Books, she is dedicated to connecting readers of all backgrounds with the perfect book. A Lafayette, CA native and current resident, she often escapes into the stunning hills for long hikes. DiabloWriters.org

Sigrid Nunez was a Finalist for the 2019 Simpson/Joyce Carol Oates Prize. She has published seven novels including *A Feather on the Breath of God*, *For Rouenna*, *The Last of Her Kind*, and, most recently, *The Friend*, which received the 2018 National Book Award for Fiction. Her other honors and awards include four Pushcart Prizes, a Whiting Award, a Berlin Prize Fellowship, the Rome Prize in Literature, and the American Academy of Arts and Letters Rosenthal Foundation Award. Nunez is also the author of *Sempre Susan: A Memoir of Susan Sontag*. Among the journals to which she has contributed are the *New York Times*, the *Wall Street Journal*, the *Paris Review*, *Threepenny Review*, and *Harper's*. She lives in New York City. https://sigridnunez.com/

Joyce Carol Oates is Joyce Carol Oates. She was the Simpson Project Writer-in-Residence at the Lafayette Library and Learning Center (2018, 2019), and is a member of the Simpson Literary Project Board. She is the Roger S. Berlind Distinguished Professor of the Humanities at Princeton University, and the recipient of numerous awards, including the National Book Award, the PEN/Malamud Award for Excellence in Short Fiction, and recently the 2019 Jerusalem Prize. She is the prolific author of novels, short stories, memoirs, poetry, and nonfiction; and, as legions of readers around the world appreciate, an author of unparalleled range, depth, and accomplishment. Her most recent novel is *My Life as a Rat*.

Lori Ostlund was a Finalist for the 2017 Simpson/Joyce Carol Oates Prize. She is the author of *After the Parade* (Scribner, 2015), which was shortlisted for the Center for Fiction First Novel Prize, and was a Ferro-Grumley Award finalist and a Barnes and Noble Discover Great New Writers pick. Her first book, a story collection entitled *The Bigness of the World* (UGA Press, 2009; reissued by Scribner, 2016), won the 2008 Flannery O'Connor Award, the Edmund White Debut Fiction Award, and the 2009 California Book Award for First Fiction. Stories from it appeared in the *Best American Short Stories* and the *PEN/O. Henry Prize Stories*. Lori has received a Rona Jaffe Foundation Award and a fellowship to the Bread Loaf Writers' Conference. She is a teacher and lives in San Francisco with her wife and cats, though she spent her formative years in Minnesota, cat-less. loriostlund.com

Genaro Padilla is a founding member of the Simpson Literary Project. Professor of English at UC Berkeley, he is Chair Emeritus of the English Department and Vice Chancellor Emeritus, UC Berkeley. He is also the author of *The Daring Flight of My Pen: Cultural Politics and Gaspar Perez*

de *Villagra's Historia de la Nueva Mexico, 1610,* and *My History, Not Yours: The Formation of Mexican American Autobiography.*

Alexis Peters is a student of San Leandro High School (San Leandro, California). She has a distinct interest in surrealist art, which serves as her inspiration to view the world from another perspective and convey that through her writing.

Anne Raeff was a Finalist for the 2019 Simpson/Joyce Carol Oates Prize. Her second novel, *Winter Kept Us Warm,* was published in February 2018 and won a Silver Medal from the California Book Awards. Her short story collection, *The Jungle Around Us,* won the 2015 Flannery O'Connor Award for Short Fiction. The collection was also a finalist for the California Book Award and was on the *San Francisco Chronicle's 100 Best Books of 2017 list. Clara Mondschein's Melancholia,* also a novel, was published in 2002. Raeff's stories and essays have appeared in *New England Review, ZYZZYVA,* and *Guernica* among other places. Raeff is proud to be a high school teacher and works primarily with recent immigrants. She lives in San Francisco with her wife and two cats. Finally, she is happy to announce that her third (still untitled) novel, which is set largely in Nicaragua and examines the long-term effects of colonialism, revolution, and war, will be published in the spring of 2020 by Counterpoint Press. http://www.anneraeff.com/

Laura Ritland was a 2018 and 2019 Simpson Fellow, teaching at Girls Inc. in Oakland, California. She is a PhD student in English at UC Berkeley, and the author of *East and West,* a book of poetry, which was shortlisted for 2019 the Pat Lowther Memorial Award and nominated for the 2019 Gerald Lampert Memorial Award. Her poems have appeared in *The Fiddlehead, CNQ, The Walrus, Maisonneuve, Arc Poetry Magazine,* and *The Malahat Review.* She currently divides her time between Vancouver and California.

Vanessa Smith is a seventeen-year-old proud Latina. Growing up in the Bay Area, Vanessa got a lot of exposure to so many beautiful and unique people. However, along with all the beauty, came some pain. Vanessa was bullied throughout most of her life, but despite this she always tried to keep a positive mindset. Dance was her first love. She has been dancing Ballet Folklorico Mexicano for eleven years now, and her life would not be the same without it. However, once she discovered poetry, she knew that dance and poetry were her two outlets from the world, where she could just be herself.

David Wood has taught English at Northgate High School since 1984, and is a member of the Simpson Literary Project Board; he also served on the jury for the Simpson/Joyce Carol Oates Prize. He was a board member and board president of the celebrated Aurora Theatre Company, and now serves on the Advisory Board for the Kalmanovitz School of Education at Saint Mary's College of California. A Yale graduate and University of Chicago M.A., he estimates he is coming up on his hundredth year of teaching.

2019 SIMPSON/JOYCE CAROL OATES
LITERARY PRIZE LONGLIST

Tom Barbash

Marie Benedict

Liam Callanan

Susan Choi

Charmaine Craig

Patrick deWitt

Leif Enger

Jonathan Evison

David Francis

Kim Fu

David Burr Gerrard

Lauren Groff

Dara Horn

Silas House

Maria Hummel

Laird Hunt

Mat Johnson

Tayari Jones

Katie Kitamura

Rachel Kushner

Laila Lalami

Ariel Lawhon

Chang-Rae Lee

Douglas Light

Sam Lipsyte

Valeria Luiselli

Ben Marcus

Lee Martin

Daniel Mason

Madeline Miller

Celeste Ng

Idra Novey

Sigrid Nunez

Helen Phillips

Anne Raeff

Shoba Rao

David Rocklin

Jess Row

Julie Schumacher

B. A. Shapiro

Tatjana Soli

Rene Steinke

Amor Towles

Laura van den Berg

Lidia Yuknavitch

Leni Zumas

Simpson Literary Project

The Simpson Literary Project relies on the generous contributions of individuals and institutions, businesses, corporations, and family foundations dedicated to the advancement of literacy, storytelling, the art of teaching, creative writing, authors, readers of all generations, and literature.

All proceeds from *Simpsonistas* go to The Simpson Literary Project.

To make a donation, please use this link
https://www.lllcf.org/simpson-donation/

Or contact Diane Del Signore, Executive Director
diane@simpsonliteraryproject.org

The Lafayette Library and Learning Center Foundation (LLLCF) administers the Simpson Literary Project in accordance with laws governing tax-exempt organizations under Sec. 501(c)(3).

The Simpson Literary Project
Lafayette Library & Learning Center Foundation
Suite 214
3491 Mt. Diablo Boulevard
Lafayette, CA 94549